	Heroin	Barbiturates	Tranquilizers	Amphetamines
Effects	Euphoria, drowsiness, constricted pupils	Similar to alcoholic intoxication, constricted pupils	Similar to alcoholic intoxication, depressed reflexes	Intense stimulation, increased alertness, insomnia, euphoria, excitation
Tolerance	Yes	Yes	Yes	Yes
Physical dependence potential	High	High	Moderate	Possible
Psychological dependence potential	High	High	Moderate	High
Duration of effects	3 to 6 hours	1 to 16 hours	4 to 8 hours	2 to 4 hours
Overdose	Slow and shallow breathing, convulsions, coma, possible death	Possible coma and death	Stupor, coma and death in extreme cases	Agitation, hallucina-tions, convulsions, possible death
Special notes	One of the most addictive substances known	Withdrawal is dangerous and can cause death, can be par-ticularly dangerous when mixed with alcohol, belligerant behavior sometimes noted	Abrupt stop in use can cause serious withdrawal symptoms	Extreme abuse can produce paranoid behavior

Preface

Drug abuse in all its many and varied forms is one of the most taxing and involved problems that face today's professional law enforcement officers. Little is known of its causes or cures, and its costs, both direct and indirect, are truly staggering.

As is the case with many of society's more complex problems, the police bear a large responsibility for finding workable solutions for handling drug abuse. In many areas of this country the police are the only agency of local government actively engaged in attempting to control the drug trade and its inevitable spin-off of crime, corruption, and social decay.

This book is written to try to help them in that dangerous and often discouraging task. I have tried to include in it information that I would have found useful when I served as a police officer. The basic test that I have applied when deciding what to include has been twofold: (1) Will this information help the officer to make his or her cases? and (2) Will it help him or her to avoid some of the many errors that I made when handling drug cases?

For clarity in presentation this book is divided into three main sections:
1. The Drugs
2. Investigation
3. Treatment

The first section describes the drugs which are most commonly abused in this country. It tells how they are produced, where they come from, what they look like, how they are sold, what their effects are, and how their abusers can be recognized.

The second section explains some of the most common enforcement techniques that can be used to combat the drug trade. Procedures covered include the use of informants, undercover operations, search and seizure, buys, and raids. This section also includes a chapter on the relationship between organized crime and the drug trade.

The final section outlines some of the more important treatment methods used in this country and some of the more important aspects of how heroin addiction has been treated in Great Britain. Although there is no formally codified "British System," the approach in Great Britain to dealing with heroin addicts has followed a different path from methods used in the United States. For reasons of discussion and analysis I have therefore included a chapter on this subject.

The first two of the three appendixes give important background information that is too detailed to be included in the main body of this text. The third appendix describes emergency medical techniques—important information for anyone working with drug abusers. The glossary emphasizes the street language of the drug world.

It was a conscious decision on my part to not include the subject of alcoholism in this text, although it too can be considered a form of drug abuse. Alcoholism poses a substantially different problem for the law enforcement officer. Unlike drug abuse, use of alcohol is socially acceptable; it involves a different class of people for the most part; it does not involve investigative techniques but affects a different social category, particularly the family; and it is not influenced by organized crime. Lastly, the problem of alcohol abuse is dealt with primarily by a different type of law enforcement officer—the patrol officer—rather than the narcotics officer or investigator.

Throughout the book the historical aspects of this country's drug abuse problem have been stressed. This is not just because they happen to make interesting reading. Rather, it is so that the students may get some idea of the chain of events that has led up to the regretable condition in which we find ourselves today. For only by seeing the errors of our past can we plan intelligently for today.

I would like to acknowledge with gratitude the following people, without whose assistance this project would never have been possible: Mr. John R. Bartels, Jr., Former Administrator, Drug Enforcement Administration; Mr. Alan B. Bernstein, United States Customs Service; Capt. Houston Bigelow, Metropolitan Police Department, Washington, D.C.; Dr. Ben Coffman, U.S. Department of Agriculture; Mr. Stephen W. Cooley, Law Enforcement Assistance Administrator; Mr. John T. Cusack, Drug Enforcement Administration; Mr. Luther M. Dey, Eastman Kodak Company; Mr. Cornelius Dougherty, Drug Enforcement Administration; Dr. Robert Dupont, Director, National Institute of Drug Abuse; Dr. Walter A. Gentner, U.S. Department of Agriculture; Mrs. Sarah Goodman, Attorney at Law, San Diego, Calif.; Mr. Michael Harris, Smithsonian Institution; Mr. Edward E. Johnson, Executive Office of the President; Mr. James Judge, Drug Enforcement Administration; Mr. William Mason, U.S. Customs Service; Mr. Charles Warren, U.S. Customs Service; Mr. James Wilder, Drug Enforcement Administration; Mr. Harold Wise, U.S. Customs Service; Mr. Jerry V. Wilson, Former Chief, Metropolitan Police Department, Washington, D.C.; Mr. Mark A. Zelinger, Second Genesis, Alexandria, Virginia.

Part 1
THE DRUGS

Chapter 1

THE PROBLEM OF DRUG ABUSE

The tasks confronting law enforcement officers today are as complex and varied as modern society itself. Each new technological wrinkle devised to bring us a "better life" is accompanied by a series of problems—many of which eventually become the police officer's concern. Take, for example, the marvelous work of Henry Ford and his followers. To them we can be thankful for the transportation revolution. We went from horse and buggy to 300-horsepower Corvettes in little more than a generation. And with this great leap forward came one of the biggest headaches for the police—traffic in all its congested, snarling forms. Or take credit cards, one of the true commercial revolutions. Hand in hand with the "cashless society" there has appeared a whole new breed of criminals, the celluloid thieves. Or consider the computer. With the advent of the electronic era it seems that everything we are or do has been reduced to a punched card or a magnetic impulse. Sure enough, one of the by-products of the digital age is a whole new generation of computer criminals who specialize in bilking the magnetic monsters of millions.

In the fields of health and medicine, we have also experienced a series of revolutions. As with our other advances in the twentieth century, these have contributed to the expansion of the world of crime. Today drug-related crime is a major concern of every police officer.

In the last few generations incredible strides have been made toward unlocking the basic secrets of human existence. At every turn we have managed to delve still deeper into the fundamental mechanisms of existence. We have decoded more and more of the chemical riddles whose answers reveal the very secret of life itself. From this understanding we have been able to make great strides in medicine. Once we began to understand the fundamental life-giving processes, we were able to probe the true causes of a host of the illnesses and disorders that have plagued us since the dawn of time. In short order some of the great scourges of humanity, such as smallpox, measles, dysentery, malaria, yellow fever, and polio, were, for all practical purposes, eliminated. No longer did we have to let every disease run its natural, and all too often fatal, course.

Now we could do something, armed with perhaps our most important weapon in the war for survival, as a species—modern medicine.

As our understanding of diseases and their courses grew, so did the number of drugs available to fight them. Each year we added more and more compounds to our arsenal. Since the early 1900s thousands of new drugs have been developed in the accelerating race for better ways to treat illnesses, and the pace shows no signs of slowing. In fact, it has been estimated that between 1970 and 1980 there will be an astonishing hundredfold increase in the number and types of drugs that affect the mind.[1]

Undoubtedly, people have gained much from this pharmacological explosion (Figure 1-1). They have also inherited a plethora of problems—many of which have become the concern of today's police officers.

The drug-abuse problem is one of the most exasperating and complex challenges that faces society today. The following chapters will explore some of its aspects as they apply to the law enforcement function.

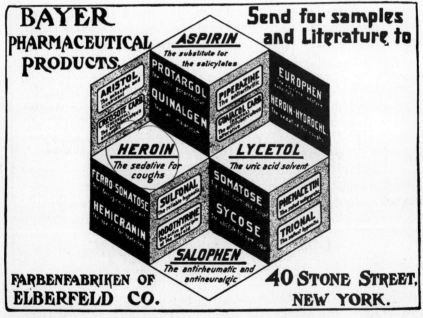

FIGURE 1-1
Heroin, perhaps the most troublesome drug ever discovered, was at first hailed as a wonder drug. It was at times even prescribed as a cure for morphine addiction.

There are several reasons why a comprehensive understanding of the drug-abuse problem and what can be done to combat it is important to today's police officers. The first can be summarized in the timeless adage, "Know thy enemy." If law enforcement people are going to be effective in combating the drug-abuse problem, they must have a thorough understanding of it. They must know how the drugs are made, where they come from, how they are smuggled, who deals in them, what they look like, how they affect users, how they are packaged, what tests can be used for them, and a host of other technical facts.

The second reason why it is vital to know all about drug abuse is closely related to the first. Drug enforcement is big business. Each year federal, state, and local authorities spend hundreds of millions of dollars on activities related to drug enforcement (Figure 1-2). The federal government alone spends an estimated $350 million on enforcement and related supply-reduction effects annually. Even at the local level drug enforcement can prove to be exhorbitantly expensive. Drug investigations can involve thousands of hours of police time. Obviously,

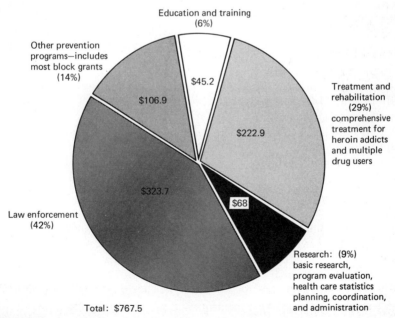

FIGURE 1-2
Fundings for federal drug-abuse programs in 1976. Figures are in millions of dollars. [From Strategy Council on Drug Abuse, Federal Strategy for Drug Abuse and Drug Traffic Prevention, 1975 (Washington, D.C.: GPO, 1975)]

with such enormous commitments of money, time, and energy, it is vital that the officials who bear the responsibility for drug enforcement activities be thoroughly familiar with all aspects of the problem.

There is another reason why law enforcement officials must be thoroughly familiar with every aspect of drug abuse: the public relies on them as a source of factual information and advice. Each year civic and community organizations turn to their police departments for advice about and information on the drug problem in their communities. Each year speakers provided by law enforcement agencies address literally thousands of different audiences on the problem of drug abuse. As a grizzled, old supervisor once commented, "The public may get mad at us when things are going okay, but when they have a problem, they come running." Of course, he was right. Once the general public became aware of the enormous scope and seriousness of the drug problem, once they found out that their children were using drugs, they immediately turned to the most logical source of information and advice—the police. This reliance of the public on the police necessitates that police departments respond by accepting the responsibility of doing all that they can to assist the public. Law enforcement officers must take the time and make the effort to learn all that they can about the drug problem, its causes, and its many implications.

BASIC DEFINITIONS

To be understood, terms must be clearly defined and they must be defined in language that has meaning for the listener. If there ever was a field in which that is important, it is drug abuse. Police, social workers, psychiatrists, parole officers, counselors, abusers, worried parents, just to name a few, are all involved, and they all have to communicate with each other. Obviously, if they are not using the same words, if they are not talking about the same things, communication is impossible.

In a field as emotionally charged and as politically sensitive as drug abuse, it is not an easy matter to separate fact, as it is delineated by the definitions that are assigned to terms, from emotional bias and prejudice. The words that we use to describe or define anything do not exist in a vacuum. They exist within the cultural context in which they are used. Consequently, they can, and often do, reflect the particular prejudices and biases of the setting in which they are being used. In other words, the words we use to describe something often are shaped by and shape the way in which we view that something.

For example, consider the two terms "drug-dependent person" and "dope fiend." The former represents or connotes a humanitarian, medically oriented approach to one who is a heavy drug user. The latter carries with it an element of strong social disapproval. There is nothing wrong with either disapproving of or taking a compassionate view of an individual who uses drugs. Where the problem develops is when such personal value judgments creep into and bias a supposedly rational and unbiased discussion of the topic. At that point one begins to operate with biases rather than facts.

To ensure that there is no misunderstanding as to what is meant by the terms used in this text, the following paragraphs define those terms basic to any consideration of drug use.

Drug

In its broadest sense a *drug* may be defined as any compound that affects the functioning of an organism. Drugs may cause changes in both the bodily processes and behavior. In this sense the air that we inhale, the food that we eat, and the water that we drink are all drugs. However, in this book the discussion is restricted to the major drugs of abuse. For convenience in discussion they have been classified into six groups:

1. Heroin and other opiates
2. Cocaine and other natural and synthetic stimulants
3. Hallucinogens, both natural and synthetic
4. Depressants, such as the barbiturates and minor tranquilizers
5. Cannabis preparations, such as marijuana and hashish
6. Inhalants, such as glue and nitrous oxide

Nicotine and alcohol, the two most widely used drugs in this country, have not been included in this discussion. While it is true that both present a clear and ever-present danger to their users, the public's attitude and, as a result, social policy toward them differ markedly from the substances discussed in this text. Since both alcohol and nicotine are not considered to be a significant social peril by the majority of people in this country, they can be obtained legally; they are licit drugs. With a few minor exceptions, most of the drugs considered in this volume are not openly available. They must be purchased on the black market; they are illicit drugs. As such, they present a wide range of problems for the entire criminal justice system.

Drug Abuse

It is difficult to define to anyone's complete satisfaction the term "drug abuse." It is one that must, to a large degree, reflect a moral judgment.

The word "abuse," by its very nature, implies wrongdoing. What some members of society regard as abuse may well be regarded as legitimate behavior by others. In the final analysis what is considered to be abuse frequently is what the group that is dominant in any particular society at a given time considers it to be. This, in turn, implies that when one group loses its domination and another takes its place, the nature of what is and is not considered abusive may well change.

Our history is rich with examples of this sort of fluctuation. Classic among them is Prohibition. Since our earliest frontier days we have been a nation of drinkers. The winning of the West and the building of saloons went hand in hand. Clearly, the consumption of vast quantities of some of the hardest liquor ever brewed was not considered by the majority to be abusive; it was an accepted and socially sanctioned fact of life.

However, a minority of citizens did not agree, and they were determined to make the United States a nation of teetotalers. At first these Prohibitionists were a small and politically insignificant minority. Gradually during the nineteenth century their ranks and influence swelled. By 1846 the first statewide Prohibition act had been passed in Maine. Led by such firebrands as William Jennings Bryan and Carrie Nation, the movement gained increasing support. It reached its culmination on January 16, 1920, when the Volstead Prohibition Act became federal law. America was by act of Congress "dry." The Prohibitionists' views of what constituted abuse at last prevailed, but not for long.

Within a few short years America's drinkers were able once again to exert sufficient political pressure so that their particular notion of right and wrong prevailed. On December 5, 1933, the Volstead Act was repealed, and liquor once again flowed freely. Once more what was and was not abuse was defined according to the likes and dislikes of those with sufficient political power to have their way.

In the light of these considerations it is not easy to pin down with scientific exactitude what is meant by drug abuse. No single definition will be totally satisfactory to everyone. The one that follows is most in keeping with both current scientific knowledge and prevailing public attitude toward it. It defines *drug abuse* as the use of a substance in such a way that it leads to such personal and/or social consequences as impaired physical or mental health, impaired maturation, loss of productivity, and involvement in socially disruptive or illegal activities.

This definition implies such specific behavior on the part of drug abusers as:

1. The use of drugs in forms, styles, or situations that are illegal

2. The use of drugs without appropriate medical supervision or in excess of accepted standards of self-medication
3. The use of drugs in such a way that users lose control of their ingestion or the resulting behavior
4. The use of drugs in pursuit of potentially hazardous states of consciousness or moods

Tolerance

As the "law of peanuts" goes, "The more you eat, the more you want." The same, unfortunately, is true of many drugs. The more they are used, the greater the reliance on them and the need for them— thus the greater the demand for them. At the root of this pattern of increasing need is the physiological mechanism called "tolerance."

Tolerance is usually defined as the ability of an organism to become used to increasing amounts of a substance upon repeated exposure to it. The biochemical mechanism responsible for this is not fully understood. We do know that in the case of some drugs, such as heroin, the body chemistry adjusts quite rapidly to the presence of the drug. As a result, each time that addicts use the drug it has a diminishing effect upon them and they experience less of a thrill from it. Consequently, if they are to continue to experience any sort of a "rush" (an intermediate exhilarating feeling) from the drug, they must continually increase the amount of the dosage. This is the reason that heroin addicts require increasing quantities of the drug in order to satisfy their craving.

It should be noted that individuals can develop different degrees of tolerance to different effects of a given drug. Again to use heroin as an example, users quickly develop a marked tolerance to its ability to produce the intense initial, orgasmic rush. However, only a minimal tolerance develops to the drug's gastrointestinal effects. As a result, most addicts suffer constipation for as long as they continue to use the drug.

A condition called *cross-tolerance* occurs with some drugs. Individuals who are tolerant to the effects of one drug are also tolerant to those of another. Methadone and heroin are good examples of this. Persons who are enrolled in methadone-maintenance programs quickly develop a tolerance to many of the effects of the drug. At the same time they develop a tolerance to many of the effects of heroin.

Withdrawal

The concept of tolerance is closely related to that of *withdrawal*. As the body adjusts to the presence of drugs, as tolerance develops, subtle changes occur in the body's chemistry. Should the user stop taking drugs, the body must once again make a chemical adjustment—this time back to a drug-free state. This period of readjustment may produce a cluster of characteristic physical reactions and behavior that are collectively referred to as a withdrawal syndrome. This syndrome can range from a comparatively mild set of symptoms as is the case with most amphetamines to the extreme discomfort that is often associated with heroin withdrawal. In the case of some drugs, such as the barbiturates, withdrawal can have fatal consequences.

Dependence

There are two types of drug dependence—physical dependence, referring to the body's need for a drug, and psychological or psychic dependence, referring to the mind's need for a drug.

Physical dependence can be defined as an altered physiological state brought about by the repeated administration of a drug that necessitates continued administration of the drug in order to prevent the appearance of withdrawal symptoms. In other words, physical dependence is said to exist when stopping the use of a drug will bring on withdrawal symptoms.

Psychological dependence, or as it is sometimes called, psychic dependence, refers to a craving or strong psychological need for the pleasurable mental effects produced by a drug. Those who are psychologically dependent upon a drug prefer the mental effects that it produces to a normal state; they find the mental state induced by the drug necessary to their well-being.

Drugs differ in their potential for producing physical and psychological dependence. Some drugs, such as heroin, can produce both an acute physical and psychological dependence. Other drugs, such as cocaine, may produce a strong psychological dependence. Most authorities agree that a true physical dependence is not produced by cocaine.

Addiction

Although similar to physical dependence, *addiction* is not synonymous with physical dependence. It is often used in reference to narcotics. Other drugs such as the barbiturates can produce physical dependence. However, narcotics addiction involves something more. It implies an overwhelming craving for an involvement with a drug to such an extent that the getting and using of it preempts all other interests and activities. Addiction involves a totally drug-centered lifestyle. The compulsive getting and using of narcotics completely pervades the addict's entire life.

RESPONDING TO THE DRUG PROBLEM

It is one thing for an individual or society as a whole to admit that a problem exists. It is quite another not only to do something about it but also to get general agreement on what to do. For years law enforcement and health officials, and an increasing segment of the general public, have known that drug abuse in all its varied forms is a serious problem. Libraries are crammed full of reports and studies about it, and articles constantly appear in the popular press that decry the terrible toll that drugs have exacted from our society. On this one point almost everyone who has looked into the matter is in agreement—we have a serious problem. Beyond that, however, there is a vast sea of conflicting theories, notions, and opinions of how to attack the problem. Assemble a panel of a dozen or so authorities in the field of drug abuse and ask them what to do about the problem, and you can be sure of getting a dozen different answers.

At one end of the spectrum are those who view drug abuse as solely the concern of the criminal justice system. Their position is usually stated as follows: Drug abusers initiate their habit of their own free will. Both abusers and the dealers who supply them know that their activities are not sanctioned by society—that they are illegal. Therefore, they have no right to complain when society takes whatever enforcement steps are needed to protect its own best interests. The proper response is to deter abusers and dealers by arresting them and giving them long prison sentences. This will accomplish two desirable objectives. First, it will deter others from using and dealing in drugs. Second, it will get users and dealers off the street and behind bars where they cannot victimize the rest of society.

At the other end of the spectrum are those who consider drug abuse to be solely a medical problem. They view drug abusers as sick people—people who are entitled to the same sympathy, compassion, and social support as given to those who are afflicted with any other terrible disease. Drug abuse is classified as either an illness in and of itself or as symptomatic of some massive underlying disorder. The proponents of this approach view medical and social treatment of drug abusers as the only proper social approach. In their opinion imprisoning drug abusers is no more justified than imprisoning people suffering from cancer.

Past experience, however, has clearly demonstrated that policies and procedures based on either of these extremes are doomed to sure and certain failure. Instead, it has become increasingly obvious that what is needed is a balanced approach to the drug problem—one that seeks through enforcement and other means to reduce the supply of drugs available and at the same time seeks to reduce the demand for them through treatment and rehabilitation.

A wide range of activities at the federal, state, and local levels are aimed at reducing the volume of illicit drugs available to abusers. All these efforts have several basic objectives in common. They seek to make it difficult to obtain illicit drugs as well as to increase the risk and price involved in processing, consuming, and dealing in them. In time, it is hoped, these efforts will decrease the ranks of the drug abusers by discouraging experimenters (the potential new users) and by causing some present users to abandon or at least to reduce their consumption because of fear of arrest, the inconvenience involved in obtaining supplies, or the increased costs involved.

A number of closely related and often overlapping activities are directed toward reducing the available supplies of illicit drugs. These are outlined in the discussion that follows.

Law Enforcement

The primary function of law enforcement efforts in the drug area is to *arrest* suspected drug traffickers and to *remove* their supplies from the illicit market. These efforts involve a wide range of agencies at all levels—local, state, federal, and international.

The key federal legislation pertaining to drug abuse is Public Law 91-513—the Comprehensive Drug Abuse Prevention and Control Act of 1970, or as it is commonly called, the Controlled Substances Act. This act is the cornerstone of the federal government's efforts in the treatment and control of drug abuse. The federal agencies charged with enforcing it are the Food and Drug Administration (FDA) of the Department of Health, Education, and Welfare and the Drug Enforcement Administration (DEA) of the Department of Justice.

Under the act all controlled substances are placed in one of five schedules—the most dangerous in Schedule I, the least in Schedule V.

SCHEDULE I
A.   The drug or other substance has a high potential for abuse.
B.   The drug or other substance has no currently accepted medical use in treatment in the United States.
C.   There is a lack of accepted safety for use of the drug or other substance under medical supervision.

SCHEDULE II
A.   The drug or other substance has a high potential for abuse.

B. The drug or other substance has a currently accepted medical use in treatment in the United States or a currently accepted medical use with severe restrictions.

C. Abuse of the drug or other substance may lead to severe psychological or physical dependence.

SCHEDULE III

A. The drug or other substance has a potential for abuse less than the drugs or other substances in Schedules I and II.

B. The drug or other substance has a currently accepted medical use in treatment in the United States.

C. Abuse of the drug or other substance may lead to moderate or low physical dependence or high psychological dependence.

SCHEDULE IV

A. The drug or other substance has a low potential for abuse relative to the drugs or other substances in Schedule III.

B. The drug or other substance has a currently accepted medical use in treatment in the United States.

C. Abuse of the drug or other substance may lead to limited physical dependence or psychological dependence relative to the drugs or other substances in Schedule III.

SCHEDULE V

A. The drug or other substance has a low potential for abuse relative to the drugs or other substances in Schedule IV.

B. The drug or other substance has a currently accepted medical use in treatment in the United States.

C. Abuse of the drug or other substance may lead to limited physical dependence or psychological dependence relative to the drugs or other substances in Schedule IV.[2]

In deciding on which schedule applies to a drug, factors considered include the drug's actual or relative potential for abuse; the scientific evidence of its pharmacological effect; the current scientific knowledge about it; the history and current pattern of abuse; the scope, duration, and significance of abuse; the risk to public health; the psychological and physical dependence liability; and whether the substance is an immediate precursor of any substance already controlled by the act. From time to time, as new information comes to light or new abuse patterns are discovered, drugs are moved to a different schedule.

The Controlled Substances Act imposes numerous controls on those involved in the manufacture, obtaining, and selling of drugs that fall under its jurisdiction (see Table 1-1). The chief of these follow:

TABLE 1-1
CONTROL MECHANISMS OF THE CSA

Schedule	Registration	Record keeping	Manufacturing Quotas		Distribution Restrictions	Dispensing Limits
I	Required	Separate	Yes		Order forms	Research use only
II	Required	Separate	Yes		Order forms	Rx: written; no refills
III	Required	Readily retrievable	No but	Some drugs limited by Schedule II quotas	DEA registration number	Rx: written or oral; with medical authorization, refills up to 5 times in 6 months
IV	Required	Readily retrievable	No but	Some drugs limited by Schedule II quotas	DEA registration number	Rx: written or oral; with medical authorization, refills up to 5 times in 6 months
V	Required	Readily retrievable	No but	Some drugs limited by Schedule II quotas	DEA registration number	OTC (Rx drugs limited to MD's order)

SOURCE: Drug Enforcement Administration, *Drugs of Abuse*, chap. 7, "The Controlled Substances Act" (Washington, D.C.: GPO, 1976), pp. 30–31.

1. REGISTRATION. Each company, dealer, or dispenser who handles controlled substances must be officially registered with the DEA. Each is assigned a registration number which must be used in all transactions involving controlled substances.
2. RECORD KEEPING. Full records must be kept of the manufacture, sale, and inventory of all controlled substances. This makes it much easier for investigators to trace their flow through the system and to detect their diversion into illicit channels.
3. MANUFACTURING QUOTAS. The FDA and DEA working together can limit the amount of the more dangerous of the controlled substances that may be produced in a given year.

Import-Export		Security	Manufacturer/ Distributor Reports to DEA	Criminal Penalties for Trafficking (First Offense)	
Narcotic	Non-narcotic			Narcotic	Non-narcotic
Permit	Permit	Vault type	Yes	15 years/ $25,000	5 years/ $15,000
Permit	Permit	Vault type	Yes	15 years/ $25,000	5 years/ $15,000
Permit	Notice	Surveillance	Yes: Narcotic No: Non-narcotic	5 years/ $15,000	5 years/ $15,000
Permit	Notice	Surveillance	No: Narcotic No: Non-narcotic	3 years/ $10,000	3 years/ $10,000
Permit to import Notice to export	Notice	Surveillance	Only Narcotic No: Non-narcotic	1 year/ $5,000	1 year/ $5,000

4. DISTRIBUTION. All steps in the distribution ladder from manufacturer to dispenser are carefully regulated. Detailed records must be made of all transactions, and a copy of each transaction must be forwarded to the DEA.

5. DISPENSING TO PATIENTS. Very strict guidelines govern the conditions under which drugs may be dispensed to either patients or researchers.

6. IMPORT AND EXPORT. The DEA closely monitors all international transactions involving drugs. The agency must be informed of each transaction and the terms.

7. STORAGE-FACILITY SECURITY. The security requirements for

areas in which controlled substances are stored are carefully spelled out. The more the substance is subject to abuse, the more stringent are the security requirements.

8. REPORT TO DEA. Detailed reports regarding inventories of and transactions involving the most dangerous of the controlled substances must be made on a regular basis.

9. PENALTIES FOR TRAFFICKING. The penalties for trafficking in the various controlled substances are given in detail. These range for the first offense from a possible fifteen years in jail and a $25,000 fine for dealing in the more dangerous drugs to one year in jail and a $5,000 fine for dealing in the less dangerous drugs. Second and subsequent offenses are punishable by twice the penalty for the first offense. The act carefully distinguishes between those who sell drugs for profit and those who possess them for their own use. Possession of any of the drugs covered by the act for one's own use is always a misdemeanor for the first offense. It is punishable by up to a year in jail and a $5,000 fine.

BORDER INTERDICTION.   Two agencies share the burden of making sure that our borders remain as impervious to drug smugglers as possible (Figure 1-3). These are the U.S. Customs Service and the Bureau of Immigration and Naturalization.

REGULATORY FUNCTIONS.   This category includes those numerous activities that are designed to monitor and regulate the legal distribution of drugs. These are carried out at both the state and the federal level.

INTELLIGENCE GATHERING.   All drug authorities at all levels are involved in gathering data about drug abuse. Their activities range from the penetration of illegal drug trafficking organizations to the use of satellite photography to spot illegal poppy patches in the wilds of Mexico. Cooperation and communication among these groups are the rule generally rather than the exception.

INTERNATIONAL ASSISTANCE.   In the international sphere the United Nations has been a focal point for drug programs. The programs cover a wide range of activities such as economic assistance, the development of substitue crops to replace the opium poppy, and the providing of training, technical assistance, and equipment to foreign governments.

FIGURE 1-3
Smugglers have tried every conceivable way to get drugs past our
borders. In this case morphine base was being smuggled inside a
wooden table top. (*U.S. Customs Service*)

CAUSES OF DRUG ABUSE

Why do people abuse drugs? What is the overpowering attraction of
the "chemical turn on"? These are questions that are frequently asked
and never satisfactorily answered.

Drug abuse is one of the more complex and baffling of vices. Each
year some of the world's most eminent scientists and physicians pour
out hundreds, if not thousands, of learned papers on the subject. Yet
the most basic question of all—what causes drug abuse?—still remains
unanswered.

All that can be said with any degree of certainty in answer to this
query is that we do not know. Of course, we can make a number of
broad generalizations. For example, drugs are used and abused for one
of two fundamental reasons: either to reduce pain or to increase pleasure. However, beyond this level the issues start to get fuzzy.

When discussing the causes of drug abuse, when seeking the answers to the many "whys" involved, we should keep certain basic considerations in mind. Among the most important of these is the notion of *multiple causation*. From the evidence that we now possess, it seems most unlikely that there is any one single cause that is responsible for drug abuse. Rather, it appears that it is brought on by the combination of a number of factors. These factors originate both within the minds and bodies of those who abuse drugs and within the environment in which they live.

It also seems likely, in the light of current research, that the various internal and external factors that produce drug abuse are additive. That is to say, they build upon and reinforce each other. And past experience seems to indicate that there is no one given set of circumstances, no one combination of factors, that invariably assures that someone will turn to drugs. In other words, a given set of circumstances that may produce drug abuse with one individual may not with another.

Because of the many variables involved and their complex relationships, it is clearly impractical and impossible to attempt to build a meaningful drug abuser's personality profile. There simply is no such creature as the "typical drug abuser." For every abuser who does fit a particular theoretical profile, there will be one who does not.

Though we can neither pinpoint the causes of drug abuse nor predict with accuracy who will and will not turn to drugs, we can suggest a number of factors that may contribute to an individual's abuse of drugs. For purposes of discussion these factors have been grouped into two basic categories:

1. *External* factors that stem from the individual's environment.
2. *Internal* causes that originate within the individual user's own mind and/or body.

External Factors

To some extent we are all products of our environment. From the very day of our birth until the last spark of life has left us, what we do and how we do it is shaped and molded by the environment in which we exist. How we face life, how we respond to the challenges that confront us, how we interrelate with others are all to some degree determined by where we live and the people with whom we come in contact during our day-to-day existence. Our response to drugs is no exception to this pattern. Whether or not individuals abuse drugs, and if they do, the particular ones with which they become involved, the manner in which the drugs are used, and the effects of the drugs are all influenced by their environment.

One such external factor that contributes to drug abuse is the *availability* of drugs to potential abusers. Whether or not drugs are readily available can and does have an enormous effect on how widely they are abused. We tend to view drug abusers in terms of the stereotyped "dope fiend," who will stop at nothing, who will do any-thing, who will go anywhere in search of a fix. True, there is a small group of abusers who are so enslaved to drugs that they will go to almost any length to obtain them, but these people are the exception rather than the rule. For many others drug abuse is an occasional sort of thing, a take-it-or-leave-it phenomenon. If the drugs are readily avail-able they will use them or experiment with them; if not, they will not. If the experimenters like the results, they will in all probability continue to use them. However, if drugs are not abundant, it is unlikely that they will go to any great trouble to find them.

Peer-group pressure is another external factor that has a great im-pact on whether or not individuals become involved with drugs. Most abusers begin experimenting with drugs in their teens—a time when they are particularly sensitive to pressure from their friends and as-sociates. For teenagers a sense of being part of things, of belonging to a group, is terribly important. In many cases youngsters will do any-thing, including use drugs, in order to be accepted by their peers.

Closely related to peer-group pressure is the general spirit of youthful rebellion that is so much a part of today's scene. For many youths drug abuse has become the ultimate symbol of their rebellion against the adult world—against the system. Drug abuse has assumed the role of a symbolic protest against all that the older generation stands for. It has become a symbol of protest against all that these youths feel is wrong with America. For many such youthful protesters drug abuse has also become the ultimate way of "driving parents crazy" or gaining their attention. As one marijuana smoker noted, "Nothing I did made a difference to my old man. I couldn't get through to him. He just kept on doing his thing and making his wads of money. He never paid any attention to anything I did or said. Then I got into the dope thing, and that brought him around. He did not know what the hell to do then. Man, did I ever give him a spin. He knew I was around then."

Finally, when we are discussing the external factors that contribute to drug abuse, it is important to remember that we are a drugged cul-ture. We are a nation of pill takers. Each year Americans consume millions upon millions of doses of an incredible variety of pills and potions. We take drugs to put us to sleep, to get us up, to prevent pregnancies, to induce pregnancies, to sharpen our wits, to dull our nerves, to stop our headaches, to regulate our bowels, to cure our diseases, to clear our sinuses, and to do just about anything else with our bodies that can be imagined. Living in such a chemical culture, is it any wonder that a good number of individuals take it upon themselves to add a few illicit substances to our socially sanctioned pharmacological cornucopia?

Internal Factors

Are we agents of our own free will, or are we, as a species, at the mercy of basic psychopharmacological drives whose origins and mechanics are for the most part beyond our present limited understanding? Are we truly able to control our own behavior, or are we the slaves of our own metabolism? To what extent are drug abusers merely individuals consciously seeking to satisfy their own desires for gratification and pleasure, and to what extent are they the helpless victims of their own aberrant physiologies? These are the questions that we must answer if we are ever to understand the nature and relevance of the causes of drug abuse that originate within the users themselves.

Unfortunately, we still have a very long way to go before we can provide the answers to these questions with any degree of certainty. Our understanding of how the chemistry of the brain influences behavior is, at best, marginal. We do know that various biochemical factors can exert a powerful influence on behavior. For the most part, however, our knowledge of how or why they do so is pitifully inadequate.

For example, it has been demonstrated experimentally that the genetic makeup of some animals affects their susceptibility to addiction. Various strains of rats have been bred that are either extremely difficult or very easy to addict to morphine.[3] Whether or not similar genetic factors operate upon humans is not known at this time.

At present it is also impossible on the basis of the information available to understand the relationship of metabolism to addiction. Some authorities contend that addiction is brought about by or is symptomatic of a metabolic disorder. The proponents of this approach generally view addiction as the product of a severe maladjustment of the body's internal chemistry.

Other researchers speak of the causes of addiction in terms of "receptors." These hypothetical components of the brain are thought to be sensitive to stimulation from various chemicals, among them the opiates. They, in turn, are believed to activate or influence the manner in which the central nervous system functions. The suggestion has been made that either some individuals have a greater number of receptors that are sensitive to drugs, such as heroin, or the receptors of some people are more sensitive than those of others to drugs. The validity of these theories has yet to be proved or disproved.

Moving somewhat away from the area of direct biochemical causation, we enter the limitless never-never land of the psyche. Here we come face to face with the vast, and for the most part unchartered, area of our innermost needs and drives. It is within this framework that such theories of the causes of drug abuse are expounded as "People take drugs because they seek immediate gratification" or "Drug abuse is an attempt to escape frustration."

Indeed, it is from the relationship of the psyche to drug abuse that we can gain a good deal of insight into some of the causes of the abuse. For example, it has been shown that many drug abusers are essentially immature. They have never mastered the skills that are required to cope in a mature, rational manner with the problems, anxieties, and frustrations that life so freely hands out. They feel inadequate and unable to deal with the pressures that surround them. Many are extremely passive and dependent in their relationships with others. For them drugs can and do provide a temporary source of adequacy—a feeling of being able to cope.

For others drugs provide a means of escape. By the same token, many drug abusers are essentially hedonistic. They endlessly seek out pleasurable experiences. For them drugs are a means to an end; they provide the ultimate in instant gratification.

Still other abusers appear to be drawn to drugs out of simple curiosity. They want to see what effects drugs will produce. This is particularly true of many youthful abusers. In most cases their curiosity to try new things, to experience new sensations, is a healthy sign. However, when it carries over into the realm of drugs, it can have tragic consequences.

A search for personal or religious insight causes some other individuals to turn to drugs. This motivation during the 1960s prompted the rage for LSD and a plethora of other hallucinogens in order to achieve "enlightenment." Of course, the use of chemicals to reach altered states of consciousness is nothing that is new to our culture or times. Since the dawn of history humans have used any number of assorted mushrooms, seeds, barks, and roots in an attempt to reach a state of mind that allows them best to communicate with the gods and forces of nature. Needless to say, the question of when a genuine, though at times misdirected, quest for a religious-mystical experience turns into clear-cut drug abuse is one that can be debated endlessly.

IN CONCLUSION

Drug abuse is a complex problem. Those involved in combating it must be familiar with a number of disciplines. The following chapters will describe the most important of these disciplines. Each of the major drugs of abuse will be reviewed in some depth. Then some of the more important investigative techniques that can be applied to a drug case will be outlined. Finally some of the current theories pertaining to the causes and treatment of drug abuse will be reviewed.

NOTES

[1]Oakley S. Ray, *Drugs, Society and Human Behavior* (St. Louis: Mosby, 1972), p. 3.

[2]Drug Enforcement Administration, *Drugs of Abuse*, chap. 7, "The Controlled Substances Act" (Washington, D.C.: GPO, 1976), p. 28.

[3]Oakley S. Ray, p. 5.

Chapter 2
NARCOTICS

The social cost of narcotics abuse in the United States is staggering. This is true in terms of both dollars lost and lives ruined. A federal study gives some idea of the staggering price America pays for its narcotics problem.

1. The dollar costs of drug abuse (the majority of which involves heroin) is estimated to be *at least* $10 billion annually.
2. Each year in excess of 15,000 individuals lose their lives in drug-implicated circumstances.[1]

And the number of people whose entire lives center around obtaining drugs for their insatiable needs runs into the tens of thousands. The enormity of such costs to society is difficult to grasp.

Before discussing narcotics, it is necessary to define precisely what is meant by the term in the context of this chapter. In current usage the term *narcotics* refers to a family of drugs that are derived from opium, the dried sap of the opium poppy *(Papaver somniferum)*. It also includes those synthetic and semisynthetic compounds that are chemically similar and produce similar results. In addition to opium, the more common narcotics are heroin, morphine, codeine, methadone, and meperidine. All these drugs act as depressants upon the central nervous system.

The definition just given is the strict scientific one. But in legal terminology this definition has been expanded by the Controlled Substances Act of 1970 to include the powerful stimulant cocaine as well as coca leaves and derivatives of both of them.

USES AND EFFECTS

Though narcotics have been known and used for thousands of years, the exact manner in which they act upon the body is still not fully understood. We do know that they depress the central nervous system and that they affect the major sensory areas of the brain. They also appear to alter the manner in which impulses are transmitted by the nervous system. Beyond these basic generalities little can be said about their effects with any degree of certainty.

When used in therapeutic doses, narcotics relieve pain. They also help to reduce anxiety, relax muscles, calm the body, and produce drowsiness and sleep. In addition, they are used as cough suppressants and to relieve diarrhea. Narcotics are capable of producing a euphoric exaggerated sense of well-being and contentment. It is this quality that makes these drugs so attractive to drug abusers.

The body rapidly builds up a tolerance to many of the effects of narcotics, and their users can (and frequently do) develop extreme physical and psychological dependence on them to maintain the effects desired. This leads to taking ever-increasing dosages. If this drug taking is interrupted, habitual users will undergo often severe withdrawal symptoms.

Overdoses are an ever-present threat to narcotic abusers. They occur most frequently (1) with novices who are not familiar with the effects of drugs, (2) when several different drugs, such as narcotics and barbiturates or narcotics and stimulants, are used together, (3) when drugs of unknown purity are used, and (4) when toxic drugs, such as strychnine, have been used to adulterate or "cut" the narcotics.

A mild overdose may simply put the user to sleep. Larger amounts, however, may cause a fatal respiratory failure or cardiovascular collapse.[2]

THE EARLY HISTORY OF NARCOTICS

The saga of narcotics reaches back to the dawn of history. Archaeologists think that the opium poppy's seemingly miraculous powers were first discovered by the simple Neolithic farmers who roamed the mountains bordering the eastern shores of the Mediterranean Sea. Knowledge of its cultivation seems to have spread from Asia Minor across the length and breadth of the ancient world. Clay tablets left almost 6,000 years ago by the Sumerians, an ancient Babylonian people, refer to opium as the "plant of joy."

The earliest mention of the medical use of opium is believed to be in the Ebers papyrus—an Egyptian medical treatise that dates to the sixteenth century B.C. It suggests the drug as a means of quieting crying babies, a recommendation made by many of America's patent medicine manufacturers in the late 1800s!

Opium enjoyed wide popularity in Greece, and it is from the Greek word *opion*, meaning "poppy juice," that the term is derived (Figure 2-1). The famous Greek physician Galen prescribed opium as a cure for such diverse ailments as epilepsy, venomous bites, fevers, melancholy, and "all pestilences." Apparently, it was also a culinary treat, for Galen mentioned that opium candies and cakes were sold widely.

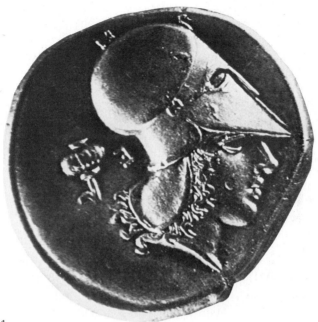

FIGURE 2-1
Ancient Greek coin showing an opium poppy seedpod.

In the period that followed the death of the prophet Mohammed, the Arabs forged a mighty empire that included most of Europe and Asia Minor. The holy writings of the Koran forbade the use of all forms of alcohol. As a substitute, opium and hashish became the principal social drugs of the servants of Allah. The writings of the Arab physician Biruni contain what is considered to be the first written description of opiate addiction. As the Arab empire spread, so did the poppy. By the tenth century the Arabs had carried the use of opium to both China and India.

As the enlightenment of the Renaissance broke through Europe's Dark Ages, the works of the ancient Arab and Greek physicians formed the basis of all medical learning. Thus it is not surprising that opium eventually became one of the most important drugs in the European physician's medicine chest.

In England the noted seventeenth-century physician Thomas Sydenham, regarded as the father of modern clinical medicine, developed one of the most popular of the opium-based medicines—laudanum. Made from opium, saffron, cinnamon, cloves, and wine, laudanum was prescribed for a range of maladies that extended from gout to the "pox." In time it became the standard remedy both in the British Isles and in the colonies.

The Isolation of Morphine

A new era in the history of opium began in 1804. It was then that the young German chemist Frederick Sertürner opened the modern era of alkaloid chemistry by successfully isolating the most important active ingredient of opium. He named the new substance morphine, after Morpheus, the Greek god of dreams. Now, at last, physicians possessed a pain-killer of known reliability and strength—it was ten times stronger than opium. But, as history so graphically illustrates, Sertürner's accomplishment soon was found to be a double-edged sword. On the one hand, the wonder drug did, and still does, provide relief from the agonies of pain for untold numbers of the suffering. On the other hand, it, and the related drugs that followed, would soon enslave millions of unfortunates in the shackles of addiction.

The Hypodermic Needle

The year 1853 marks the next important date in the history of narcotics use and abuse. It was in that year that a Scotsman, Alexander Wood, succeeded in perfecting the most efficient drug-delivery system known, the hypodermic needle (Figure 2-2). Until then morphine had been taken orally, and because much of it was broken down by the patient's digestive system before it entered the bloodstream, its pain-killing potential was severely limited. Now, for the first time, physicians had at their disposal a means to introduce the drug directly into the patient's bloodstream. When morphine is administered in this manner, its pain-killing properties are greatly increased. So, alas, is its power to entrap the unwary. In a cruel twist of history, Wood's wife became the first person to develop an injected-morphine habit. Eventually she was to die from an overdose—the hypodermic needle's first victim.

Use of Morphine and Other Opiates in the American Civil War

Five years after Wood perfected the hypodermic needle, injected morphine was introduced into American medicine by Fordice Baker and George Thompson. It was just in time for the Civil War.

Morphine was by far the most effective pain-killer available to surgeons of both the Blue and the Gray. In addition, opium preparations were widely used during the Civil War to combat dysentery and diarrhea. It was not until the years following the war that the awful results of this indiscriminate use of opiates during the hostilities were to be realized. Then it gradually became apparent that the gallant ef-

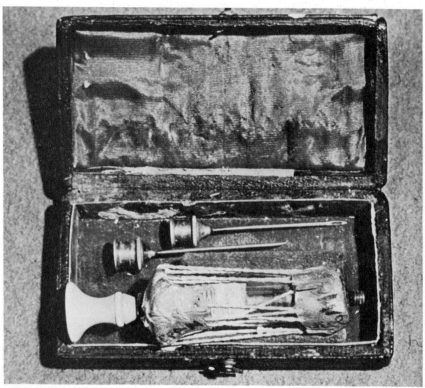

FIGURE 2-2
The advent of the hypodermic syringe marked the beginning of a
new era in narcotics abuse. Powerful opiates could now be delivered directly to the addict's bloodstream, making the drugs far
more effective and dangerous.

forts of military physicians on both sides to counteract their patients'
sufferings had resulted in widespread morphine addiction. In fact, the
problem of morphine addiction became so commonplace during the
decades following the Civil War that it came to be known as the "Army
Disease" (Figure 2-3).

GROWTH OF NARCOTICS USE IN THE UNITED STATES

While it is true that the large number of ex-soldier addicts contributed
substantially to America's growing narcotics problem, other factors
were also to blame. Among the most important was the flowering of
America's patent medicine industry.

FIGURE 2-3
The Civil War's carnage created a whole new class of ex-soldier
addicts.

Patent Medicine

In the years after the Civil War, America's patent medicine industry
boomed as never before. Thousands of pills and potions were marketed
as a sure cure for everything from "female disorders" to tuberculosis. A
general lack of sophistication on the part of the buying public, poor
health levels among the general population, and massive promotional
campaigns by patent medicine manufacturers all contributed to the
astonishing commercial success enjoyed by many of these wholly useless nostrums.

Of course, what the manufacturers of these various and assorted
snake oils did not tell the public was that most of them contained
staggering quantities of opium or morphine (Figure 2-4). The result of
this patent medicine blitz was a substantial increase in the number of
America's addicts. Many of these unfortunates were, in contrast with
our times, middle-class women who, as long as the medicines were
available, managed to function quite effectively as wives and mothers.
However, all that was soon to change.

FIGURE 2-4
Hundreds of household cures such as this one contained massive
amounts of opium. (*National Library of Medicine*)

Heroin

Science marches on, and in 1874, a British researcher, C. B. Wright,
succeeded in creating a semisynthetic opiate by boiling morphine and
acetic acid together for several hours. At first little interest was shown
in the new drug. However, during the 1890s physicians found that it
was useful in relieving the agonies of those suffering from morphine
addiction. About the same time the Bayer Company, an aggressively
managed German pharmaceutical firm, embarked on an intense sales
campaign aimed at marketing the new drug as a cough suppressant. To
this end the decision makers at Bayer felt that their new "wonder drug"
needed a short, catchy name—a name the public would remember.
They were right on one thing! The name they chose—heroin—has been
a household word ever since.

All too quickly heroin became the drug of choice for thousands of
this country's narcotic addicts. By the time its terrible dangers were
recognized, countless more thousands of unfortunates had been added
to the already swollen rolls of America's addicts. Estimates vary substantially, but it appears beyond a doubt that by the turn of the twen-

tieth century several hundred thousand Americans were addicted to
some form of narcotic drug. Such figures are quite comparable to recent
estimates, which place this country's heroin addict population at
somewhere between 250,000 and 600,000 individuals.[3]

Opium Smoking

The almost inexhaustible need for laborers caused by the explosive
expansion of the railroads also contributed to increasing the rolls of
America's narcotic addicts. During the 1880s thousands of Chinese
were brought to this country to help stretch the iron ribbons from coast
to coast. With them came the practice of opium smoking.

By the 1870s prejudice against the Chinese and their habit of
opium smoking had reached a fever pitch. In 1875 the city fathers of
San Francisco adopted an anti–opium-smoking ordinance, the first
such law in the United States. Virginia City, Nevada, followed suit
within a year. During the next decade a number of states passed similar
antiopium laws aimed at the "un-American" drug habits of the "yellow
devils."

Regulatory Legislation

Shortly after the turn of the century official concern began to develop
about America's increasingly more obvious drug-abuse problems. By
1903 medical authorities had recognized the addiction-producing qualities of heroin. During the next few years public alarm continued to
mount. In 1906 this concern resulted in the passage of the Pure Food
and Drug Act. As a result of this and subsequent acts, pharmaceutical
manufacturers were required to state what ingredients were included
in their various pills and potions. This and an energetic educational
campaign conducted by both the government and the press made
Americans aware for the first time of the enormous quantities of narcotics included in their favorite home remedies.

THE ERA OF REFORM

During the first decade of the twentieth century the spirit of reform
which permeated so much of American life was to spill over into the
area of drug abuse. Just as a few years later we decided to "make
the world safe for democracy," we now declared our intention to rid the
globe of the "scourge" of narcotics. The Philippine Islands became the
first battleground in our international war on drugs—a war that has
now lasted almost three-quarters of a century.

At the close of the Spanish-American War the American authorities in the Philippine Islands inherited from the Spanish a complex system designed to license narcotic addicts and supply them with drugs. Shortly after the end of the hostilities the War Department formed a commission to develop alternatives to the Spanish system. After studying the problem of narcotics throughout the Far East, the commission recommended that all narcotics be placed under strict international controls.

International Conferences

In February 1909, largely as the result of pressures brought to bear by Teddy Roosevelt, an international conference was held in Shanghai to consider the opium problem. The Shanghai Conference produced no treaties, only a noble resolution to the effect that "the use of opium and its alkaloids for non-medical purposes was evil, was spreading and is to be restrained."[4]

The Hague was the scene in 1911 of the second international conference on narcotics control. The result of this conference was the Hague Convention of 1912—the first international agreement on the control of narcotic drugs. Under its terms the production and trade in the opiates and cocaine was to be strictly limited to the amounts needed for medical and scientific purposes.[5] In terms of practical impact, the Hague Convention accomplished little. There was no way of using sanctions against those who violated it. With World War II the disruption to its goals was almost complete. However, the Convention did lay the foundation for other legislation that was soon to follow.

American Drug Legislation

The year 1915 marked the passage of the Harrison Narcotics Act, the basis of federal antidrug efforts until the Controlled Substances Act of 1970. Championed by Secretary of State William Jennings Bryan, the act, on its surface, appeared merely to be an attempt to bring order to the marketing of opiates. However, as time would soon show, it was destined to become the cornerstone of future federal drug control efforts.

Soon after the passage of the Harrison Act the Treasury Department issued a series of regulations that had the effect of prohibiting the dispensing of maintenance doses of narcotics to addicts. A series of court decisions followed, confirming the Treasury Department's position. Before long the government was leading the way in a vigorous "war on drugs." Soon after, state after state took up the cause and passed antidrug laws patterned after the Harrison Act.

THE CHANGING NATURE OF DRUG USE AND DRUG USERS

During the years between the passage of the Harrison Act and the outbreak of World War II several fundamental changes took place in the nature of America's narcotics problem. Though the figures available are not the most reliable, they do indicate that during this period the number of addicts in the United States probably decreased substantially. That this occurred is understandable when one considers the intense enforcement activities that characterized this period. A graphic indication of the emphasis that was placed on enforcement can be seen in prison population figures. By mid-1928 almost one-third of all the prisoners in federal penitentiaries were serving time for violations of the Harrison Act.[6]

As enforcement intensified, the character of the "average" drug user changed radically, as did the general pattern of drug abuse in this country. Intravenous injection of heroin began to be a serious problem by the mid-1920s. During the 1930s it became increasingly popular, and by the outbreak of World War II it was the rule rather than the exception. As the manner in which heroin was used changed, the cost of its use to society increased dramatically. The relatively harmless, middle-aged, middle-class housewife who personified the typical narcotic addict at the turn of the century had now been replaced by a young, urban, minority-class male. This new type of addict posed an infinitely more serious problem for society than that of only a generation before. Because injected drugs produce a more severe dependence, the new generation of addicts needed a far greater supply of drugs—a supply that had to be paid for. And in most cases crime was the only way in which the new addicts could get enough money to pay for their habits. The profits that their drug craving produced were used by the underworld to develop and entrench a vast, organized crime empire. Prostitution, extortion, gambling, and corruption all benefited from the seed money provided by the narcotics traffic.

With the shift in narcotics-use patterns, the cost to and the impact upon the individual addict became far greater. The housewife morphine addict of a generation earlier was, in spite of her addiction, usually able to function quite satisfactorily. This was not the case with the new generation of intravenous-heroin abusers. Because of the increased effects of the injected drug, addiction was far more crippling. The new addicts were completely controlled by their insatiable craving for heroin. It was the only focus in their lives, and it destroyed their lives. Their families were split apart, their potentials never realized. Their health deteriorated. Hepatitis and all the other host of diseases brought about by unsterile needles, as well as reactions to all the various types of "garbage" used to dilute heroin, took their toll.

After World War II

The international narcotics trade was almost completely disrupted by World War II. The activities of enemy submarines as well as increased wartime security on the docks reduced the flow of heroin from Europe to the United States to a trickle. The international connection was broken—for the time being.

However, long before the last shots of World War II were fired, the stage was being set for the resumption of the international drug trade on a scale never before imagined by even the most successful prewar drug dealer.

Bitter because of years of wartime persecution by Mussolini, the Mafia was all too ready to provide assistance to the Allies in their drive through Italy. Later in the tense cold war years of the 1950s, the Mafiosi were quick to ally themselves with the United States against the Communist-backed Italian labor unions. Much of the same train of events followed with the Corsican-dominated underworld in France. The Corsicans too had been influential in drug circles. They also sided with American interests against the Communists in the postwar battle for control of the key port city of Marseilles.

Whether or not these French and Italian criminal organizations, which had been the illicit drug magnates in the prewar period, received any direct aid from agencies of the United States government as a consequence of their anti-Communist activities is a topic that is still hotly debated. Regardless, the fact remains that in the years immediately after World War II the international drug connection was firmly reestablished. Drugs again became plentiful in the ghettos of America's major cities.

By 1948 the United States was on the brink of a serious postwar heroin problem. By 1953 international drug traffic reached such proportions that the United Nations passed a protocol calling for the worldwide control of opium production. This was followed in 1961 by the United Nations Single Convention on Narcotic Drugs.

THE DRUG EXPLOSION OF THE 1960s AND 1970s

The early 1960s saw America's drug problem go from bad to worse— and still worse. By 1965 the United States was staggering under the

impact of an epidemic increase in drug abuse. Federal authorities estimated that during 1965 almost 5,000 kilos (kilograms) of heroin were
smuggled into the United States—double the amount of only five years
before.[7] During the seven years from 1965 to 1972 the incidence (new
use) rate of heroin was to multiply by a factor of ten. Cases of drug-
related hepatitis were to increase about ninefold during the same
period.[8]

As the epidemic intensified, a number of radical changes occurred
in this country's drug-abuse patterns. Since the implementation of the
Harrison Act, drug abuse, for the most part, was a phenomenon associated with the inhabitants of America's urban ghettos. The "typical"
heroin abuser was a minority male who lived in the slums of one of the
large cities. Heroin, and for that matter all drug abuse, was a problem
that the popular mind associated with "them" and not with "nice"
people.

By the early 1960s, however, it became alarmingly obvious that
"their" problem had become everybody's problem. Drug abuse had
spread to the middle classes.

By applying the same epidemiological techniques that health
specialists used to track the spread of such diseases as diphtheria and
yellow fever, authorities have been able to trace the spread of drug
abuse during this period. The epidemic appears to have begun among
minority populations living in major urban areas on both coasts such as
New York, Washington, and Los Angeles. It then spread to youthful
nonminority populations in the same areas. Next it spread to such other
major population centers as Boston, Phoenix, Miami, and Detroit. Finally, during the early 1970s heroin abuse reached America's smaller
cities.[9]

Federal Countermeasures

The federal government launched a major multifaceted assault on drug
abuse in 1969. This effort was designed to reduce both the supply of
narcotics available to abusers and their demand for narcotics. During
the last few years this massive effort has achieved a number of notable
successes. It has also met with some dismal failures.

In October 1970, the Comprehensive Drug Abuse Prevention and
Control Act was passed. It was the first major reworking of federal drug
laws since the Harrison Act of 1915. The 1970 act was designed to
stimulate "increased research into and prevention of drug abuse and
drug dependence; to provide for treatment and rehabilitation of drug
abusers and drug-dependent persons; and to strengthen existing law
enforcement authority in the field of drug abuse."

In an attempt to intensify and coordinate international drug control efforts, a Cabinet Committee on International Narcotics Control was organized in August 1971. This committee combined the efforts of the Departments of State, Justice, Treasury, Defense, and Agriculture, the Central Intelligence Agency, and the United States delegation to the United Nations.[10]

Supply-reduction efforts were centralized both at home and abroad. In July 1973 the drug enforcement responsibilities of ten federal organizations were combined under the control of a newly formed Drug Enforcement Administration (DEA). This agency was made responsible for spearheading federal antidrug enforcement activities. Massive federal assistance was also made available to state and local authorities. Training programs were set up, and technical assistance and specialized equipment were made available. Cooperative federal, state, and local enforcement efforts were undertaken.

Overseas supply-reduction efforts were similarly intensified. Programs designed to strengthen international drug enforcement were given a high priority. DEA agents were assigned to overseas posts to assist foreign governments in their efforts to control drug trafficking and smuggling.

The United States also greatly stepped up its drive to encourage opium-producing nations to either eliminate or more closely control opium poppy cultivation. In 1967 the Turkish government announced plans to reduce gradually opium poppy cultivation. From 1968 through 1971 poppy cultivation in Turkey was cut back from twenty-one to four provinces. Finally, as the result of intense diplomatic pressure from the United States, the Turkish government announced that it was banning all opium poppy cultivation at the end of the 1972 fall harvest. In return the United States was to provide technical assistance and over $35 million in foreign aid to attempt to develop satisfactory substitute crops.

All the while major efforts were also being made to reduce the demand of America's addicts for illicit drugs. A wide range of treatment, prevention, and vocational rehabilitation programs were initiated. Federal expenditures were dramatically increased, especially in the area of treatment. Whereas in 1966 the total federal expenditure for treatment was $16 million, by 1975 this had grown by a factor of over twenty to $375 million.[11]

In 1972 the Drug Abuse Office and Treatment Act was passed. It called for the creation of the Special Action Office for Drug Abuse Prevention. This office was charged with the responsibility of developing policies that coordinate the efforts of all the various federal agencies that deal with drug-abuse prevention.

The "Turning Point"

By mid-1972 it appeared that the massive efforts of the last seven years were finally paying off. All the signs were encouraging. In the major East Coast cities where an estimated one-half of the heroin users lived, heroin was becoming increasingly hard to obtain. Such traditional barometers of heroin abuse as the number of narcotic-related hepatitis cases reported, the frequency of overdose deaths, the age of first heroin use, the number of new users in treatment, the number of persons arrested who use drugs, and the purity and cost of heroin all seemed to indicate that the upswing in heroin abuse that had plagued this nation for so many years had at last been interrupted.

Optimism became the order of the day. Here, finally, was proof that when a concerned nation was prepared to commit the necessary resources, the drug problem could be licked. The "corner had been turned" on drug abuse—or so it was thought!

Mexican Mud

By the early summer of 1974 authorities around the nation became aware that something was wrong—terribly and unmistakably wrong. Instead of continuing to improve, the drug problem was worsening. Gains that had been so dearly won were being lost. Demand for treatment was increasing at an alarming rate. The cost of heroin remained the same or decreased. This indicated replenished supplies. Hepatitis cases, seizures, and drug-related arrests also began to climb. All too obviously, "smack" was back.

What had happened to rekindle the problem? Nothing, really, other than the triumph of the laws of supply and demand. In the world of drugs there is one basic, inescapable rule—where a demand exists, a supply will spring up from somewhere to fill it.

For a number of years poppies grown in Mexico had made a sizable, if not major, contribution to the supply of heroin available in this country. By 1972 it was estimated that approximately one-third of the heroin in the United States originated in Mexico.[12] As soon as the authorities were successful in smashing the French-Corsican drug rings and Turkey ceased poppy cultivation, Mexican drug traffickers stepped in to fill the void. And fill the void they did! By 1974 Mexico was supplying more than three-quarters of the heroin (known due to its brown color as "Mexican Mud") available in the United States. By 1975 authorities estimated that the share had increased to over 90 percent (Figure 2-5).

Close proximity and a long common border that is relatively easy to cross and is extensively crossed have added to the problem that

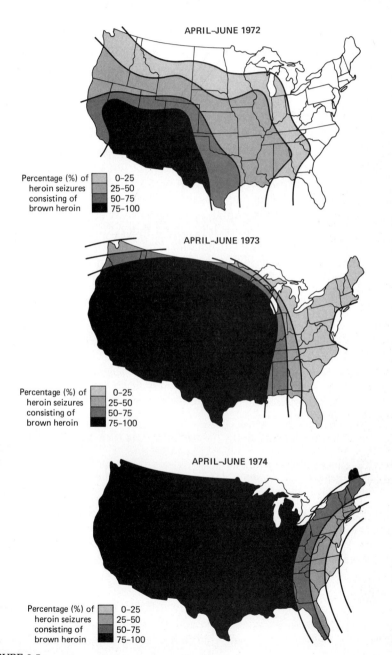

FIGURE 2-5
As European heroin became harder to obtain, the void in the
United States was filled by the smuggling of Mexican brown he-
roin (Mexican Mud).

authorities face in keeping Mexican heroin from entering this country. During the last few years cooperation between officials of this country and those of Mexico has increased dramatically. But nevertheless "Mud" continues to pour in.

LOOKING AHEAD

Our past history can, if nothing else, teach us one valuable lesson: There are no easy answers to the drug problem. During the half a century or so since the Harrison Act was passed, we have tried a number of different approaches to controlling drug abuse. None of them have been particularly successful. And, at the present time, the indications are that no single strategy will be completely successful in eradicating narcotics abuse from our soil. However, it is hoped that continued constant vigilance by law enforcement authorities, the medical profession, legislators, and aroused and aware citizens can make an impact on the drug problem and can lead to its reduction to at least manageable proportions.

NOTES

[1]Strategy Council on Drug Abuse, *Federal Strategy for Drug Abuse and Drug Traffic Prevention, 1975* (Washington, D.C.: GPO, 1975), p. 15.

[2]Louis S. Goodman and Alfred Gilman (eds.), *Pharmacological Basis of Therapeutics* (New York: Macmillan, 1970), p. 243; David E. Smith and George R. Gay, *It's So Good, Don't Even Try It Once* (Englewood Cliffs, N.J.: Prentice-Hall, 1972), pp. 51–53.

[3]Strategy Council on Drug Abuse, p. 17.

[4]Geoffrey Marks and William Beatly, *The Medical Garden* (New York: Scribner, 1971), p. 26.

[5]David E. Smith and George R. Gay, p. 56.

[6]Richard C. Schroeder, *The Politics of Drugs: Marijuana to Mainlining* (Washington, D.C.: Congressional Quarterly Inc., 1976), p. 96.

[7]Horton Heath, Jr. (ed), *Drug Enforcement*, vol. 1, no. 1, U.S. Department of Justice, Drug Enforcement Administration, 1975.

[8]Domestic Council Drug Abuse Task Force, *White Paper on Drug Abuse* (Washington, D.C.: GPO, 1975).

[9]Domestic Council Drug Abuse Task Force, p. 16.

[10]Strategy Council on Drug Abuse, p. 11.

[11]Domestic Council Drug Abuse Task Force, p. 68.

[12]Domestic Council Drug Abuse Task Force, p. 18.

Chapter 3
HEROIN

Fact Sheet on Heroin

Street names
  H, horse, shit, junk, smack, Mexican Mud, skag
Drug family
  Depressant
Appearance
  Fluffy powder that ranges from white to brown in color
How used
  Injected, smoked, inhaled
Source
  Clandestine labs in Mexico, Europe, and the Far East
Medical uses
  None in this country
Control schedule
  I
Effects
  Euphoria, drowsiness, constricted pupils
Tolerance
  Yes
Physical dependence potential
  High
Psychological dependence potential
  High
Duration of effects
  3 to 6 hours
Overdose
  Slow and shallow breathing, convulsions, coma, possible death

H is for heaven, H is for hell,
H is for heroin. . . .[1]

Heroin is many things to many people. To the peasants who diligently cultivate its source, the delicately beautiful opium poppy, it is a livelihood. To the traffickers who manufacture and peddle it, it is the foundation upon which an extraordinarily profitable business empire is based. To the addict enslaved by it, it is a diabolical combination of agony and ecstasy. To those in the field of criminal justice, it is the most dangerous substance on the face of the earth.

In this country, heroin (or as it is called technically, diacetylmorphine) is usually found in the form of a crystalline powder that ranges in color from white to dark brown. It has a distinctly bitter taste and is soluble in water. Mexican brown heroin often possesses a strong, vinegarlike odor that is produced by the acetic acid that is used in its manufacture. Heroin is several times more powerful than its close relative, morphine.

On the street heroin is known by such slang names as "horse," "smack," "shit," "junk," and "Mexican Mud." Small quantities are usually packed in glassine envelopes, gelatin capsules, folded paper, or aluminum foil packages (Figure 3-1). Larger quantities may be packaged in balloons, contraceptives, rubber finger cots, or polyethylene bags.

At one time heroin was used in this country as a powerful painkiller. Its manufacture and use in medicine is now prohibited by law.

HOW USED

Heroin can be inhaled, smoked, or injected. Inhaling and smoking are common in countries where high-grade heroin is available at a rela-

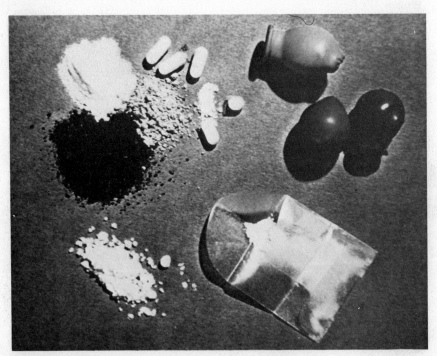

FIGURE 3-1
Heroin is packaged for street sale in a number of ways. Some of the most common are in small rubber balloons, in glassine envelopes, and in gelatin capsules.

tively modest cost. However, in this country, due to its extremely high cost and low purity, heroin is almost always injected. This method of administration assures the user the greatest possible effect from the drug. Novices sometimes inject the drug just under the skin, a practice known on the street as "skin popping." The maximum effect, however, is obtained by mainlining—injecting the heroin directly into a vein.

The usual procedure that addicts employ when mainlining is simple. First, the heroin is dissolved by heating it in a small amount of water. This is usually done in a "cooker" made from some such handy item as a spoon or metal wine bottle cap. A match or lighter provides all the heat needed.

Next, the heroin solution is drawn into some form of syringe through a bit of cotton wool or cloth that filters out some of the larger impurities. Some addicts use standard medical hypodermic needles. Others use spikes fashioned from needles and eyedroppers (Figure 3-2). Then the heroin solution is injected into a vein. A tourniquet fashioned

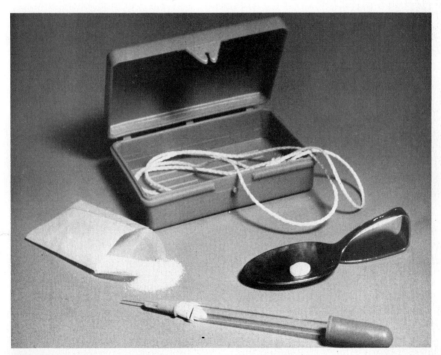

FIGURE 3-2
A typical addict's kit contains some type of syringe, a cooker made from an old spoon or metal bottletop, and something to use as a tourniquet. (Libby Wolfe)

from an item such as an old stocking, a belt, or a bit of string is often used by addicts to make their veins pop out. This makes them more accessible for injection. Though veins in the arms, hands, and elbows are most often favored (Figure 3-3), addicts will, especially if they wish to conceal their drug habit, also select less obvious veins such as those in their legs, ankles, between their toes, in their penises, and at the base of their tongues.

EFFECTS

As is true for all drugs, the effects of heroin vary from person to person. Such factors as the user's experience with drugs, age, health, mental condition, expectations, the setting in which it is taken, its purity, and adulterants used to dilute it may all influence the drug's effects. However, though individual variations are frequent, the following sequence is fairly well representative of a typical heroin experience:

The rush: Moments after the heroin is mainlined, the user will (if he or she has not developed too great a tolerance to the drug's effects) experience a "rush" or "flash" as the nervous system reacts violently to the drug's presence. Addicts describe the rush as an extraordinarily pleasurable sensation—one that is similar in many ways to a sexual orgasm, only much more intense and involving the entire body. This initial rush lasts only briefly.

The nods: Next, the user experiences a lingering state of euphoric bliss. Fatigue, tension, and anxiety fade away. Feelings of inadequacy and inferiority are replaced by a relaxed contentment. The user becomes disassociated from his or her surroundings—no matter how depressing they may be in reality. During this period the user will frequently give the appearance of being in a languid stupor—hence the slang phrase, "on the nods."

In addition to the mood-altering changes for which it is noted, heroin also produces a wide range of other effects. For example, it constricts the pupils, causes constipation, depresses the respiration rate and depth. In addition, heroin addicts of both sexes frequently experience a depressed sexual drive; in the case of female users, menstrual periods may cease.

Heroin readily crosses the placental barrier. Consequently, it can produce physical dependence in the fetus of a pregnant user. Soon after birth the newborn infant will require treatment; otherwise it will suffer withdrawal symptoms.[2] Though the condition is not difficult to treat, it can prove fatal if the proper corrective measures are not started immediately.

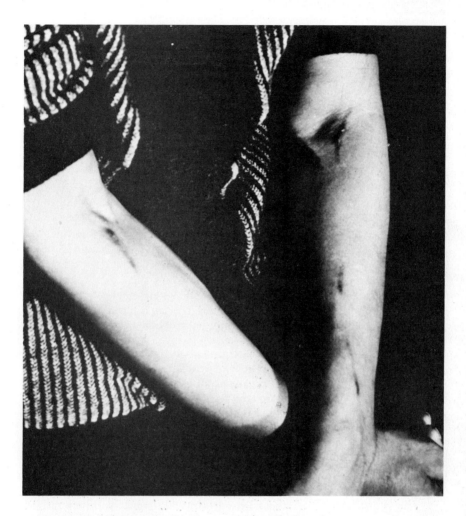

Addicts' veins are often covered with scar tissue, or "tracks," that are caused by repeated injections in the same place.

Tolerance, Dependence, and Withdrawal

Heroin is one of the most seductive drugs known. Its ability to enslave those who use it is legendary. The body quickly builds a tolerance to many of its pleasurable effects and both psychological and physical dependence develop rapidly. The results are, in all too many cases, an intense addiction which becomes the governing force in the user's life.

As tolerance to heroin mounts, the nature of the addict's relationship to the drug undergoes a distinct change. The quest for pleasure changes to a flight from pain. In the beginning, heroin produces intensely pleasurable sensations. However, as the addict continues to use the drug and tolerance increases, this changes. Each time the drug is used, the pleasure is less. Soon the rush is muted, the euphoria dulled to lethargy. But by now the user is firmly within the grasp of a physical dependence upon the drug. Unless the drug can be procured, unless the addict can "shoot up" every few hours, withdrawal is sure to set in. At this stage heroin is no longer being used to provide gratification. Instead, it is being used to ward off the agonies that are sure to follow if the addict stops.

The severity and nature of the withdrawal symptoms that a sudden stop in heroin use brings on vary considerably according to the makeup of the addict and the severity of his or her habit. However, the following account is fairly typical. It was given by a young female addict who died of an overdose several weeks later.

> I started to get sick, quick, real quick. At first I just retched a lot; then I started to vomit. I had such bad stomach cramps that I couldn't stop vomiting. Soon I didn't have anything left to vomit, but the dry heaves kept on. By that time I was all cramped up and I had the cold sweats. I cried and I screamed a lot, but that didn't do no good. Nobody gave a good God damn. My eyes were running—so was my nose. I had awful gas and then I got terrible diarrhea. I crapped all over myself all the time, but I couldn't help that. All of a sudden I'd get real hot, then real cold. My body was covered with goose bumps. I couldn't sleep, and I'd just lay there and I couldn't think. It was like hammering inside my head. I was dizzy, and I ached all over. My legs cramped up, but whenever I tried to move, I'd hurt even more. I would have given anything in the world for some shit. I would have given you my soul for a nickle bag. '

The symptoms associated with withdrawal usually follow a rather predictable timetable[3]:

1. Symptoms become increasing severe for the first twenty-four or thirty-six hours after the last use of the drug.
2. They then begin to decrease in severity and within seventy-two hours they will have subsided to a large degree.
3. Within seven to ten days the major symptoms of withdrawal will almost all have disappeared. However, minor symptoms such as nervousness, anxiety, instability, and insomnia may last for anywhere from several months to a year. It is not unusual for addicts to experience a periodic craving for narcotics years after they last used them.

EXTENT AND PATTERNS OF ABUSE

It is impossible to know with any degree of certainty the number of heroin users in the United States. The most carefully worked out estimates are exactly that—estimates. Since it is obviously impossible in a society as large and complex as ours to identify each and every heroin user, every attempt to estimate the prevalence of heroin abuse must be viewed as at best an uncertain approximation. The following figures on heroin abuse should be viewed with these comments in mind.

In the *White Paper on Drug Abuse* the Domestic Council Drug Abuse Task Force estimates that currently there are "several hundred thousand daily chronic [heroin] users not currently in treatment."[4]

The same report also goes on to estimate that there exists in this country a heroin "core problem" composed of 400,000 compulsive heroin users who are currently suffering (or causing others to suffer) adverse consequences from the drug.[5]

Another federal study estimates that the number of heroin addicts in this country ranges anywhere from 250,000 to 600,000.[6]

In a recent survey on drug-abuse patterns in this country, 1.3 percent of the adults and 1.0 percent of the youths questioned admitted that they had used heroin at least once. However, only 0.1 percent of the adults and a still smaller percentage of the youths said that they had used the drug during the month prior to the interview.[7]

An analysis of DAWN III figures shows that heroin is the third most frequently mentioned drug, being exceeded only by diazepam (such as Valium) and the alcohol-in-combination category.[8]

Use with Other Drugs

Heroin addicts frequently use other drugs as well. As one middle-aged mainliner has said, "Man, I use anything I can get my hands on. Smack is my thing, but if I can't cop it, I take whatever I can get. One thing I ain't, is particular."

Barbiturates and other sedatives are used to enhance the effect of heroin that has been overly "cut" (adulterated) and as a substitute when it is not available. Addicts who are attempting to "dry out" from heroin also use barbiturates to ease withdrawal symptoms.

Cocaine and heroin are sometimes taken together in a combination known as a "speedball." Cocaine is said to heighten heroin's rush, and heroin is supposed to reduce the unpleasant side effects sometimes associated with cocaine use.

Amphetamines are used by some addicts to prevent themselves from slipping too deeply into the nods and to give them energy to find their next "fix."

Other opiates, such as methadone, are substituted for heroin when it is not available. They are also used to reduce withdrawal symptoms.

An interesting profile of secondary drug-abuse patterns among heroin users is provided by John Langrod of Columbia University. In a study of 422 institutionalized male heroin users he found the following secondary drug-use pattern:

Drugs Used	Percent Using Drug More Than 6 Times	Percent Using Drug 6 times or Less	Total Percent Ever Using Drug
Marijuana	86	6	92
Cocaine	47	19	66
Hashish	44	14	58
Barbiturates	34	11	45
Amphetamines ("bombitas")	33	10	43
Methadone ("dollies")	26	11	37
Morphine	16	11	27
Methedrine ("speed")	16	10	26
Airplane glue	14	8	22
LSD	11	8	19
Opium	8	10	18
Demerol	9	8	17

SOURCE: John Langrod, "Secondary Drug Use among Heroin Users," *The International Journal of Addictions*, vol. 5, no. 4, pp. 611–635, December 1970.

Recognizing the Abuser

Is there any way of recognizing a heroin abuser on the street? This question is frequently asked by those just entering the fields of narcotics enforcement and treatment. The answer, unfortunately, is no. Short of laboratory tests, there is no positive way of telling whether or not an individual is using heroin or any other narcotic. However, there are a number of signs that may indicate heroin abuse. These include:

1. Constricted or "pinned" pupils of the eyes that fail to respond when a light is shone into them.
2. Scars (tracks) or discolorations over the veins caused by repeated intravenous injections.
3. Abscesses caused by infected needles.
4. Stuporous, lethargic behavior (the nods).
5. A generally rundown physical appearance. Heroin abusers frequently ignore their personal hygiene and nutritional needs.

RECOGNIZING
THE ABUSER: HEROIN

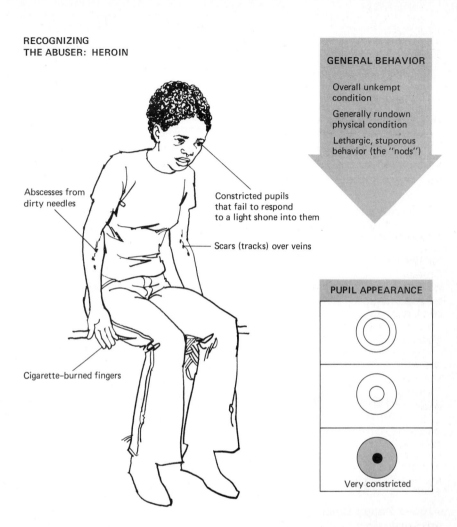

GENERAL BEHAVIOR

Overall unkempt
condition

Generally rundown
physical condition

Lethargic, stuporous
behavior (the "nods")

Abscesses from
dirty needles

Constricted pupils
that fail to respond
to a light shone into them

Scars (tracks) over veins

Cigarette–burned fingers

PUPIL APPEARANCE

Very constricted

PARAPHERNALIA

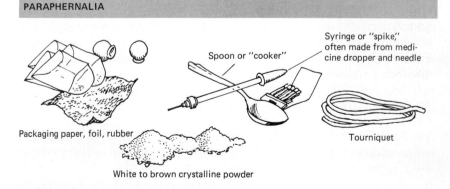

Syringe or "spike,"
often made from medi-
cine dropper and needle

Spoon or "cooker"

Packaging paper, foil, rubber

Tourniquet

White to brown crystalline powder

FIGURE 3-4
Common signs of heroin abuse.

6. Cigarette-burned fingers. Abusers are frequently in a semicomatose condition during which they suffer from a diminished perception of pain.
7. Early signs of withdrawal such as a runny nose, sweating, and anxiety.
8. The presence of narcotics paraphernalia such as needles, syringes, cookers, strings or cords that are used as tourniquets, and capsules, envelopes, or paper or foil packages with traces of white powder.

HEROIN PRODUCTION

> You know, it's kind of hard to believe that such a pretty little plant can screw up so many millions of people.[9]

Though the details vary from country to country, the basics of heroin production remain essentially the same the world over (Figure 3-5). Fundamentally, the process includes:

1. Cultivation of the opium poppy and collection of raw opium from its unripe seedpods
2. The conversion of the opium to more concentrated morphine "base"
3. The acetylation of the morphine base into heroin

Opium Poppy Cultivation

The opium poppy, *Papaver somniferum*, is a showy, annual plant that is or has been grown over almost all of the world from latitudes 56° N to the equator. It can be cultivated in almost any soil and at any altitude at which normal food crops are grown. Healthy plants can reach a height of 3 to 4 feet (Figure 3-6). The flowers are large, some of them reaching a diameter of 4 to 5 inches. They range in color from a pure white to a deep, rich red or purple. Under favorable growing conditions an acre will support from 40,000 to 60,000 plants and yield enough opium to make about 1 kilogram of heroin.

Poppy seeds are usually sown in the late spring after the ground has warmed. Opium can be harvested 90 to 120 days later. In some areas, such as Mexico, farmers are able to harvest two or three crops a year.

A few days after the last petals have fallen from the flowers, the backbreaking business of collecting the opium begins. First the unripe seedpods are carefully slit with a special knife to a depth of several

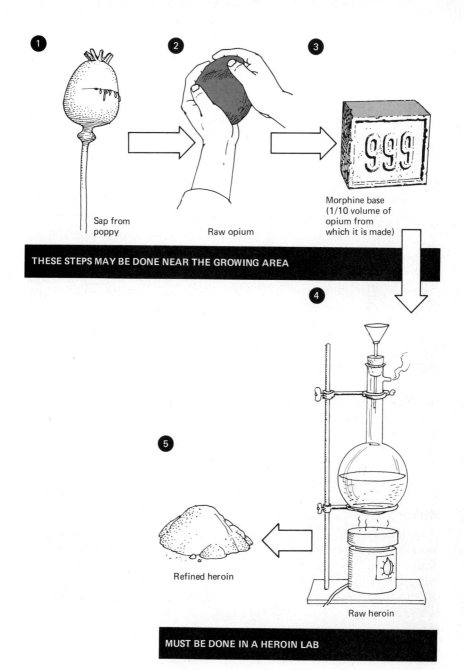

THESE STEPS MAY BE DONE NEAR THE GROWING AREA

Sap from poppy

Raw opium

Morphine base (1/10 volume of opium from which it is made)

Refined heroin

Raw heroin

MUST BE DONE IN A HEROIN LAB

FIGURE 3-5
The basic steps in heroin production are the same the world over: (1) Sap from the opium poppy seed-pod is collected. (2) It dries into raw opium. The raw opium is dissolved in water, and (3) the morphine base is collected. This is treated with various chemicals to yield (4) raw heroin, which is washed and further purified to yield (5) refined heroin.

FIGURE 3-6
The opium poppy provides the raw material for the world's heroin
supply. *(U.S. Department of Agriculture)*

millimeters. This is usually done in the late afternoon or early evening.
During the night the milky white sap or, as it is technically called,
latex, oozes out onto the surface of the pod, where it congeals into a
brown, sticky substance with a consistency similar to that of wet clay.
This sticky mass is raw opium. In the morning, the workers return to

the fields and gently scrape the opium from the poppy pods with a blunt knife.

Opium harvesting is tedious, backbreaking, and time-consuming labor. An acre of poppies can be expected to yield about 10 kilos of opium. On the average it takes a worker 40 hours or more to collect each pound. For their labors farmers can expect to receive, depending on the state of the world market, somewhere between $25 and $100 per kilo.[10]

At the present time eight countires—Bulgaria, India, Iran, Japan, Pakistan, Turkey, the U.S.S.R., and Yugoslavia—produce almost all of the world's supply of licit opium. India is by far the largest producer. In 1972 India recorded a harvest of just under 1,000,000 kilograms. This was followed by Iran and the U.S.S.R., which reported almost 400 and just over 100,000 kilograms, respectively. These figures can be presumed to be quite accurate as producer nations are required by treaty to submit production data to the United Nations.

Almost all of the world's licit opium supply is used to produce pharmaceutical products such as morphine and codeine. The fact remains that though we are able to triumph technologically to such a degree that we can put people on the moon, we still cannot synthetically produce a pain-killer that is as effective and free from unwanted side effects as the products of the opium poppy.

For the past several years the world's pharmaceutical needs have outstripped opium production. Poor weather conditions and other factors combined to have a devastating effect on the 1973 poppy crop in the U.S.S.R. and India. Because of this shortfall, the United States government had to release over 200 metric tons of its emergency stockpile of opium and morphine to American pharmaceutical firms. Without this action it is likely that production of opiate-based pain-killers would have ground to a halt.

Data from Congressional testimony by John Bartels, then Director of the Drug Enforcement Administration, gives an overview of the scope and what happens to the world's opium production.[11] This testimony also points up the almost limitless supplies of opium available to the world's drug traffickers.

THAILAND.

An estimated 150 to 200 tons of opium comes from the Thailand border provinces of Chiang Mai, Chiang Rai, Mae Hong Son, and Nan. Processed opium, in the form of smoking opium, is consumed in Southeast Asia, although some of it is now finding its way to Europe and the United States. Number four injectable heroin is sent to European and American markets. Number three smoking heroin ("red rock") is appearing in increasing quantities in Europe and North America, used principally by local Chinese populations.

PEOPLE'S REPUBLIC OF CHINA.

The P.R.C. produces about 100 tons of opium legally each year, apparently under very strict controls. None of the allegations of widespread international trafficking of P.R.C.-originated opium could be substantiated, although minor amounts may be smuggled across the border into adjacent areas of Laos and Burma.

HONG KONG.

Hong Kong is a major transit point for all opiates. Laboratories there tend to specialize in smoking heroin, but some injectable is also produced.

SOUTH KOREA.

A small amount of illicit opium is produced in South Korea. Most of the opium is probably used by South Korean addicts.

MEXICO.

Total production is estimated at between 5 and 15 tons. Although there is evidence of growing heroin abuse in Mexico, it is believed that nearly all Mexican heroin finds its way into the United States.

AFGHANISTAN.

Estimates of opium production in Afghanistan, all of which is illicit, vary. The best estimates are between 100 and 200 tons.

IRAN.

Since the reintroduction of legal opium production in Iran in 1969, production, which is carried out under very strict supervision, has varied between 8 and 217 tons. All this is produced for distribution to Iranian addicts and there is no evidence of significant diversion.

PAKISTAN.

Twelve tons of opium were produced legally in Pakistan in 1973, but a much larger and undetermined amount was produced in tribal areas outside the government's control. Estimates of this range from 32 to 170 tons, with the higher figure probably being more accurate. Destinations for some recent narcotics shipments originating in Karachi were reported to be Europe, Hong Kong, and the United States. Although most of these "narcotics" were probably hashish, some opium may well have been included.

TURKEY.

There was no licit opium production in Turkey in the 1974 crop year. Some minor illicit production may have occurred in a region about 100 miles northeast of Ankara. During the period of the ban (July 1972 to July 1974) both opium and morphine base continued to flow into illicit international channels from Turkey. Opium shipments, mostly to Egypt, sometimes amounted to more than 1 ton. Both the opium and the morphine base shipments derived from illegal opium stockpiles accumulated over many years before the imposition of the 1972 ban.

With the resumption of legal production beginning with the summer of 1975 harvest, an increase in both illegal opium and morphine base (all of which is illegal) shipments can be expected, drawn mainly from illegal stockpiles rather than current production. This could amount to 25 to 35 opium tons equivalent yearly over the next several years.

INDIA.
Announced production for the current crop is 1,050 tons. No illicit production is reported. As much as 100 tons of Indian licit opium production may be diverted into illicit trade, with most of it being consumed locally.

BURMA.
Between 350 and 400 tons of opium are produced in Burma's Shan and Kachin states. A substantial part of this opium is consumed locally; this varies with the export price that can be obtained at the time the opium is available. Local consumption is in the form of raw opium, which also makes up the greater part of the opium exported. About 6 tons of opium are produced in the Chin state of Burma. Bost of this is sold to traders from India and Bangladesh.

ECUADOR.
An undetermined amount of opium is grown illegally in Ecuador and converted into heroin there. Available information is insufficient to support an estimate of either opium or heroin production. No information is available on where either is consumed.

PERU.
Opium fields have been seen in Peru, but there is no information available on production figures or on the destination of any opium or heroin produced there.

YUGOSLAVIA.
As a signatory to the 1974 pact, Yugoslavia is entitled to produce 100 tons of opium. Actual production varies between 3 and 4 tons yearly. There is no evidence of illicit production or significant diversion of legally produced opium.

Morphine Base
The next step in the heroin manufacturing process is the conversion of the raw opium gum into the more concentrated morphine base (Figure

3-7). This is a relatively simple process that requires little in the way of special skills or equipment.

First, a vat of water is heated. Any relatively large container will serve. Old oil drums, discarded bathtubs, and galvanized buckets have all been used. Next, the raw opium is added, and the solution is stirred until all the opium is completely dissolved. Then, ordinary lime, such as that used in farming, is added. It causes most of the impurities present with the raw opium to settle to the bottom of the container while the morphine stays dissolved in the solution.

This morphine-rich solution is then filtered and heated for a second time. Ammonia is then added, and this causes the morphine to precipitate out. It is then collected by filtration and dried. When dried, the base usually constitutes about 10 percent of the volume of the opium from which it was extracted. Obviously, this reduced volume is helpful to the drug traffickers who must smuggle it to clandestine laboratories where it will be converted to heroin.

FIGURE 3-7
Raw opium is converted to the more concentrated morphine base, shown here.

Heroin Laboratories

The conversion of base to heroin is a good deal more complex than the previous steps. The labors of skilled underground chemists are required if the process is to be completed without either blowing the laboratory to bits or ruining the batch of morphine base being processed (Figure 3-8).

In summary, the procedure is as follows. Equal quantities of morphine base and acetic anhydride are heated together for several hours. The reaction that results produces an impure form of heroin. Next, this crude heroin is washed with both water and chloroform. This step removes a number of the impurities from it. Then sodium carbonate is added. This causes particles of heroin to precipitate out of the solution. These are filtered out and purified in a solution of alcohol and activated charcoal. This is then purified by the use of alcohol, ether, and hydrochloric acid, and the resulting high-grade heroin is collected by filtration.

Underground chemists lead lives that are both profitable and dangerous. The acids and other active chemicals with which they work

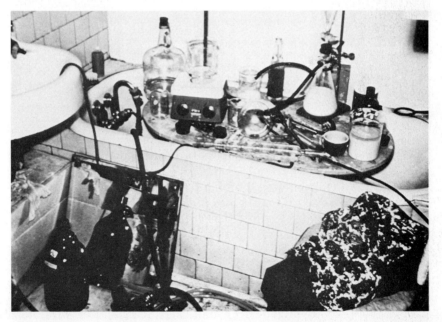

FIGURE 3-8
Even relatively simple heroin laboratories, such as this French one, are capable of producing millions of dollars worth of the drug. (Drug Enforcement Administration)

exact an awful toll upon their skin, lungs, and other vital organs. The danger of explosion is ever present. One wrong move and the whole operation will, quite literally, "go through the roof." To this must be added the risks of arrest and imprisonment as well as the general specter of violence which is such a part of the narcotics trafficking scene.

Offsetting these risks, however, are the enormous profits that are to be made. Joseph Cesari was, until his recent capture by French authorities and subsequent suicide, one of the most famous heroin chemists. He was reputed to be the dean of the several dozen underground lab operators who plied their trade around Marseilles. Cesari was under contract to the lords of the French-Corsican underworld. But, because of the dangers involved, he, like most heroin chemists, only worked four or five times a year. When he did work, however, his output was prodigious. He was known to have produced as much as 17 kilos of pure heroin within a two- or three-day period. For his services he was paid well in excess of $100,000 per year.[12]

INTERNATIONAL HEROIN TRAFFICKING PATTERNS

The heroin that ends up in the veins of America's addicts comes from three main sources (Figure 3-9):

1. The Turkish-French Connection
2. The "Golden Triangle" of Southeast Asia
3. Mexico

Before we look at each of these sources in detail, one important point should be noted. It takes very little heroin to meet the demands of America's addicts. All the drug needed to supply every addict in this country for an entire year could easily be transported in a single medium-sized airplane. Experts at the Drug Enforcement Administration calculate that the average addict needs approximately 50 milligrams of heroin a day to support his or her habit. So, depending on the purity of the drug and the number of addicts in this country (estimated at somewhere between 250,000 and 600,000), it only takes somewhere between 3 and 12 tons of heroin to supply America's addicts for a year.

The implications of this are staggering. In order to successfully stop the flow of heroin into this country, authorities are faced with the problem of preventing a large group of determined, experienced, and in many cases, very intelligent drug traffickers with almost unlimited financing behind them from slipping a relatively small amount of easily concealable powder across our borders—borders that altogether are over 96,000 miles long and crossed by millions of travelers and hun-

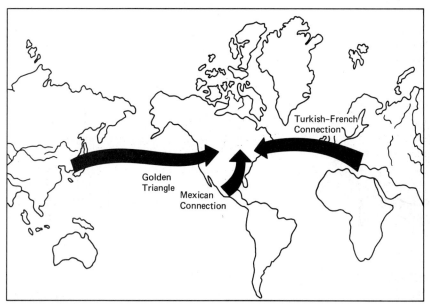

FIGURE 3-9
The heroin used in this country comes from three major sources:
Mexico, the Golden Triangle area of Southeast Asia, and the
Turkish-French Connection.

dreds of millions of pounds of cargo each year. When viewed in the
light of these facts and figures, the scope of the problem that authorities
face becomes only too apparent.

Turkish-French Connection

For many years opium poppies grown in the desolate, windswept
Anatolian Plateau of central and western Turkey were the source of
most of the heroin smuggled into the United States. Each year Turkish
peasants held back a portion of their opium crop from the official government marketing system to sell, at a far better price, to illicit drug
traffickers. The traffickers in turn smuggled it across the border into
Syria, where it was converted into the less bulky and more easily concealed morphine base. The base was then smuggled either by sea or
across Europe to one of the many heroin laboratories located in southern France.

For many years drug traffickers preferred to use the sea route. The
base could be easily hidden aboard one of the hundreds of vessels that
regularly ply the waters between such ports as Istanbul or Beirut and
Marseilles. Later, many of the traffickers switched to the overland route

from the Middle East to Europe. One of their favorite tactics was to conceal morphine base in the thousands of TIR trucks that carry meat, produce, and other products from Turkey and neighboring countries such as Lebanon and Syria to northern Europe. These transcontinental trucks were designed to expedite the flow of international traffic; they are examined and sealed by customs officers at their origin and then allowed to pass over subsequent borders without any additional inspection. Obviously, with such a system, it was a relatively simple matter to conceal a few kilograms of morphine base among tons of legitimate cargo.

Once the base was converted into heroin, a variety of routes were used to smuggle it into the United States. Some was sent directly from France. A favorite technique was to conceal it in automobiles that were being shipped here. Other routes led from Europe to Canada and then to the United States. Still other traffickers preferred to route the drug by way of Mexico or other Latin American countries such as Brazil and Panama.

During the early 1970s a series of events combined to effectively smash the Turkish-French Connection. Intense international enforcement efforts resulted in the jailing of a large number of important French and Corsican drug traffickers. Key drug figures throughout Europe, Latin America, and in this country were successfully put out of business. At the same time intense diplomatic pressure was brought to bear on the Turkish government. As a result, in 1972 Turkey finally banned all cultivation of the opium poppy. This ban had the effect of drying up illicit opium supplies. As a result, the Turkish-French Connection share of America's heroin market dropped dramatically. In the mid-1960s federal authorities estimated that Marseilles laboratories supplied about 80 percent of the heroin available on the streets of America. By 1975 this had slipped to a mere 10 percent.

In July 1974 the Turkish government announced the resumption of opium poppy cultivation. It stressed, however, that the renewed cultivation would be carried out under the most stringent government controls. Diversion of any opium from government marketing channels into the black market would not be tolerated. This announcement was greeted with much skepticism by United States officials, many of whom were all too familiar with the ineffectiveness of past Turkish government control efforts. However, current evidence indicates that Turkish efforts have, indeed, been successful in preventing the diversion of any appreciable quantities of opium into the black market.

The key to this success is the adoption by the Turkish government of the poppy straw method of opiate extraction. In this process the entire poppy seedpod and part of the stem is sent intact to a processing plant. There the morphine and other desired alkaloids are chemically extracted. In addition to adopting the straw process, the Turkish government also took exceedingly strong measures to see that peasants did not try to bypass the control system by collecting opium before the poppy straw was harvested.

Golden Triangle

This area, which includes the wild, mountainous regions of eastern Burma and Northern Laos, and Thailand, is the world's largest producer of illicit opium. It is estimated that somewhere between 600 and 750 tons of illicit opium are produced by tribes inhabiting this region each year. This enormous production does not, however, have much of an impact on the American heroin market. Much of the opium is used medicinally by the native hill tribes who grow it. The rest is converted into so-called popular Asian number three or smoking heroin.

It is thought that opium growing was introduced into the area by Chinese who fled their homeland in the nineteenth century to avoid political persecution by rival factions. During the colonial period opium growing was encouraged by the Europeans as an important source of revenue.

The particulars of Asian heroin production and trafficking are not as well understood as their European or Mexican counterparts. Limited Western contact with the area, its remote nature, and the fact that much of it is under the control of insurgent factions combine to make fact finding difficult at the least. However, the following overview gives some idea of the situation.

Today opium production throughout most of the Golden Triangle area seems to be under the control of the Kuomintang. This group, numbering several thousand, is essentially a private army made up of remnants of Chiang Kai-shek's Nationalist Chinese Army who fled into the area to escape the victorious Communist forces in the late 1940s. The Kuomintang support and arm themselves with the profits that they make from the opium trade. Their primary role is to collect the opium from the hill tribes who harvest it and then transport it under heavy guard to market.

During the early spring great caravans laden with tons of raw opium and escorted by hundreds of heavily armed Kuomintang guards wind their way down the tortuous mountain trails that lead from the opium-producing highlands to the plains below. This is the first step in a journey that will finally end in one of the many heroin labs located in and around such cities as Bangkok and Hong Kong. There the opium will be converted into either the granular number three smoking heroin that is the mainstay of the Asian trade or the more refined number four or white heroin that is in demand in this country and Europe.

The manufacture and distribution of Asian heroin is managed and controlled by the Chiu Chou. These tightly run Chinese crime syndicates have had their hand in every known vice and criminal activity since the early 1800s. They arrange for the purchase of the raw opium from the hill tribes, oversee its conversion into heroin, and set up the international smuggling network that moves it from country to country.

The war in Vietnam facilitated the establishment of major Asian drug smuggling connections. To some extent we still feel the effect of these today. A relatively small but steady stream of heroin from Southeast Asia still enters this country. Some comes by way of Europe with Brussels and Amsterdam favorite transshipment points; other shipments enter directly or via Canada, particularly through the city of Vancouver.

A thorny issue in the Southeast Asian heroin picture is to what extent drug traffickers in the area were and are aided by various agencies of the United States government. It has been charged that such agencies as the Central Intelligence Agency, the State Department, and the military establishment have been, at times, a party to the Southeast Asian drug trade. At the least, the accusers charge, the government looked the other way when it became obvious that high-ranking officials in friendly Asian governments were deeply involved in heroin trafficking. At worst, it is charged, the government actively supported these drug trafficking activities by providing aid such as helicopters and aircraft to transport the drugs and armed protection for drug trafficking operations. Needless to say, all the government agencies mentioned have hotly denied the accusations.

Mexican Connection

During the past few years Mexico has rapidly become the main source of the heroin found in this country. In 1971 it was estimated that less than 10 percent of the heroin used by America's addicts originated in Mexico. The Drug Enforcement Administration now believes that Mexico dominates the United States market, providing 90 percent of the heroin available.

To a large extent the dominance of Mexican brown heroin can be explained in simple terms of supply and demand. During the early 1970s when the French Connection was shattered and the Turkish ban on poppy growing was imposed, America was left with a core problem of at least 250,000 active heroin addicts. Some of the luckier addicts entered treatment programs and were able to kick their habit. Others switched to more available drugs. But for many addicts, perhaps hundreds of thousands of them, there was no escape from the slavery of addiction. Their dependence was too great, their cravings too all-consuming.

The situation was not lost on the lords of the drug trade. Profits of the magnitude that heroin represented were not to be dismissed lightly. Other major heroin sources were needed and needed quickly. That is when Mexico entered the picture on a large scale.

For years the opium poppy had been cultivated on a small scale in Mexico. Some of the Chinese who came to the United States in the second half of the nineteenth century to work in the mines and on the railroads eventually made their way to Mexico. They carried with them the custom of opium smoking and their knowledge of poppy cultivation. Before long a small but thriving opium trade whose principal business consisted in satisfying the needs of the Chinese was established. During World War II, when European drug supplies were cut off by Hitler's submarines, the Mexican opium merchants sensed new profits and branched out into heroin. After World War II, most addicts quickly reverted to the superior and now freely available European white heroin. However, the Mexican Connection continued to operate on a small scale, especially in areas close to the United States–Mexican border.

Mexico's role as a major transshipment point for European heroin bound for the United States also helped to lay the groundwork for the rapid expansion of its heroin-producing capacity. For years large quantities of the heroin that originated in the laboratories of Marseilles were shipped into this country by way of Mexico. Many drug traffickers thought it safer to try to smuggle it in by this route rather than directly from Europe. Thus, by the time the demand for Mexican heroin exploded, well-established drug smuggling organizations with strong ties to our underworld were already operating.

The brisk trade in Mexican marijuana also contributed to the speed with which Mexican heroin became widely available in this country. Since the early 1960s the Mexican marijuana trade expanded from a trickle to a multimillion-dollar torrent. By the time the Turks banned the poppy, literally thousands of smugglers were engaged in the highly profitable business of smuggling tons of "grass" across the border from Mexico. These smugglers ranged from small, part-time, one-person operations to sophisticated multimillion-dollar concerns outfitted with the latest aircraft and vessels. As the demand for Mexican heroin grew, many marijuana smugglers made the obvious move of adding it to their "product line."

The nature of the countryside also was a factor in the rapid expansion of the Mexican heroin industry. Heroin production is centered in the wild and remote Sinaloa and Durango states. The poppies are grown in small plots among the peaks and valleys of the rugged Sierra Madre mountains. There are few trails and even fewer roads in this region. On-the-ground travel through the densely wooded hills is by foot or mule. Obviously, terrain as difficult as this puts severe limits on the effectiveness of any enforcement activity. It is exceedingly difficult to spot the small fields in which opium poppies are grown. And, once they are located, about the only way to reach most of them is by helicopter.

Political unrest in Mexico also was a factor in the expansion of the heroin trade. Much of the countryside where the opium poppy is grown is frequented by, and to some extent is under the control of, insurgent groups. These rebels, like their counterparts in the Golden Triangle of Southeast Asia, regard the products of the opium poppy as a source of legitimate money and weapons.

Today Mexico is the primary target of the United States war on heroin. Close cooperation has been established between Mexican and U.S. authorities. In October 1972 the former Director of the Drug Enforcement Administration, John Bartels, met with the Attorney General of Mexico, Pedro Ojeda-Paullada, and other ranking officials. As a result of this and other high-level exchanges, a policy of mutual assistance in drug enforcement was forged. As the Mexican government increased its efforts against drug traffickers, the United States did everything it could to be of assistance. Technical advisers were sent to work with Mexican enforcement officials. The border between the two countries was "hardened" through increased patrol and the installation of electronic sensing devices designed to spot would-be smugglers. Equipment such as light aircraft, jeeps, helicopters, and communications gear was provided to Mexican authorities for use in their antiheroin efforts.

It is too early to evaluate the real impact of these efforts. Though it is true that major strides have been made—for example, over 6,000 opium poppy fields have been destroyed—Mexican heroin is still freely available on the streets of America. Only time will tell if the intense battle that is being waged by both governments will be successful in smashing the Mexican Connection.

DISTRIBUTION SYSTEM

Once heroin arrives in the United States, it flows into a multilayered, extremely profitable illegal distribution and marketing system. At the top of this system are the major drug importers upon whose orders large shipments of heroin cross our borders. At the bottom are the street dealers, many of whom are themselves addicts. In between are various levels of wholesalers, jobbers, and midlevel dealers who characterize any well-organized marketing arrangement. Because of its covert nature and because of continual shifts in the supply and demand patterns this distribution system is difficult to describe with any degree of accuracy. Nevertheless, the following will provide a general overview of how it functions.

The marketing process begins when a major drug dealer in this country arranges with a foreign supplier for a multikilo shipment of heroin. At going prices, the dealer will pay in the vicinity of $20,000 per kilo for heroin that is bought in bulk—say 50 or 100 kilos at a time. After the heroin enters this country, it will change hands several times in its pure form. (Today this ranges from 75 percent to 100 percent pure, depending upon its source.) By the time the individual wholesalers take delivery of their portion of the shipment, the price will have increased to about $40,000 per kilo.

Depending upon their level in the system and the customers to whom they intend to resell the heroin, the wholesalers will now dilute the drug to 25 to 50 percent purity. A wide variety of substances are used for this dilution. Three of the most common are quinine, mannite, and lactose. Quinine is said to heighten the rush that the addict feels when the drug first enters the veins. Mannite, a mild laxative widely used in Europe, inflates the volume of the adulterated mixture, a procedure called "fluffing." Lactose, a common milk sugar frequently used in baby formulas, gives extra bulk to the mixture.

The cutting process generally is done in heavily guarded "mills" or "factories." These are set up in out-of-the-way places such as isolated motels, hotel rooms, tenements, parking garages, warehouses, lofts, boats, and private homes. The work in these mills is demanding and tedious, and the threat of raids by either the police or rival dealers out to "score a free load" is ever present. But the pay is good. It is not uncommon for mill hands to receive more than $100 a day for their labors.

The procedure used to cut heroin is simple and is usually carried out on an assembly-line basis. The first worker measures out the exact quantities of heroin and adulterants that are to be mixed. The next mixes them together, frequently by passing them through either a common kitchen sieve or a stocking pulled taut over a coat-hanger frame. Another worker uses a measuring spoon to portion out exact doses of the adulterated drug and places them in a package (Figure 3-10).

FIGURE 3-10
Heroin is cut, or diluted, in simple mills such as this one. Common adulterants include lactose, mannite, and quinine.

Heroin is packaged for sale in several different ways. In some areas it is found on the street in small glassine envelopes; in others, in gelatin capsules. In still others, it is put in folded paper or metal foil packs. The individual packages are then bundled together in preparation for distribution to the street dealers.

The cutting process is the key to the enormous profits that are made in heroin. At each rung in the distribution ladder the heroin is diluted and rediluted. By the time it finally reaches the user, it is generally less than 5 percent pure, and as the purity of the drug goes down, the profits made from it go up. By the time the same kilo of heroin for which the importer paid $20,000 finally reaches the street in its diluted form, its worth will have risen to over $1,000,000.

LEGAL CONTROLS

Heroin is included in Schedule I of the Controlled Substances Act of 1970. In addition to a wide range of opiates and opium derivatives this schedule also includes marijuana and such hallucinogens as LSD, peyote, and mescaline. In order to be included in Schedule I it must be shown that:

1. The drug or other substance has a high potential for abuse.
2. The drug or other substance has no currently accepted medical use in treatment in the United States.
3. There is a lack of accepted safety for use of the drug or other substance under medical supervision.

OTHER OPIATES

Methadone

During World War II German doctors were severely hampered in their treatment of the wounded by a lack of morphine. The Allies had cut off their supplies almost completely. In response to this crisis methadone, a synthetic narcotic, was developed. It first became available in this country in 1947, and it is currently marketed under such trademarks as Amidone and Dolophine. On the street methadone goes by such slang names as "meth," "dollies," and "dolls." It is usually found either in tablet form or as a clear, viscous solution.

Methadone can be either injected or taken orally. Though chemically different from morphine and heroin, it has many of the same effects. In medicine it is used as a pain-killer, to reduce the discomforts of narcotic withdrawal, and in the detoxification and maintenance of heroin addicts.

When abused, methadone produces many of the same symptoms as heroin, such as drowsiness, anxiety, impaired coordination, depressed reflexes, constricted pupils, loss of appetite, and constipation. When used medically, methadone rarely produces euphoria. However, the larger doses that are characteristic of abuse are capable of producing pronounced euphoric effects. Methadone abusers develop a tolerance to the drug as well as both physical and psychological dependence upon it. The withdrawal symptoms associated with methadone are generally considered to be less severe than those produced by heroin, and they develop more slowly. However, they frequently are more prolonged. (For a discussion of the use of methadone in the treatment of heroin addicts, see Chapter 16.)

Codeine

When heroin is not available addicts will frequently turn to codeine. In medicine codeine is used as a cough suppressant and a mild pain-reliever. Though it occurs naturally as one of the many alkaloids found in opium, most medicinal codeine is produced synthetically from morphine.

Though codeine is less potent than morphine, addicts can develop a moderate physical and psychological dependence upon codeine. Withdrawal from it produces symptoms that are similar to but considerably less severe than those associated with heroin. Sometimes called "school boy," codeine is found in both tablet and liquid form. It is often combined with other pain-relievers such as Emperin analgesic. It is either taken orally or injected. Some of the more common commercial preparations containing codeine are Robitussin A-C, Cheracol, and Elixir of Terpin Hydrate with codeine.

Meperidine

Introduced in 1939, meperidine was the first of the synthetic narcotics. Though very different chemically from morphine, it is similar in potency. Next to morphine, meperidine is probably the most widely used pain-killer today.

Meperidine is available in both tablets and liquid form. It usually does not produce euphoria; consequently it is not particularly popular among addicts. Most commonly abused by hospital personnel, meperidine is capable of causing mild physical and psychological dependency.

Morphine

First isolated in 1803 by Frederick Sertürner, a young German pharmacist, morphine is one of the natural constituents of raw opium. It is one of the most effective pain-relievers known. There is a high potential for both physical and psychological dependence associated with morphine abuse. Its effects upon the body closely parallel those of heroin.

Morphine is available in solution, powder, or tablets. On the street it is called such names as "M," "dreamer," "white stuff," "unkie," "Miss Emma," "monkey," "morf," "hocus," and "melter." Occasionally bricks of morphine base are smuggled into this country. These are usually 4 by 3 by 1 inch in size and they frequently have a trademark such as the number 999 or a tiger embossed upon the top surface of the brick.

IN CONCLUSION

Narcotic drugs in general and heroin in particular pose the most troublesome drug problem to this country. While stepped-up treatment and enforcement programs have met with a number of outstanding successes, there is little indication that we will truly "turn the corner" on this country's narcotics problem anytime in the near future.

NOTES

[1]Isador Chein et al., *The Road to H* (New York: Basic Books, 1964), p. 26.

[2]National Clearinghouse for Drug Abuse Information, *Neonatal Narcotic Dependence*, U.S. Department of Health, Education, and Welfare Report Series 29, no. 1, p. 1 (Rockville, Md.: The Clearinghouse, 1974).

[3]National Clearinghouse for Drug Abuse Information, *Heroin*, U.S. Department of Health, Education, and Welfare Report Series 33, no. 1, p. 10 (Rockville, Md.: The Clearinghouse, 1975).

[4]Domestic Council Drug Abuse Task Force, *White Paper on Drug Abuse* (Washington, D.C.: GPO, 1975), p. 20.

[5]Domestic Council Drug Abuse Task Force, p. 30.

[6]Strategy Council on Drug Abuse, *Federal Strategy for Drug Abuse and Drug Traffic Prevention 1975* (Washington, D.C.: GPO, 1975), p. 17.

[7]Herbert I. Abelson and Ronald B. Atkinson, *Public Experience with Psychoactive Substances* (Rockville, Md.: National Institute on Drug Abuse, August 1975), pp. 9–10.

[8]Drug Enforcement Administration and National Institute on Drug Abuse, *Drug Abuse Warning Network, Phase III Report* (Washington, D.C.: GPO, 1976), p. 4.

[9]U.S. Narcotics agent standing in a field of opium poppies in Mexico.

[10]Richard C. Schroeder, *The Politics of Drugs: Marijuana to Mainlining* (Washington, D.C.: Congressional Quarterly Inc., 1975), p. 103.

[11]U.S. House of Representatives, Committee on Interstate and Foreign Commerce, *Heroin Trafficking and Addiction Oversight, Hearing before the Subcommittee on Public Health and Environment* (Washington, D.C.: GPO, 1974), p. 16.

[12]Staff and editors of Newsday, *The Heroin Trail* (Long Island, N.Y.: Newsday Inc., 1973), pp. 75–77.

Chapter 4
DEPRESSANTS

Fact Sheet on Barbiturates

Street names
Barbs, reds, yellow jackets, goofballs
Drug family
Depressant
Appearance
Usually brightly colored capsules
How used
Swallowed, injected
Source
Diversion on legitimate stocks, smuggled, overprescribing
Medical uses
Central nervous system depressant; to relieve anxiety, to treat insomnia
Control schedule
II (most commonly abused forms)
Effects
Similar to alcoholic intoxication, constricted pupils
Tolerance
Yes
Physical dependence potential
High
Psychological dependence potential
High
Duration of effects
1 to 16 hours
Overdose
Can cause coma and death
Special notes
1. Withdrawal is particularly dangerous, can cause death.
2. Barbiturates can be particularly dangerous when mixed with alcohol.
3. Belligerent behavior is sometimes noted.

Fact Sheet on Tranquilizers

Street names
Val, big E, lib
Drug family
Depressant
Appearance
Tablets and capsules
How used
Swallowed
Source
Overprescribing, street sales
Medical use
To relieve anxiety

Control schedule
IV (most commonly abused forms)
Effects
Depressed reflexes; similar to alcoholic intoxication
Tolerance
Yes
Physical dependence potential
Moderate
Psychological dependence potential
Moderate
Duration of effects
4 to 8 hours
Overdose
Stupor, coma, and death in extreme cases
Special notes
1. Abrupt stop in use can cause serious withdrawal symptoms.
2. Most widely prescribed drugs in Western world
3. Widespread abuse

Each year Americans consume an estimated 300 tons of barbiturates.[1] Tranquilizers are even bigger business. During 1974 almost 20 million prescriptions for Librium were filled. These added up to more than a billion capsules, worth $120 million. In the same year, over 50 million prescriptions were filled for Valium, dispensing almost 3 billion tablets worth $500 million. This probably made Valium the most commonly used drug in the Western world.[2]

Several types of depressants are subject to widespread abuses. The most common are:

1. *Barbiturates*, such as phenobarbital (Luminal), amobarbital (Amytal), pentobarbital (Nembutal), secobarbital (Seconal), and thiopental sodium (Pentothal sodium)
2. *Nonbarbiturate hypnotics*, such as glutethimide (Doriden), methyprylon (Noludar), and methaqualone (Parest, Quaalude, Sopor, Somnafac)
3. *Minor tranquilizers*, such as meprobamate (Miltown, Equanil), chlordiazepoxide (Librium), and diazepam (Valium)
4. *Miscellaneous drugs*, such as chloral hydrate, ethyl alcohol, and chloroform

These drugs are grouped together because they have a depressing effect on the central nervous system. In medicine they are used mainly to relieve anxiety and insomnia. A number of them are also used as general or preliminary anesthetics and to relieve some of the symptoms of epilepsy.

Depressants have a broad range of effects on users, ranging from mild intoxication and euphoria to complete stupor, coma, and, in extreme cases, death. As with all drugs, the effects of a given depressant upon an individual will vary widely, depending on several factors. These include the user's psychological makeup, mood, and tolerance as well as the potency and the amount of the drug taken.

The body quickly develops a tolerance to many of the effects of depressants. Most of these drugs, if not all, can cause both physical and psychological dependence. Withdrawal from depressants can produce delirium, convulsions, and death.

Because depressants are so readily available and because they are prescribed in such staggering quantities, their regulation is a difficult task. They are easily attainable from black market sources at relatively low prices. Enough barbiturates for an all-day "drunk" can be purchased in many areas for less than $10.

Many depressant abusers obtain their drugs through legitimate medical channels and consequently never come in contact with the authorities. This makes it impossible to precisely gauge the extent of current abuse in this country. However, figures from health and enforcement agencies give some idea of the scope of the problem. One analysis of reports made to the Drug Abuse Warning Network (DAWN) found that depressants accounted for 37 percent of the drugs reported between July 1973 and January 1974.[3] Another analysis of DAWN figures showed that depressants were mentioned in 44 percent of the emergency room reports filed, 40 percent of the inpatient reports, 35 percent of the medical examiner reports, and 25 percent of the crisis center reports.[4]

Depressant abuse is not confined to any particular segment of society. Amphetamine abusers take them to control overstimulation. Students take them to get high at a party. Heroin abusers rely on them to give their fix an extra impact. Businessmen and housewives use them to cope with the tensions and anxieties of the modern world. The desperate use them as a favored method of suicide.[5]

Women are more likely to abuse depressant drugs than men. An analysis conducted between July 1973 and March 1974 by the Drug Enforcement Administration indicates that depressant abuse was found among 45 percent of the women and 28 percent of the men who came to the attention of the Drug Abuse Warning Network. This difference is largely because women use more tranquilizers than men.[6]

Types of abuse vary as widely as types of abusers. A large number of automobile accidents are caused by drivers who have taken depressants, especially in combination with alcohol. Accidental self-poisonings are common among depressant abusers. Withdrawal from some barbiturates is especially dangerous and often fatal. Depressants are frequently abused along with other drugs, such as heroin or amphetamines. This polydrug abuse can cause particularly serious health problems.

BARBITURATES

Among the most useful and commonly prescribed depressants are the barbiturates (Figure 4-1). When abused, they become some of the most dangerous drugs available today. A 1975 White House study ranks their abuse second only to that of heroin and amphetamines in terms of adverse consequences produced.[7]

Barbiturate abusers run a high risk of developing both psychological and physical drug dependence. Severe abuse can lead to overtly hostile and aggressive behavior—behavior that is dangerous to abusers and those around them.

Barbiturates are often taken in conjunction with alcohol and other drugs, such as amphetamines and heroin. Such mixed abuse is extremely hazardous. For example, the combination of barbiturates and alcohol can be fatal.

Development

From earliest times physicians have sought to find remedies that provide relief from anxiety and insomnia. During the nineteenth century opiates were the favorite remedy. Hundreds of different preparations containing opium were sold. However, because of their high addiction potential, these preparations created more problems than they cured. Bromide was another drug that was frequently prescribed to relieve tension and induce sleep. But its potential for causing severe poisoning greatly limited its usefulness.

Largely because of the drawbacks associated with other drugs, alcohol became the most widely prescribed cure for anxiety and insomnia. But its use also presented problems. Those who had "taken the pledge" objected to it and strenuously called for its discontinuance as a prescription. Those in the opposite camp regarded the doctor's directions as a glorious excuse for staying perpetually drunk.

Against this background it is easy to see why the introduction in 1903 of Verinol, the first barbiturate, was looked on with relief by both physicians and the general public alike.[8] Since Verinol was introduced,

SHAPE AND COLOR	STREET NAME	TRADEMARK
 Red	Red bird Red Big red	Seconal (secobarbital)
 Red–blue	Rainbow Blue boy	Tuinal (secobarbital and amobarbital)
 Yellow	Yellow Yellow jacket	Nembutal (pentobarbital)
 Blue	Blue Blue boy	Amytal (amobarbital)

FIGURE 4-1
Dosage forms of commonly abused barbiturates.

over 2,500 derivatives of barbituric acid have been developed. At the present time about a dozen are in common medical use. Most often they are prescribed to relieve anxiety, reduce tension, and induce sleep. Occasionally they are used in the treatment of epilepsy or as anesthetics.

Classes of Barbiturates

Depending upon the duration of their effects, barbiturates are divided into four classes:

1. *Long-acting barbiturates* move slowly through the bloodstream to the brain. As a result, they are slow in taking effect. Because it takes a relatively long time for them to be broken down and eliminated by the liver and kidneys, they produce a deep sleep that lasts for six to ten hours.[9] Luminal and Tuinal are popular long-acting barbiturates.
2. *Intermediate-acting barbiturates* begin to take effect in about half an hour and last up to six hours. Barbiturates in this category, such as Amytal, are widely prescribed for insomnia.[10]
3. *Short-acting barbiturates* take hold within fifteen minutes and remain effective for two to three hours. Nembutal and Seconal are two of the commonly used drugs in this group.
4. *Ultrashort-acting barbiturates,* such as Pentothal, usually begin to act within ten minutes but only stay in effect for approximately fifteen minutes.

The most frequently abused barbiturates are those in the short- and intermediate-acting categories.

Tolerance, Dependence, and Withdrawal

The body rapidly develops a tolerance to the effects of barbiturates. This is especially true when they are injected. Consequently, the abuser needs ever-increasing quantities of them in order to experience their effects. In the case of severe abuse this can lead to a particularly dangerous situation. As the amount of barbiturates a user must take to get high increases, the amount needed to produce a fatal dose also increases, but at a slower rate. As a result the abuser is soon in the position where there is very little difference between the dose that produces the desired effects and the one that kills (Figure 4-2).

The massive doses that characterize severe barbiturate abuse can produce pronounced physical dependence. Psychological dependence can develop at any level of use.

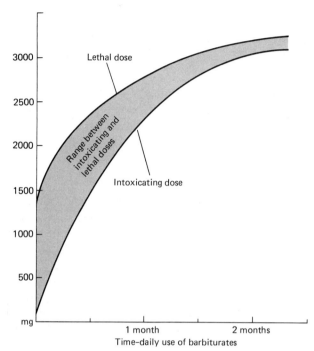

FIGURE 4-2

As more and more barbiturates are consumed, the difference be-
tween lethal and intoxicating doses of barbiturates grows smaller.
This can result, all too easily, in fatal overdoses. [*From David E.
Smith and Donald R. Wesson,* Uppers and Downers *(Englewood
Cliffs, N.J.: Prentice-Hall, 1973), p. 91*]

    Anyone who becomes dependent upon barbiturates and then stops
taking them will experience withdrawal symptoms. The intensity of
these symptoms is determined by the duration and severity of the
abuser's dependence as well as by individual differences.

    In general, the withdrawal process for a barbiturate abuser follows
a set pattern:

1. For the first few hours the patient's condition will seem to improve.
2. Anywhere from eight to twelve hours after the last dose the patient
   will begin to experience nervousness, anxiety, and insomnia. This
   may be accompanied by an overall weakness and a headache.
   These symptoms usually peak within twenty-four hours or so.
3. Within thirty-six to seventy-two hours after the last dose convulsions and delirium may set in. At this stage the patient may lapse
   into a fatal coma.

4. If the patient survives the preceding crisis, a period marked by delusions and hallucinations similar to alcoholic delirium tremens (DTs) may follow.[11]

Abuse Patterns

There is no single phenomenon, no single pattern that can be labeled as the barbiturate-abuse problem. Patterns of misuse range in severity from the mild abuse typified by a student trying to get through exam week to the intense intravenous abuse characteristic of those deep into the drug scene.

BARBITURATES AND ALCOHOL. Teenagers and young adults abuse barbiturates in much the same way as they abuse alcohol. They take them to get high—to provide social "lubrication." This practice can be extremely dangerous if the barbiturates are taken with alcohol.

Barbiturates interfere with the normal metabolism of the body. When they are mixed with alcohol, both they and the alcohol quickly reach toxic levels. In addition, when the two are taken together, they have what doctors call a "synergetic effect." That is, the combination of their effects when taken together is far greater than their effects if they were consumed separately (Figure 4-3). Thus, relatively small doses of barbiturates and alcohol taken together can prove fatal.[12]

CHRONIC INTOXICATION. Most often chronic barbiturate abuse is found among thirty- to fifty-year-olds from middle-class-family backgrounds. In many cases their drug histories are the same. They began by taking barbiturates that their physicians had prescribed to alleviate insomnia or anxiety. As their tolerance to the drugs increased, they took larger and larger doses. Soon they found that they "couldn't get along without them."

Chronic abusers often get their drugs through legitimate medical channels. To avoid suspicion, they will obtain prescriptions from several different physicians and fill them at different drugstores.

INTRAVENOUS ABUSE. Heavy barbiturate abusers usually inject the drug. They prefer this method of ingestion because it produces the desired orgasmic sensation or rush. Injection is a particularly dangerous practice. The body rapidly develops a tolerance to barbiturates when they are injected. In addition the risk of infection is high because of the unsterile conditions under which the drugs are injected. Serum hepatitis and other infections, such as tetanus, syphilis, and malaria, are another problem for the heavy drug shooter.[13]

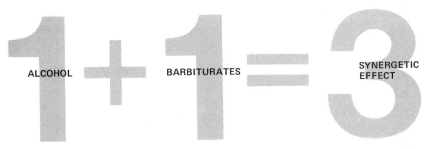

FIGURE 4-3
Barbiturates are particularly dangerous when used with alcohol.
The effects of the two together are far more potent than the effects
of a similar amount of the two used by themselves.

POLYDRUG ABUSE.   Barbiturates are often abused in conjunction
with other drugs. Amphetamine abusers rely on them to maximize that
drug's rush and to ease the agonies of withdrawal. Barbiturates are also
popular among some heroin abusers who are in methadone maintenance programs. They have found that though methadone blocks the
euphoric effects that they crave, barbiturates will still produce such a
high.

Results of Abuse

Morose, irritable, and quarrelsome behavior accompanied by general
emotional instability commonly characterize severe barbiturate abusers.[14] In extreme cases overtly aggressive behavior and paranoid delusions may develop.[15] Many experienced police officers will swear that
the "barb freak" can be one of the most difficult types of drug abusers to
handle. A study conducted by the Drug Enforcement Administration
supports this viewpoint. It found that barbiturate abusers had the highest aggravated assault rate (11.3 percent) of any category of drug abusers.[16]

Overdoses of barbiturates are a favorite method of committing
suicide, especially among women. During 1973 they were the cause of
death for 1,400 suicides; 870 of the victims were women.

Extent of Abuse

Barbiturate abuse is a widespread problem. Because many middle-class
abusers are treated privately and never come to the attention of the
authorities, it is impossible to judge accurately the full extent of the
abuse. It has been estimated that there are approximately 300,000 compulsive barbiturate abusers in the United States.[17] Reports made to the
Drug Abuse Warning Network also give some idea of the magnitude of

the problem. Between July 1973 and June 1974 barbiturates were the most commonly mentioned drugs in a DAWN analysis of medical examiner reports because of their being the direct cause of many suicides and other fatalities. In the same period they were the second most commonly mentioned drugs in both DAWN's hospital emergency room reports and its inpatient reports.[18]

It is difficult to gauge with any degree of accuracy how widespread barbiturate abuse is among today's youth. There are not enough data available to make any but the broadest generalizations. However, the figures that are available do give some idea of the problem's scope. In 1969 the National Commission on Marijuana and Drug Abuse found that 6 percent of the junior high school students interviewed admitted using depressants (the majority of which may be assumed to have been barbiturates) at least once. In 1972 junior high school students were again asked about the use of depressants. This time the figure for those answering affirmatively rose to 8 percent. Of the senior high school students interviewed in 1972, 16 percent admitted using barbiturates at least once, and a poll of college students taken the same year found a usage rate of 14 percent.[19]

Recognizing the Barbiturate Abuser

There is no foolproof way of telling, o.. ure street, whether or not someone is under the influence of barbiturates. However, there are certain signs. Generally, the signs of barbiturate and alcoholic intoxication are similar—with one important difference. The barbiturate abuser will not have the odor of alcohol on his or her breath or clothing. Some conditions to look for when trying to determine if a person may be a barbiturate abuser are:

1. General incoherence.
2. Disorientation.
3. Staggering and stumbling.
4. Drowsiness. (The abuser may appear to be in a complete stupor.)
5. Slurred speech.
6. Constricted pupils. (Dilation may occur in overdoses.)
7. Irritability and restlessness.
8. Belligerence.
9. Depressed reflexes.
10. Slow, shallow respiration (Figure 4-4).

The general behavior of "barb drunks" is similar to that of alcoholics. Their thought processes are muddled, and they neglect their personal appearance.

RECOGNIZING
THE ABUSER: BARBITURATES

Slurred speech

Drowsiness

Shallow, depressed
respiration

GENERAL BEHAVIOR

Stumbling, staggering,
disoriented, "drunken"
behavior

PUPIL APPEARANCE

Constricted

PARAPHERNALIA

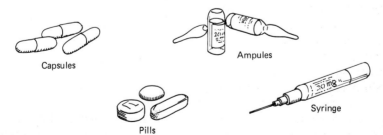

Capsules

Ampules

Pills

Syringe

FIGURE 4-4
Common signs of barbiturate abuse.

A graphic portrayal of the complete deterioration that so often accompanies this pattern of abuse is given in a passage from *Naked Lunch* by William Burroughs:

> The barbiturate addict presents a shocking spectacle. He cannot coordinate, he staggers, falls off bar stools, goes to sleep in the middle of a sentence, drops food out of his mouth. He is confused, quarrelsome and stupid. And he almost always uses other drugs, anything he can lay his hands on: alcohol, benzedrine, opiates, marijuana. Barbiturate users are looked down on in addict society: "Goof ball bums. They got no class to me." . . . It seems to me that barbiturates cause the worst possible form of addictions, unsightly, deteriorating, difficult to treat.[20]

Sources of Supply

Most black market barbiturates come from two sources. They are either smuggled into the United States from abroad or diverted from legitimate domestic production and distribution. Currently, diversion seems to account for the largest share of the illegitimate supply. Some authorities believe that as much as 80 percent of the barbiturates found on the street have been diverted from legitimate channels.[21]

SMUGGLING.   The largest part of the barbiturates smuggled into this country enter via Mexico into the Southwest, particularly southern California. Authorities in that part of the country have seized enormous quantities of "reds," unmarked orange and red capsules containing sodium secobarbital. Intelligence sources indicate that the drug is shipped legitimately in bulk to Mexico, where it is packaged into capsules and slipped across the border into the United States.

DIVERSION.   Most barbiturates enter the black market through the diversion of legitimate supplies (Figure 4-5). Since millions of barbiturates are legitimately prescribed by physicians each year, it is extremely difficult to plug all the leaks in the manufacturing and distribution pipeline. Authorities cannot accurately determine the volume of barbiturates that find their way into illicit hands. However, the extent of the problem is illustrated by some federal audit figures. In the one-year period between April 1971 and April 1972, thefts of barbiturates from storage facilities resulted in the diversion of over 7 million dosage units. During the same period unauthorized sales (such as a pharmacist selling to a customer without a prescription or a wholesaler selling to someone who is not authorized to deal in barbiturates) resulted in the diversion of another 6.4 million dosage units.[22]

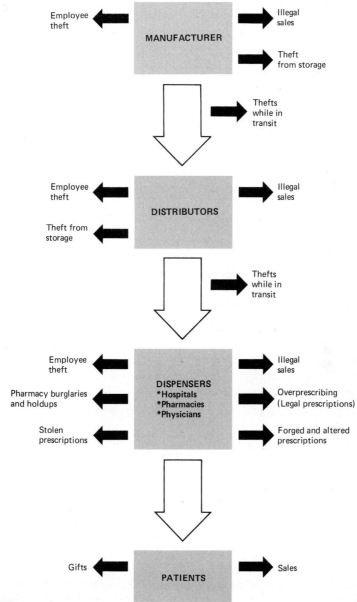

FIGURE 4-5
Barbiturates are diverted into the illicit market at numerous points
in the licit distribution system.

Barbiturates can be diverted into illicit channels at any point in the manufacturing or distribution process. Unscrupulous manufacturers, distributors, and dispensers can peddle them illegally. Dishonest employees can pilfer them. Highjackers can "rip them off" by the truckload. Prescriptions can be stolen, forged, or altered.

Pharmacy burglaries and holdups are a particularly serious diversion problem. There were over 6,300 such incidents during 1974, resulting in the loss of over 28 million dosage units of dangerous drugs. Many of these were barbiturates and related substances.

Overprescribing by physicians is one of the more complex forms of diversion. Obviously, doctors must have a great deal of freedom in prescribing drugs that they deem necessary to their patients' welfare. Yet past experience has shown that overprescribing contributes materially to the availability and abuse of such drugs as barbiturates, tranquilizers, and amphetamines. This is especially true among so-called respectable middle-class abusers.

Legal Controls

The most commonly abused forms of barbiturates are listed under Schedule II of the Controlled Substances Act of 1970. Other drugs in this schedule include cocaine, methamphetamine, and opium and many of its derivatives.

TRANQUILIZERS

In addition to barbiturates, several other families of depressants are commonly used and abused in this country. The effects of some are quite similar to the effects of barbiturates; others act in ways that are quite different.

Tranquilizers, or antianxiety agents as they are sometimes called, are not only the most widely used of the depressants, but also among the most widely used drugs in the Western world. In normal doses they decrease anxiety and tension, without causing fatigue or drowsiness. Depending on their effects, these drugs are categorized as either major or minor tranquilizers.

The major tranquilizers are used to treat those suffering from many forms of severe mental illnesses. While these drugs do not cure the conditions for which they are prescribed, they do provide relief from many severe and debilitating symptoms. At present, major tranquilizers do not present serious street-abuse problems. However, their potential overuse in institutional settings is a question that generates a great deal of discussion among doctors and laypeople alike.

The era of minor tranquilizers began in the 1950s with the introduction of meprobamate, marketed under such trademarks as Miltown and Equanil. Billions of tablets are sold annually. Other commonly known minor tranquilizers are chlordiazepoxide (Librium), diazepam (Valium), and benactyzines (Phobex, Suavitil, Anarex).

Scientists do not fully understand how these drugs affect the nervous system. They appear to act on the brain in such a way as to somehow insulate an individual from the external stimuli that are producing anxiety and stress.

Tolerance, Dependence, and Withdrawal

As with barbiturates, the body develops a tolerance to the effects of minor tranquilizers. Abusers can also develop both a physical and psychological dependence upon them. An abrupt stop after repeated, intense abuse may produce such serious withdrawal symptoms as convulsions, coma, psychotic behavior, and, in extreme cases, death.[23]

Extent of Abuse

The abuse of minor tranquilizers is extensive. In the period from July 1973 to March 1974 they were the most frequently mentioned category of drug in a DAWN report. In a 1975 report on drug abuse released by the White House it was estimated that between 400,000 and 490,000 individuals in this country regularly take tranquilizers for nonmedical purposes.[24]

Sources of Supply

Most abusers obtain minor tranquilizers from legitimate sources rather than from the black market. A 1974 DAWN study showed that 58 percent of the tranquilizer abusers interviewed obtained their drugs via legitimate prescriptions. Less than 6 percent obtained their tranquilizers through such means as street buys, forged prescriptions, or theft.

Legal Controls

The most commonly abused minor tranquilizers are listed in Schedule IV of the Controlled Substances Act of 1970. This schedule also contains such other drugs as chloral hydrate and meprobamate.

MISCELLANEOUS DRUGS

The rest of the extensive family of depressants is made up of miscellaneous drugs, each of which functions a little bit differently. Among these are chloral hydrate, glutethimide, and methaqualone.

Chloral Hydrate

One of the oldest of the sleep-inducing drugs, chloral hydrate was first synthesized from alcohol in the 1860s. In many ways its effects upon an individual parallel those of alcohol. The body develops a tolerance to the drug, and there is a moderate psychological and physiological dependency potential. Withdrawal symptoms are similar to the delirium tremors experienced by alcoholics.

Glutethimide

When it was first introduced in 1954, glutethimide (sold under the trademark Doriden) was thought to be a safe, abuse-free substitute for barbiturates. However, time has proved that it is merely another central nervous system depressant that exhibits few, if any, advantages over barbiturates. Its effects generally last from four to eight hours. Because of its long-acting effects, overdoses are particularly dangerous and difficult to reverse. All too often severe abuse results in death.

Methaqualone

One of the more faddishly popular street drugs, methaqualone, was introduced in India in 1950. At first it was hailed as a safe substitute for barbiturates, but experience has shown that this claim was overly optimistic. Some of the trademarks under which methaqualone is marketed are Quaalude, Sopor, Parest, Optimil, and Somnafac. On the street it is frequently called "lude" or "soaper."

Methaqualone is taken orally. Small doses produce feelings of general calm and well-being. Larger quantities can cause a euphoric high. Some of the adverse reactions that accompany its abuse include headache, menstrual disturbance, dryness of the mouth, nosebleed, depersonalization, dizziness, skin eruptions, numbness, pain in the extremities, diarrhea, and loss of appetite.

There are no signs that methaqualone is produced illicitly. All indications are that street supplies are obtained through diversion of licit supplies into the black market and by legitimate prescriptions.

Methaqualone seems to be particularly popular with students. Its abuse seems to have begun on college campuses in the Midwest and then spread to college campuses on the East and West Coasts.

Several factors contributed to methaqualone's popularity. Originally it was thought to have a low dependence potential. It was also rumored to be an aphrodisiac (love) drug. And finally, while increased enforcement efforts on the part of federal, state, and local authorities had greatly decreased the supply of many other drugs, methaqualone was readily available.

The body develops a tolerance to methaqualone, and there is a high potential for both psychological and physical dependence.

IN CONCLUSION

Both barbiturates and tranquilizers present a serious drug-abuse threat. They are comparatively easy to obtain on the street, and they are potentially lethal when abused, particularly in conjunction with alcohol. In addition, because they are so widely prescribed, many of those who use them to excess do not feel that their misuse bears the stigma of drug abuse. Because of this combination of factors, continued enforcement, education, regulation, and treatment efforts are needed.

NOTES

[1]National Clearinghouse for Drug Abuse Information, *CNS Depressants*, U.S. Department of Health, Education, and Welfare (Rockville, Md.: The Clearinghouse, 1973), p. 8.

[2]Drug Enforcement Administration, *Drugs of Abuse*, vol. 2, no. 2, Spring 1975, (Washington, D.C.: GPO, 1975), p. 20.

[3]Drug Enforcement Administration, *Drugs of Abuse* (Washington, D.C.: GPO, 1974), p. 68.

[4]Drug Enforcement Administration, *The Supply, Distribution and Usage Patterns of Drugs of Abuse* (Washington, D.C.: GPO, 1974), p. 79.

[5]Drug Enforcement Administration, *Drugs of Abuse*, vol. 2, no. 2, Spring 1975, pp. 14–15.

[6]Drug Enforcement Administration, *DAWN 2 Analysis* (Washington, D.C.: GPO, 1974), pp. 255–256.

[7]Domestic Council Drug Abuse Task Force, *White Paper on Drug Abuse* (Washington, D.C.: GPO, 1975), p. 33.

[8]Edward M. Brecher and Consumers Union Editors, *Licit and Illicit Drugs* (Boston: Little, Brown, 1972), p. 247; Richard R. Lingeman, *Drugs from A to Z: A Dictionary* (New York: McGraw-Hill, 1969), p. 16.

[9]For a more extensive discussion of long-acting barbiturates, see Richard R. Lingeman, p. 16; and Franz Bergel and D. R. A. Davies, *All About Drugs* (New York: Barnes & Noble, 1970), p. 120.

[10]For additional data on intermediate-acting barbiturates, see Franz Bergel and D. R. A. Davies.

[11]*Drug Abuse: A Guide for Law Enforcement Officers* (Philadelphia: Smith Kline & French Laboratories, 1968), pp. 8–9.

[12]Kenneth L. Jones, Louis W. Shainber, and Curtis O. Byer, *Drugs and Alcohol* (New York: Harper & Row, 1969), p. 48.

[13]David E. Smith and Donald R. Wesson, *Uppers and Downers* (Englewood Cliffs, N.J.: Prentice-Hall, 1973), pp. 87–90.

[14]National Clearinghouse for Drug Abuse Information, *CNS Depressants*, p. 11.

[15]National Clearinghouse for Drug Abuse Information, *Sedatives: Some Questions and Answers*, U.S. Department of Health, Education and Welfare, (Washington, D.C.: GPO, 1971), p.2.

[16]*A Study of Current Abuse and Abuse Potential of Sedative-Hypnotic Derivatives of Barbiturate Acid with Control Recommendations* (Washington, D.C.: U.S. Department of Justice, November 1972), p. 65.

[17]Domestic Council Drug Abuse Task Force, p. 33.

[18]*Quarterly Statistical Brochure* (Rockville, Md.: National Institute on Drug Abuse, 1975), pp. 30–33.

[19]National Commission on Marijuana and Drug Abuse, *Drug Use in America: Problem in Perspective* (Washington, D.C.: GPO, 1973), p. 80.

[20]William Burroughs, *Naked Lunch* (New York: Ballatine, 1973), p. 251.

[21]Domestic Council Drug Abuse Task Force, p. 57.

[22]*A Study of Current Abuse*, pp. 80–88.

[23]For more details on tolerance, dependence, and withdrawal of the minor tranquilizers, see Robert E. Taylor, Theodore F. Karla, and F. Gerald St. Souver, *The Police Officer's Guide to Narcotics and Dangerous Drugs* (privately published, n.d.); Robert M. Julien, *A Primer of Drug Action* (San Francisco: Freeman, 1975), p. 58; and John M. Davis, Edward Bartlett, and Benedict A. Termini,"Overdoses of Psychotropic Drugs: A review, I, Major & Minor Tranquilizers," *Diseases of the Nervous System*, vol. 29, no. 3, pp. 157–164, March 1968.

[24]Domestic Council Drug Abuse Task Force, p. 23.

Chapter 5

AMPHETAMINES

Fact Sheet on Amphetamines

Street names
Dexies, uppers, bennies, West Coast turnarounds
Drug family
Stimulant
Appearance
Capsules, tablets, white crystalline powder, liquid
How used
Swallowed, injected
Source
Diverted from legitimate channels, stolen, clandestine labs
Medical uses
Short-term weight reduction, overactive children, narcolepsy
Control schedule
II (most commonly abused forms)
Effects
Intense stimulation, increased alertness, excitation, insomnia, euphoria
Tolerance
Yes
Physical dependence potential
Possible
Psychological dependence potential
High
Duration of effects
2 to 4 hours
Overdose
Agitation, hallucinations, convulsions, possible death
Special notes
Extreme abuse may produce paranoid behavior.

The amphetamines are a large and potent family of central nervous system stimulants. Included in the group are such drugs as dextroamphetamine, methamphetamine, and amphetamine itself.[1] On the street the various family members carry descriptive name tags—"speed," "bennies," "West Coast turnarounds," "dexies," and "uppers," to name only a few (Figure 5-1).

All amphetamines are synthetic. Since these drugs, when abused, are extremely dangerous, their legal manufacture is limited in this country to a relatively small number of companies, all of whom are strictly regulated and controlled by the government. Amphetamine abuse can lead to an intense psychological dependence. In severe cases

SHAPE AND COLOR	STREET NAME	TRADEMARK
 SKF A91 Pink	Benny	Benzedrine (5 milligrams)
 SKF E19 Orange	Dexy	Dexedrine (5 milligrams)
 SKF D93 Green	Dexy	Dexamyl (5 milligrams)
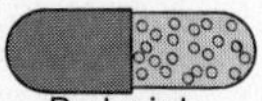 Red–pink (spansule capsule)	Benny	Benzedrine (15 milligrams)
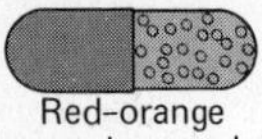 Red–orange (spansule capsule)	Dexy	Dexedrine

FIGURE 5-1
Dosage forms of commonly abused amphetamines.

of abuse, it can also lead to violent and self-destructive behavior. The question of whether or not any degree of physical dependence can develop has not been completely resolved.

Amphetamine abuse is sufficiently widespread in the United States to merit grave concern. The Domestic Council Drug Abuse Task Force in its *White Paper on Drug Abuse* estimated that between 400,000 and 490,000 stimulant abusers are "in trouble." These are the people who take amphetamines regularly for nonmedical purposes. The council stated that "chronic intensive medically unsupervised use of amphetamines and barbiturates probably ranks with heroin use as a major social problem."[2] A survey by the National Institute of Drug Abuse found that 6 percent of the adults and 5 percent of the youths questioned admitted to the nonmedical use of stimulants.[3] Drug-use figures reported by DAWN for the period April 1974 through April 1975 indicated that amphetamines ranked twelfth in the list of drugs mentioned.[4]

HISTORY

When compared to some other drugs such as the opiates and cocaine, the amphetamines are "Johnny-come-latelys." However, in the brief time span that they have been available, they have created more than their fair share of problems for medical and enforcement authorities as well as for those who abuse them. Although they were initially synthesized in 1887, it was not until 1927 that the first significant investigation into their therapeutic uses was conducted, and it was not until 1932 that a patent for their discovery was awarded to Dr. G. Alles. In return for royalties Dr. Alles assigned their production rights to the Smith Kline & French pharmaceutical company.[5]

In the early 1930s Smith Kline & French introduced the Benzedrine (the company's trademark for amphetamine) bronchial inhaler as an over-the-counter item (Figure 5-2). Because of the ability of Benzedrine to dilate bronchial tubes, it soon won wide acceptance among those suffering from such respiratory ailments as asthma. By the mid-1930s amphetamines had also been found to be useful in combating narcolepsy, a relatively rare disease characterized by compulsive sleep. By the end of the decade their appetite-suppressing qualities made them popular among those attempting to lose weight.

The first nonmedical use of amphetamines is thought to have occurred during the Spanish Civil War in the late 1930s, when they were issued in ship survival packs. Soon after World War II broke out, both the Allies and the Axis powers were taking advantage of the stimulant

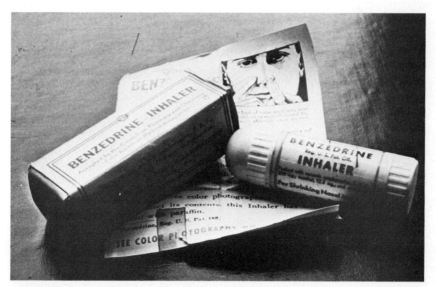

FIGURE 5-2
Benzedrine inhalers were widely abused until their sale was placed under stringent control.

properties of amphetamines and issuing them to soldiers as well as production workers on the home fronts.

Almost immediately after their introduction into the medical marketplace in the 1930s, the abuse of amphetamines began. As early as 1937 a group of students at the University of Minnesota reported that amphetamines were the ideal cram drug. The drug's stimulant qualities were just what was needed to keep the candle burning at both ends during those critical days and nights before important examinations. By the mid-1940s, alarmed authorities reported widespread misuse of Benzedrine inhalers. An abuser would break open an inhaler, remove the amphetamine-impregnated paper that it contained, and soak the paper in anything from fruit juice to beer. The resulting "cocktail" provided the desired stimulant kick.

The United States is not the only country to have experienced a serious amphetamine-abuse problem. During World War II the Japanese government provided millions of amphetamine tablets to both military personnel and civilians in an effort to obtain increased productivity. After the war large stockpiles of amphetamines were made available to the general population. Their misuse quickly grew to alarming proportions. For example, in 1954 it was estimated that as many as 15 million Japanese could be classified as abusers. In that same year the Japanese police arrested over 55,000 individuals for amphetamine abuse. Finally, sufficient alarm developed in official circles, and in 1955 Japan instituted a major enforcement and educational program that succeeded in reducing the problem to at least manageable proportions.[6]

MEDICAL USES

Until the early 1970s when they were placed under rigorous control by the federal government, amphetamines were widely prescribed in this country. One authority listed thirty clinical uses for them. Dozens of different compounds containing them were noted. The 1976 edition of the *Physicians' Desk Reference to Pharmaceutical Specialties and Biologicals* listed the trademarks of over fifty stimulants of the amphetamine type.

Perhaps the most commonly prescribed use of amphetamine was to alleviate depression and fatigue. When taken in therapeutic doses, amphetamines produce (at least initially) a pleasurable sense of mental and physical stimulation. Users report that their mood is elevated and fatigue seems to disappear. They also frequently experience a feeling of increased initiative and self-confidence. They are ready to take the world "by the tail." In short, amphetamines are "just what the doctor ordered" (and unfortunately in the past that was all too often the truth) to give the lift needed to get through the day.

Amphetamines were also widely prescribed in weight-reduction programs. As early as 1939 their hunger-suppressing qualities had been reported.[7] For many millions of America's obese, amphetamines appeared to be the miracle answer to their problem. All they had to do was to down a few pills and their hunger would disappear as if by magic. But all too soon this miracle proved to be another of life's cruel illusions. Again, human physiology got in the way of the drug manufacturers' wondrous claims. Since the human body rapidly develops tolerance to the appetite-suppressing qualities of amphetamines, the drugs become useless within four to six weeks.

Finally, during the latter part of the 1960s, alarm caused by a growing recognition of widespread misuse of the amphetamines resulted in congressional hearings, and in 1970 the Federal Drug Administration severely restricted their use in medicine. Amphetamines may now be used only to treat narcolepsy and hyperkinetic (overactive) children, and as a part of short-term weight-reduction programs.

ABUSE

Amphetamine abuse is found in varying forms at all levels and in all segments of our society. Truck drivers take amphetamines to stay awake on long hauls. Executives and housewives swallow them for a lift. "Speed freaks" inject them for the rush that they produce. Frequently those who abuse barbiturates and other depressant drugs take them as part of a vicious "upper-downer" cycle (Figure 5-3).

Generally speaking, amphetamine abusers fall into one of three broad categories—occasional abusers, chronic or compulsive oral abusers, and intravenous abusers.

Occasional Abuse

Individuals who, from time to time, take relatively small, oral doses of amphetamines for a variety of reasons are considered occasional abusers. The occasional-abuse pattern is not confined to any one age or any one social, economic, or cultural group. Many youths fall into this pattern for recreational purposes. They regard pep pills as the ideal way of getting high at a party, and they use them only at a social function. Or they may take them out of simple curiosity about their effects or as the result of pressures from their friends and acquaintances. Others, especially those in high school or college, may from time to time take them to stay awake before a particularly crucial examination.

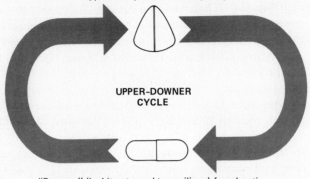

"Uppers" (amphetamines) for pickup

UPPER-DOWNER
CYCLE

"Downers" (barbiturates and tranquilizers) for relaxation

FIGURE 5-3
Amphetamine abusers frequently fall victim to a vicious upper-downer cycle. They rely on amphetamines to get them "up" in the morning. In the evening they use downers, such as barbiturates and tranquilizers, to calm their jagged nerves.

Adults similarly may resort occasionally to amphetamines for a wide range of reasons. Exhausted executives may swallow them in order to get through a difficult day at the office; housewives may now and again use them to ward off depression. Drivers may rely on them to stay awake on a long trip. Those who follow this pattern of occasional abuse generally obtain their drugs from friends and acquaintances rather than from black market sources.

Chronic Oral Abuse

A pattern of chronic oral abuse is considerably more damaging than the occasional pattern. It is characterized by a compulsive, day-to-day reliance on the mood-elevating and fatigue-defeating qualities of amphetamines. It appears to be most common among middle-aged housewives, businessmen, and executives. Abusers of this type generally suffer from a strong psychological dependence upon the effects of the amphetamines, and they frequently resort to them three or four times a day. Though this level of abuse tends to remain quite stable, it may gradually increase over a period of time. For such abusers amphetamines are a way of life. Without these drugs they are haunted by depression and foreboding. With them they feel that they are able to cope with the tasks that confront them.

One of the great dangers of this abuse pattern is the frequency with which it leads to the establishment of an extremely dangerous upper-downer amphetamine-barbiturate abuse cycle. Abusers in the clutches of this cycle rely on amphetamines for the lift that they feel is essential to get through the day. When evening comes, they resort to barbiturates or other depressants to slow themselves down so they can sleep. Morning starts the vicious cycle again. The severe medical problem that this behavior can produce as well as the chance of overdoses make this cycle particularly hazardous.

Intravenous Abuse

The compulsive, high-dose, intravenous use of amphetamines characterizes this pattern of abuse. Though in terms of absolute numbers the abusers in this pattern are relatively few, their often bizarre behavior and the violence to which they sometimes resort have served to focus a good deal of notoriety upon them.

Intravenous amphetamine abuse seems first to have attracted the public's attention in California during the early 1960s.[8] It is a particularly serious type of abuse that is usually characterized by an action phase, during which the abuser repeatedly consumes large quantities of drugs, and a reaction or "crash" phase, which sets in when drug taking stops (Figure 5-4).

ACTION-REACTION CYCLE

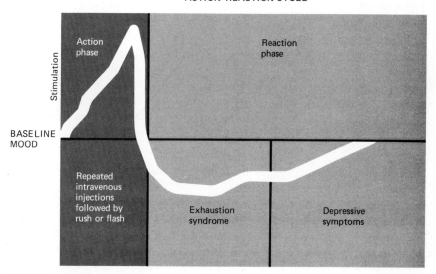

FIGURE 5-4
Severe amphetamine abusers frequently react in a cyclic manner. During the action phase of the cycle, they receive violent stimulation. This is followed by the reaction depressive phase, which occurs when the effects of the drug wear off. (*Drug Enforcement Administration*)

ACTION PHASE. During the action phase of the cycle abusers repeatedly inject large doses of methamphetamine (or, as it is called on
the street, "speed," "crack," or "crystal") into their veins. If methamphetamine is not available, they will frequently substitute other stimulants such as dissolved amphetamine tablets. The doses used are often
hundreds of times larger than those normally prescribed by a physician. Whereas the usual therapeutic dose for these drugs ranges from
2.5 to 10 milligrams, speed freaks will often inject from 500 to 1,000
milligrams at a time. They will continue to inject themselves every
three or four hours during their "run" (amphetamine binge), which
may last anywhere from a few hours to several days.

Immediately after injecting speed, abusers experience an exhilarating, orgasmic sensation, or rush. This is followed by a period marked
by hyperactivity, exuberance, excitation, talkativeness, enthusiastic
self-confidence, and euphoria. At this point no task seems too large, no
challenge too great. These symptoms are almost identical to those produced by cocaine, with one major exception—they last far longer.

Frequently when abusers are in the midst of a run, they will go for
days without eating or sleeping. During this period they may exhibit
patterns of meaningless compulsive behavior. For example, one speed
freak stirred a pot of spaghetti continually for hours on end. Another
abuser spent all day and night meticulously dusting and scrubbing his
room.

As abusers continue to inject themselves and the drug level in their
system increases, they may in some cases develop decidedly paranoid
behavior patterns that closely resemble those of the stereotyped dope
fiend. If they get to this stage, typically they become deeply suspicious
of the motives and actions of others. They may become convinced that
they are being followed—that someone is "out to get them." Their
mood can change instantaneously from warm and enthusiastic friend-
ship to raging hostility. Bizarre notions and terrors can overwhelm
them. For example, it is not unusual for hard-core abusers to become
convinced that bugs or some other vermin are crawling under their
skin. Raw sores and scars testify to the frantic scratching and picking
that such abusers will indulge in to free themselves of these imaginary
bugs. They may also experience both visual and auditory hallucinations.

The combination of extreme overactivity, paranoid suspicion, and
lowering of impulse control can produce, at times, belligerent and violent behavior. The files of many a law enforcement agency contain
cases in which abusers in the grip of an amphetamine panic have at-
tacked, maimed, and sometimes killed for no apparent reason. Though

such occurrences are rare, it is prudent to keep them in mind whenever dealing with anyone who appears to be under the influence of amphetamines.

REACTION PHASE.   The reaction phase of the cycle begins when the abuser stops his or her drug taking. This can happen for a number of reasons. Abusers may become utterly exhausted and find it physically impossible to continue on drugs. Or they can become so utterly possessed by paranoid fears that they can no longer function. Or, as usually happens, they simply run out of drugs.

As the effects wear off, abusers begin to crash. They are overcome by exhaustion; it is not uncommon for abusers to sleep eighteen to twenty hours at a time without interruption. Upon awakening, they will often fall into the grip of severe depression, fatigue, and apathy. These symptoms can last for days and even, in particularly severe cases, weeks. During this crash abusers frequently turn to depressants such as heroin and barbiturates to ease their suffering. Though not common, crash-related suicides have been reported.

Tolerance, Dependence, and Withdrawal

Abusers can develop a tolerance to and an intense psychological dependence upon amphetamines. Authorities are divided on the question of physical dependence. Some feel that withdrawal from amphetamines does not produce sufficiently serious or noticeable symptoms to warrant claiming that the body is physically dependent upon them. Others, however, argue that the characteristic fatigue, apathy, and depression that accompany amphetamine withdrawal clearly indicate a genuine physical dependence.

Generally speaking, amphetamine withdrawal does not pose any grave physical threat to the abuser. Recovery is usually made rather rapidly after a period of abstinence and rest.

Recognizing the Abuser

Again, short of laboratory tests, there is no set pattern of behavior or exact physical characteristics that will positively identify amphetamine abusers. However, there are several common signs to look for. These include:

1.   Hyperactivity. This is often accompanied by intense anxiety, nervousness, talkativeness, irritability, and a short temper.
2.   Dilated pupils.

3. Bad breath, sometimes accompanied by raw, cracked lips.
4. Sores or lesions caused by picking and scratching at imaginary bugs.
5. Nose rubbing. Amphetamines cause the mucous membranes to dry out and itch.
6. Needle marks and scars (Figure 5-5).

SOURCES OF SUPPLY

Amphetamines enter the illicit market from three main sources—diversion of legitimately produced drugs, clandestine laboratories, and smuggling operations.

Diversion

For many years the diversion of amphetamines from legitimate production and distribution channels posed a very serious problem. Prior to the implementation of strict federal regulations, it was estimated that over 8 billion dosage units of amphetamines were manufactured each year in this country. A study in 1970 by the U.S. Department of Justice calculated that fully one-third of this production—or over 3 billion doses—was diverted from legitimate channels into the black market.[9] Amphetamines leaked from every point in the manufacturing and distribution pipeline. Some were stolen by dishonest employees, while others were hijacked from delivery trucks. Warehouses were burglarized and pharmacies broken into, and unscrupulous manufacturers, dealers, and physicians all made them available—for a price.

As part of a major effort designed to stop this wholesale diversion, the federal government placed them on Schedule II of the Controlled Substances Act in July of 1971. This forced legitimate manufacturers and distributors to install much more rigorous security and inventory control systems throughout the entire distribution network. At the same time the government also assigned production quotas that were about 80 percent less than those of the preceding year.[10]

Historically, overprescribing by physicians has posed another serious diversion problem. Abusers have often been successful in getting physicians to prescribe amphetamines for such disorders as chronic fatigue and for use in long-term weight-control programs. It has not been uncommon for abusers to obtain prescriptions from several different physicians at the same time. Some abusers have even forced themselves to eat large quantities of fattening foods so that doctors would continue to prescribe amphetamines as part of a weight-control program.

To combat the problem of overprescription, the federal govern-

**RECOGNIZING
THE ABUSER: AMPHETAMINES**

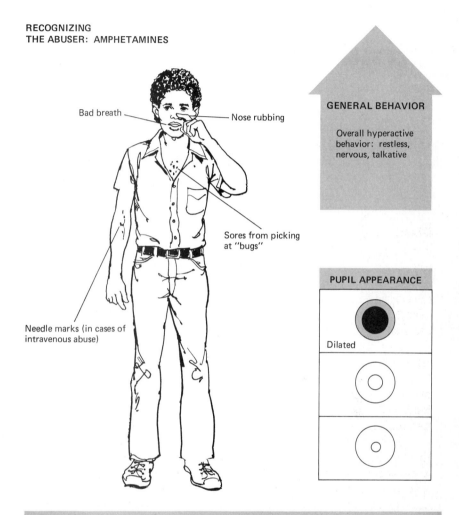

Bad breath

Nose rubbing

GENERAL BEHAVIOR

Overall hyperactive
behavior: restless,
nervous, talkative

Sores from picking
at "bugs"

Needle marks (in cases of
intravenous abuse)

PUPIL APPEARANCE

Dilated

PARAPHERNALIA

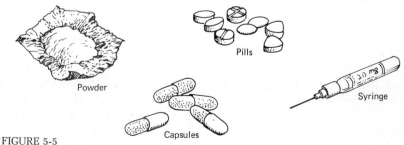

Powder

Pills

Capsules

Syringe

FIGURE 5-5
Common signs of amphetamine abuse.

ment in 1970 limited the medical uses of amphetamines to the treatment of narcolepsy, for hyperkinetic children, and as part of short-term weight-reduction programs. This, along with regulations stating that prescriptions cannot be refilled, has helped to limit diversion as a source of the drugs.

Clandestine Laboratories

During the early 1960s law enforcement authorities first became aware that clandestine laboratories were being set up for the production of methamphetamine. Such laboratories still present a troublesome enforcement problem. The chemicals needed to produce speed are not hard to obtain, and the manufacturing process is relatively easy. Moreover, the profits are substantial. At 1976 prices, a $200 investment would yield $2,500 worth of speed.

In testimony before the House Select Committee on Crime, the operator of one clandestine laboratory boasted that with an initial investment of only $200 and with overhead of just $1,800 a month, he was able to net a profit of $360,000 a year. This was not bad considering that the individual in question had never taken a chemistry course in his life. Instead he had learned how to manufacture speed while serving a forty-day sentence in jail.[11]

Smuggling

Prior to the implementation of vigorous export controls, millions of amphetamines were shipped by legitimate United States manufacturers to Mexico. They were then promptly smuggled back across the border into this country. In testimony before the House Select Committee on Crime, the scope of this problem and the devious paths taken were revealed. For example, one Chicago-based manufacturer shipped 15 million amphetamine tablets to a drugstore that allegedly was located in Tijuana, Mexico. Investigation subsequently revealed, however, that this particular drugstore did not exist. The address given was, in fact, if taken literally, the eleventh hole of the Tijuana Country Club golf course.[12]

Though federal export regulations have helped to curb many of the abuses such as the one just cited, authorities are still faced with the problem of preventing amphetamines that are manufactured in other countries from being smuggled into the United States.

As soon as federal regulations stopped the flow of United States–manufactured amphetamines into Mexico, European manufacturers stepped in to fill the void. Bulk amphetamine powder manufactured by legitimate European pharmaceutical firms is shipped by the ton to Mexico. It is then converted by underworld operators into small tablets—"minibennies," as they are called on the street. These are then smuggled by the millions across the border into the United States.

Until recently authorities have been hampered in their investigation of smuggled amphetamines because of the problems involved in tracing back to their sources drugs that were seized. However, largely due to the pioneering work of Dr. Albert Tillson of the federal Drug Enforcement Administration laboratory, it is now often possible to link a given tablet to a particular tableting machine. This allows investigators to coordinate information from different seizures and buys. Such information, in turn, is useful in pinpointing the location of clandestine manufacturing operations and in figuring out illicit distribution networks.

Dr. Tillson's method is based on the fact that the individual punches and dies that are used to compress the bulk amphetamine powder leave distinctive marks on the tablets (Figure 5-6). These die marks can be compared, much in the same manner as those that are found on bullets that have been fired. This information, along with that gained from an analysis of the tablet's contents, has helped investigators to link a particular amphetamine tablet with the machine that was used to manufacture it.

LEGAL CONTROLS

Amphetamines were first placed in Schedule III of the Controlled Substances Act of 1970, but on July 7, 1971, they were moved to Schedule II. This schedule is designed for drugs (1) that have a high potential for abuse, (2) that have a currently accepted medical use in treatment in the United States or a currently accepted medical use with severe restrictions, or (3) that may lead to severe psychological or physical dependence.

IN CONCLUSION

The amphetamines are a dangerous family of drugs that has little or no real use in medicine. As long as they remain on the market, amphetamines will probably continue to present a troublesome problem. However, there is every indication that legislation will soon be forthcoming which will greatly curtail their manufacture and hence their availability. Illicitly manufactured amphetamines will, however, undoubtedly continue to present a problem for the foreseeable future.

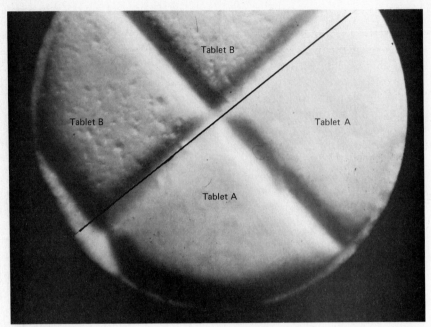

FIGURE 5-6
The punches and dies used to manufacture amphetamine tablets leave distinctive marks on the tablets. These marks can be used to link a given tablet with the machine on which it was made. Note how tablets A and B match. This proves that they were made with the same punch and die.

NOTES

[1]Louis S. Goodman and Alfred Gilman (eds.), *Pharmacological Basis of Therapeutics* (New York: Macmillan, 1970), p. 505.

[2]Domestic Council Drug Abuse Task Force, *White Paper on Drug Abuse* (Washington, D.C.: GPO, 1975), p. 23.

[3]Herbert I. Abelson and Ronald B. Atkinson, *Public Experience with Psychoactive Substances* (Rockville, Md.: National Institute on Drug Abuse, August 1975), pp. 9–10.

[4]Drug Enforcement Administration and National Institute on Drug Abuse, *Drug Abuse Warning Network, Phase III Report* (Washington, D.C.: GPO, 1976), p. 4.

[5]"Assault on Amphetamines," *Drug Enforcement*, vol. 2, no. 1, p. 26, Winter 1975.

[6]Sidney Cohen, *The Drug Dilemma* (New York: McGraw-Hill, 1969), p. 44; Oakley S. Ray, *Drugs, Society, and Human Behavior* (St. Louis: Mosby, 1972), p. 170.

[7]Oakley S. Ray, p. 161.

[8]Oakley S. Ray, p. 160.

[9]Oakley S. Ray, p. 170.

[10]Oakley S. Ray, pp. 161–170.

[11]U.S. House of Representatives, House Select Committee on Crime, *Testimony in San Francisco*, Oct. 23–27, 1969, Nov. 18, 1969.

[12]U.S. House of Representatives, House Select Committee on Crime.

Chapter 6
COCAINE

Fact Sheet on Cocaine

Street names
Coke, snow, flake
Drug family
Stimulant
Appearance
White crystalline powder
How used
Inhaled (sniffed, snorted), injected
Source
Leaves of South American coca bush
Medical use
Local anesthetic
Control schedule
II
Effects
Intense stimulation, excitation, nervousness, talkativeness, euphoria
Tolerance
Probably
Physical dependence potential
Uncertain
Psychological dependence potential
High
Duration of effects
15 to 30 minutes
Overdose
Fast, irregular respiration, extreme agitation, convulsions, coma, possible death
Special notes
Extreme abuse can produce paranoid behavior.

Cocaine, currently one of the most popular fad drugs, is a powerful natural stimulant that is extracted from the leaf of the coca bush, *Erythroxylon coca*. This medium-sized flowering shrub is a native of the rugged eastern slopes of the Andes Mountains of South America, a region in which it grows in abundance today.

HISTORY

South America
The intoxicating effects of the coca leaf were known in South America long before the arrival of the first white man. An ancient myth has it

that Manco Capac, the royal son of the Sun God, was the source of coca. He, it is said, sent it as a gift "to satisfy the hungry, fortify the weary, and make the unfortunate forget their sorrows."

Coca was unknown to Europeans until the Spanish conquistadores reached South America in the early sixteenth century. There they found the Indians chewing coca leaves "from morning until they lie down to sleep." When asked why they chewed the leaves, the natives replied that it gave them great energy and strength and kept them from hunger, a role it still fills for many Indians in Latin America today (Figure 6-1).

When the Spaniards first came to the empire of the Incas in the 1500s, it was the emperor who controlled the use of coca. When the Spanish took over the empire, they also took over the control of the

FIGURE 6-1
Inca nobles stored their precious coca leaves in golden containers such as this one. (Trustees of Harvard University)

distribution of coca leaves. This gave them a stronghold over the Indians, who, under the drug's stimulating influence, worked harder and longer and required less to eat.

Today the coca leaf is still chewed widely in the Andes regions of South America for its stimulating effects and its curtailment of hunger pangs. The ancient measurement of cocada also continues as a measure of distance. One cocada is how far a fully laden porter can travel on foot while chewing on a cud of leaves.

Europe

A Spaniard from Seville is credited with first introducing cocaine to Europe in 1580, but it was not until the nineteenth century, when doctors were searching for a local anesthetic, that general interest was focused on the powers of the coca leaf. Doctors were improving surgical techniques and needed something to deaden pain. About 1860 two German scientists, Drs. Gaedecke and Niemann, discovered that the active ingredient in the coca leaf effectively counteracted pain. They called it "cocaine."[1] Interest was stimulated in the product, although its actual use as an anesthetic was not to come for another twenty-five years.

After the 1860s the use of cocaine spread rapidly. It was not until many years later that dangers were recognized. Between 1863 and 1865 a Corsican living in Paris, Angelo Mariani, developed a tonic whose active ingredient was cocaine. He called it "Mariani wine." After trying to grow coca trees in his Paris garden and failing, he became a major importer of the leaves. His wine was hailed by doctors, royalty, and other notables as well as laypeople as a great cure-all. It was used for the treatment of everything from headaches, obesity, and depression to indigestion, gout, and heart disease (Figure 6-2).

In the 1880s Sigmund Freud, who at that time was a young, obscure neurologist, became interested in cocaine (Figure 6-3). He tried it on himself and found it to be a magical drug that lifted depression, cured indigestion, and gave him energy. Soon he was prescribing it for his patients and writing scientific papers praising its wondrous powers.

On Freud's advice, a close friend who was seriously ill substituted cocaine for morphine as a pain-killer. After a year of ever-greater doses of it, he developed a severe cocaine psychosis: a feeling of "white snakes creeping over his skin." This experience, among others, may have led Freud to give up both his use of cocaine and his praise of it by 1887.[2]

At about the same time, 1884, Dr. Carl Koller became interested in

FIGURE 6-2
Advertisements featuring notables of the age were used to inform the public of the extraordinary powers of Vin Mariani, the first of the popular cocaine nostrums.

cocaine because of the enthusiasm for its powers of his close friend Freud. Koller was an eye surgeon in search of a potent local anesthetic. He tried cocaine and it proved to be highly effective. Thereafter it was widely used as a local anesthetic, until the advent of synthetic anesthetics, such as novocaine, in the mid-twentieth century. Indeed, cocaine is still used to a limited extent in eye operations.

Perhaps the most famous user of cocaine was the fictional English detective, Sherlock Holmes. His creator, Sir Arthur Conan Doyle, may have reflected the changes in popular reactions to cocaine through his character's changing use of it. As can be seen in the following passage in an 1889 Sherlock Holmes adventure, the *Sign of the Four*, cocaine was viewed by Doyle as a relatively harmless stimulant.

FIGURE 6-3
Sigmund Freud was one of the first supporters of cocaine. Later in his career he recognized many of the dangerous qualities of the drug. *(The Bettmann Archive, Inc.)*

Sherlock Holmes took his bottle from the corner of the mantelpiece, and his hypodermic syringe from its neat morocco case. With his long, white, nervous fingers he adjusted the delicate needle and rolled back his left shirt-cuff. For some little time his eyes rested thoughtfully upon the sinewy forearm and wrist all dotted and scarred with innumerable puncture marks. Finally he thrust the sharp point home, pressed down the tiny piston, and sank back into the velvet-lined arm-chair with a long sigh of satisfaction.

Three times a day for many months I had witnessed this performance, but custom had not reconciled my mind to it. . . . "Which is it to-day." I asked,—"Morphine or cocaine?"

He raised his eyes languidly from the old black-letter volume which he had opened. "It is cocaine," he said,—"a seven-per-cent solution. Would you care to try it?"

"No indeed," I answered, brusquely, "My constitution has not got over the Afghan campaign yet. I cannot afford to throw any extra strain upon it."

He smiled at my vehemence. "Perhaps you are right, Watson." he said. "I suppose that its influence is physically a bad one. I find it, however, so transcendently stimulating and clarifying to the mind that its secondary action is a matter of small moment."

"But consider!" I said, earnestly. "Count the cost! Your brain may, as you say, be roused and excited, but it is a pathological and morbid process, which involves increased tissue-change and may at least leave a permanent weakness. You know, too, what a blank reaction comes upon you. Surely the game is hardly worth the candle. Why should you, for a mere passing pleasure, risk the loss of those great powers with which you have been endowed? Remember that I speak not only as one comrade to another, but as a medical man to one for whose constitution he is to some extent answerable."

He did not seem offended. On the contrary, he put his finger-tips together, and leaned his elbows on the arms of his chair, like one who has a relish for conversation.

"My mind," he said, "rebels at stagnation. Give me problems, give me work, give me the most abstruse cryptogram or the most intricate analysis, and I am in my own proper atmosphere. I can dispense then with artificial stimulants. But I abhor the dull routine of existence. I crave for mental exaltation."[3]

By 1891 public opinion was condemning cocaine, and Doyle turned Holmes into an addict. In 1899, ten years after his author had started him on the drug, Holmes became cured of his addiction and called the hypodermic syringe an "instrument of evil."[4]

United States

During the 1880s cocaine gained wide popularity in the United States as a wonder drug. It was taken to treat everything from sinus trouble and hay fever to colic. It was widely used as a general tonic. Cocaine was also believed to be a cure for opium, morphine, and alcohol addiction. Such respectable public figures as Dr. William Hammond, a former surgeon general of the United States Army, praised it highly and took it at each meal.[5] In 1886 Hammond announced that cocaine was the officially recommended remedy of the Hay Fever Association. It became the main ingredient in many popular products, medicinal and otherwise. The Parke Davis Company, for example, sold coca leaf cigarettes, coca ointments, tablets, and a liqueurlike coca cordial. Sales of these products boomed.

At the same time, 1886, John Styth Pemberton of Atlanta, Georgia, introduced a drink that combined coca and an extract of the kola nut—Coca-Cola. He advertised it as "the intellectual beverage . . . valuable brain tonic and a cure for all nervous affections"[6] (Figure 6-4). What today is known as America's national drink contained cocaine until 1903, when the manufacturers were forced to switch to decocainized coca leaves. Such "sanitized" coca leaves are still used as a flavoring agent in Coca-Cola.

Around the turn of the century, abuse of cocaine became widespread, and fears grew of the danger of overstimulating "social subgroups," such as foreign and black laborers.[7] Criminal and immoral acts were blamed on cocaine. Officials began to take notice of the problem, and in 1906 the Pure Food and Drug Act curtailed the use of cocaine in over-the-counter medicines. By 1914 forty-six of the forty-eight states had laws regulating its use and sale.

The Harrison Narcotics Act was passed in 1914. It was the first federal antidrug law, and it made the illegal use and sale of cocaine punishable by fine and/or imprisonment. Although this was the end of the era of easy-to-get cocaine, cocaine was still available through the black market.

An indication of its continued and popular use can be seen in one of the songs from a well-known musical comedy of the day—Cole Porter's *Anything Goes*. One line of "I Get a Kick Out of You" was

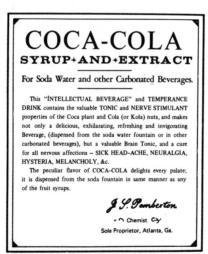

FIGURE 6-4
Coca-Cola, the most famous of the early American cocaine-based beverages, was an immediate success. Since 1903 only decocainized leaves have been used in its manufacture.

originally, "I get no kick from cocaine." It was later "sanitized" to refer to a more acceptable intoxicant—champagne.

The year 1932 initiated a thirty-year decline in the illegal importation and use of cocaine. It was not law enforcement efforts alone, however, that brought this about. Research had led to the development of a group of powerful synthetic stimulants—the amphetamines. They were far cheaper than cocaine and provided a similar "kick."

During the 1960s history was to repeat itself as cocaine made a sudden reappearance on the drug scene. Curiosity about its effects, the continual search among those involved in the drug scene for new and more potent highs, and the publicity given to it by a number of pace-setting show business superstars all contributed to the sudden upswing in cocaine's popularity.

About the same time that cocaine's popularity began to soar, stepped-up federal, state, and local enforcement efforts, as well as the imposition of rigorous production quotas by the government, were successful in severely limiting the availability of amphetamines on the street. As a result, stimulant abusers found that the once-plentiful uppers were no longer available. A good number of abusers sought to fill the void with cocaine.

A somewhat similar turn of events also took place in marijuana supply-and-demand patterns. Greatly increased surveillance at the border as well as stepped-up enforcement activity both in Mexico and in this country were, for some time, quite successful in cutting down the amount of marijuana smuggled into the United States. Consequently, a number of marijuana smugglers switched their efforts to cocaine. Not only was it less bulky, and as a consequence easier to slip over the border, but also the profits were far better. As one drug trafficker said, "Why should I mess around trying to get a pickup truck full of grass past the feds when I can slip a couple of bags of coke past them and make a hell of a lot more bread?"

During the last few years cocaine's popularity has continued to accelerate at an alarming rate. Seizures of cocaine enroute from South America have increased drastically as have undercover purchases both here and broad. Cocaine-related arrests by both state and federal authorities have also increased markedly.[8]

Today cocaine is the "in" drug—the ultimate status symbol in the drug scene. It is the way of showing that one is "with it." As one youngster said, "Coke is where it is all at. It's the only place to be if you are going to be somebody. Everybody who is together, who is anybody, is snorting coke." He then went on to explain, "Coke is where all the action is at. It's the way that you let folks know that you are with it . . . that you have *made* it. After all, you have to have it all together, you have to *be* somebody to snort flake that's worth a couple of thousand bills an ounce."

PRODUCTION

The cocaine trail begins high on the slopes of South America's rugged Andes Mountains. There, in thousands of small plots, Indian laborers tend their precious coca bushes (Figure 6-5). Today cultivation of the coca plant is legal in only two South American countries—Peru and Boliva. However, it is grown illegally in abundance in some of the more remote areas of Chile, Colombia, and Ecuador (Figure 6-6).

Both the Peruvian and Bolivian governments regard coca leaves as a vital source of foreign exchange. Thousands of tons of them are sold abroad each year for use in flavoring soft drinks and as a source of cocaine that is to be used medically. Many of the coca leaves, however, never make it into the official, government-sanctioned marketing system. Instead, the Indians sell them, at a far better price, to the numerous drug traffickers who operate near the growing areas. It is estimated that as much as 80 percent of the coca-leaf crops in Peru and Bolivia ends up in the black market.

Cocaine is extracted from the leaves of the coca bush by a relatively simple process (Figure 6-7). Every three or four months, depending on growing conditions, the Indians harvest the shiny, thumb-sized leaves. The leaves are carefully dried. The Indians then take them to one of the numerous primitive laboratories that the trafficking organization operate near the growing area.

There the leaves are soaked in a mixture of water, a petroleum distillate (such as kerosene), and calcium carbonate until an off-white sludge called "coca paste" precipitates out of the solution. This paste is raw cocaine. After being dried in the sun or over a slow fire, the paste is ready for shipment to one of the more sophisticated finishing labs where the final stage in the cocaine refinement process is carried out.

These finishing labs are run by the major drug trafficking organizations. Their locations are some of the underworld's most closely guarded secrets. Authorities have uncovered them in Ecuador, Colombia, Chile, Brazil, Argentina, and Paraguay, as well as in Peru and Bolivia. Because of the enormous volume of coca paste that is shipped from southeastern Bolivia into northern Paraguay and western Brazil, the area has been christened the Silver Triangle in contrast with the Golden Triangle opium-producing center in Southeast Asia.

The process of converting the coca paste into refined cocaine is relatively simple when compared to the chemistry of heroin produc-

FIGURE 6-5
Indians still cultivate their coca bushes in thousands of small
plots scattered throughout the Andes region of Latin America.

FIGURE 6-6
Coca-bush growing areas.

tion. Only rudimentary equipment is needed. First, the paste is dissolved in a dilute solution of hydrochloric acid. The resulting solution is then treated with potassium permanganate and sodium carbonate. At this point the cocaine precipitates out of the solution, and it is collected by filtration. The resulting cocaine is known as "rock." Depending on the skill of the chemists who operate the finishing labs, its purity will be anywhere from 70 to 86 percent. Most of the illicit cocaine that is available on the streets today is pulverized rock. Rock can be further refined into a purer form known as "flake." The purity of flake can exceed 90 percent. At the present time flake is rarely encountered on the street.

DISTRIBUTION SYSTEM

Smuggling Operations

Obviously, it is impossible to gather completely accurate figures on illicit cocaine production. However, the informed estimates of those who work closely with the problem give some idea of its magnitude. Authorities estimate the drug trafficking organizations based in Col-

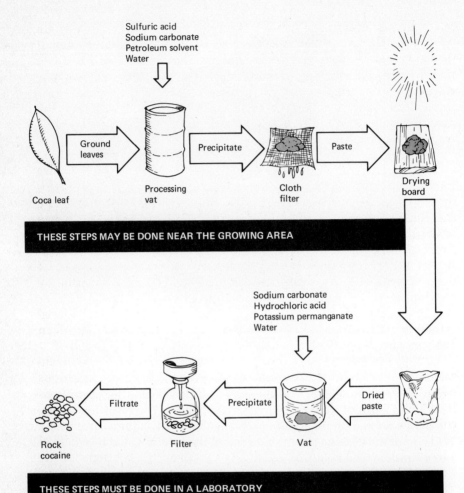

FIGURE 6-7
Cocaine production. First, the coca leaves are converted into coca
paste. Next, the paste is refined into pure cocaine.

ombia smuggle about 300 kilograms of cocaine a month to this country.
Similar groups based in Ecuador and Chile are thought to ship 50 to
100 kilos a month.

Federal authorities believe that most of the cocaine smuggled into
this country is carried by amateur couriers or, as they are called in the
trade, "mules." Typically, these couriers are students, housewives, or
tourists who are recruited to smuggle relatively small quantities, say 2
or 3 kilos, at a time. For them cocaine smuggling is a well-paying and

relatively safe way to make a lot of money in a short time. They are usually paid from $500 to $1,000 for each kilo plus their expenses. If they are unfortunate enough to be caught in the United States, it is rare that they are given anything more severe than a suspended sentence before being deported to their homeland. There they function as a walking advertisement for others who would be smugglers. After all, the money is good, and if all that the Americans do, if they catch you, is send you home again, why not give it a try?

Smugglers have tried every conceivable way of concealing cocaine. It has been found packed in hollow ski poles and picture frames; hidden in false-bottomed suitcases; packed in dolls, toy animals, and wine bottles; pressed paper thin and placed between the leaves of books; and strapped to the smuggler's body (Figure 6-8). Some have tried to fool customs officers by swallowing small pouches of it or stuffing it in their body cavities. Other enterprising smugglers even go so far as to soak their clothes in a solution of liquid cocaine and let them dry. When they get to this country, they recover the cocaine by soaking the garments in a solvent such as acetone.

Larger shipments of cocaine are usually handled by professional smugglers. In many cases sailors on vessels that call at South American ports and crew members of commercial aircraft have been involved.

Private planes are also used by the larger drug rings. This technique appears to have been perfected by the criminal organizations based in Colombia. The smuggler pilots hire a plane in the United States and file a misleading flight plan. They then fly to Colombia, collect the drug shipment, and return to the United States with it. Many of the better organized smuggling rings furnish complete logistical support for their flights. They provide depots for refueling, ground-to-air communications, and standard procedures for jettisoning the cargo if the plane gets into trouble or falls under suspicion.[9]

Domestic Sales

Most cocaine is smuggled into the United States by way of New York City, Miami, and Los Angeles. Its importation and high-level distribution are dominated by criminal groups that are believed to be controlled by Colombian, Cuban, and Puerto Rican nationals. These individuals are known to maintain close relations with their South American counterparts. Lately, however, there has been increasing evidence that the traditional organized crime groups in this country are becoming increasingly involved in the cocaine trade.

When a large shipment of cocaine arrives in the country, it is broken up and distributed among the larger customers. These are indi-

FIGURE 6-8
Smugglers have tried every imaginable means of slipping cocaine
into this country. In this case a false-bottomed wine bottle was
used. *(U.S. Customs Service)*

viduals or groups who have the resources to deal in quantities of a
kilogram or more. In the fall of 1976 a kilo was worth $20,000 to
$25,000 delivered in the United States. The wholesalers will, in turn,
break the shipment into smaller lots to be passed on to their own customers. And so the process continues until the cocaine reaches the
bottom rung of the distribution system—the street dealers. These generally peddle the drug in quantities of a gram or less. At this level
cocaine is often measured by the "spoon," a nebulous measure that
varies, depending on location, anywhere from one-sixteenth to one-
quarter of a teaspoon (Figure 6-9).

As the cocaine passes down through the distribution system from

FIGURE 6-9
Cocaine abusers frequently use small spoons to snort the drug. *(Fil Hunter)*

importer to user, two things happen: its purity goes down and its price skyrockets. Cocaine that is purchased in Latin America is anywhere from 60 to 80 percent pure, although the latter is rare. When cocaine arrives in this country, it may be sold in an unadulterated form at the wholesale level. However, once it gets below that rung in the distribution ladder, it is heavily adulterated (or as it is called on the street, "cut," "hit," or "stepped on") with such substances as dextrose, lactose, lidocaine, procaine, mannitol, inositol, and quinine. At each link in the sales chain the process is repeated, further reducing the purity of the drug. It is this cutting process that is, as in the case of heroin, at the heart of the enormous profits that are to be made from dealing in cocaine. By the time the drug finally reaches the user, it is rarely over 5 to 10 percent pure. That means that the same kilo that cost $4,000 or $5,000 in Latin America, or $20,000 delivered stateside, will yield 8 or more kilos of cut cocaine. By the time that this is sold in gram or spoon lots, its value will have risen to well over $300,000.

HOW USED

Most abusers prefer to inhale cocaine. On the street this is called "sniffing" or "snorting." There are those few abusers, however, who seek to intensify the drug's effects by injecting it intravenously.

The procedure followed in snorting is simple. First the user grinds the drug into a fine powder with a razor blade or some similar instrument. This step is important. Large granules of cocaine can become lodged in the nasal passages and cause severe irritation and inflammation of the mucous membrane. After grinding the cocaine, the user pinches one nostril shut and inhales the powder deeply through the other. Within moments the drug will have passed through the lining of the nasal passages into the bloodstream and be on its way to the brain.

Today's cocaine snorters have a wide range of paraphernalia to assist them. Miniature mortars and pestles as well as gold and sterling silver razor blades are sold for grinding cocaine into a suitable fine powder. Tiny spoons and straws, some made of silver, gold, or ivory, are also available. One of the newest entries in the cocaine paraphernalia market is the "tooter." Marketed for $25, it is purported to dispense just the right amount of cocaine for the perfect snort.

A small minority of diehard "coke freaks" prefer to inject the drug intravenously. Undoubtedly this practice heightens the drug's effects. It also greatly increases the danger associated with its use. Not only does cocaine that is injected directly into the bloodstream place a severe strain on the abuser's system, but it also markedly increases the damage that may be caused by any toxic adulterants that have been added to the drug. Furthermore, since the injections in almost all instances are done under unsterile conditions, they carry with them the potential for hepatitis and other infections.

EFFECTS

Cocaine is one of the most powerful stimulants known. Its effects are similar to those of the amphetamines; however, they do not last as long. Whereas an amphetamine high may last for several hours, the effects of a snort of cocaine usually wear off in fifteen minutes or so. The following description graphically portrays the stimulating effects of the drug.

"Cocaine produces, for those who sniff its powdery white crystals, an illusion of supreme well-being, and a soaring overconfidence in both physical and mental ability. You think you could whip the heavyweight champion, and that you are smarter than everybody. There was also that feeling of timelessness. And there were intervals of ability to recall and review things that had happened years back with an astonishing clarity."[10]

Cocaine causes an intense excitation of the central nervous system. Within moments, users begin to feel a sense of increased energy and alertness. This is generally accompanied by an overall sense of euphoria. They are "on top of the world." Their reflexes quicken and fatigue disappears. They become hyperactive, talkative, and enthusiastic, often to the point of outright grandiosity. No task seems too difficult to them. Some users also claim that cocaine has pronounced aphrodisiac qualities. Supposedly, it both heightens and prolongs sexual pleasures.

The effects of cocaine soon wear off. As the liver breaks down the drug, elation is all too quickly replaced by anxiety, depression, and fatigue. Most cocaine users feel that the intensity of the crash is directly related to the intensity of the high that it follows. As one heavy user said, "When I come down off a dynamite high, it's like sinking down all the way to the bottom of hell. I feel like the whole world is caving in on me. I can't handle it. It's one big nightmare."

Chronic Abuse

Chronic cocaine abuse over an extended period of time can greatly increase the drug's harmful effects. Symptoms similar to those associated with amphetamine psychosis have been reported. Chronic abusers can become severely agitated and overwrought. At times they experience both audible and visual hallucinations. In some instances such users become convinced that bugs or other vermin are crawling under their skin. In particularly severe cases abusers may exhibit distinctly paranoid behavior. This may be accompanied by a sense of panic as well as unpredictable bursts of violent behavior.[11]

Cocaine Poisoning

The increase in cocaine's popularity as well as variations in its purity and individual susceptibilities to the drug and the adulterants used to cut it have all contributed to a marked increase in the frequency of cocaine-poisoning cases. Cocaine poisoning usually follows a relatively predictable pattern:

1. Victims become extremely restless and excitable.
2. Their reflex responses increase, and they may experience chills or a fever.
3. Respiration is at first rapid and irregular. Later it becomes shallow and slow.
4. There may be vomiting and complaints of abdominal pain and nausea.
5. Convulsions, circulatory failure, coma, and respiratory failure may follow.

If an individual survives the initial crisis, recovery is generally quite rapid. Headaches and feelings of overall restlessness and depression may last for a few days and then subside. In rare cases, treatment of the psychosis that sometimes accompanies particularly severe abuse may require hospitalization. Follow-up treatment is also required if the psychological dependence that generally accompanies heavy cocaine abuse is to be broken.

Tolerance, Dependence, and Withdrawal

Cocaine is an extraordinarily seductive drug. Users can easily develop a strong psychological dependence on it.

The question of whether or not the body develops a tolerance to cocaine has not yet been satisfactorily answered. Some authorities believe that the body readily develops a tolerance to the effects of cocaine.[12] For example, one author reported a case in which an individual developed such a massive tolerance that he required 10,000 milligrams of cocaine a day to satisfy his craving. However, other equally qualified experts feel that a true psychological tolerance has not yet been positively demonstrated.[13]

Authorities are similarly divided on the question of physical dependence. Some researchers state flatly that the body does not develop a physical dependence upon cocaine. Others feel that the extreme depression and fatigue that occur when cocaine abuse is terminated are, in fact, withdrawal symptoms. This, they assert, indicates a genuine physical dependence on the drug. Only future research will be able to resolve these differing opinions.

EXTENT AND PATTERNS OF ABUSE

A survey conducted in 1974 found that 3.4 percent of the adults and 3.6 percent of the youths questioned said that they had used cocaine on at least one occasion. When compared with a similar survey conducted in 1972, the percentage of adults who use cocaine remained almost the same. However, the percentage of youths who admitted to using the drug had more than doubled.[14]

The frequency of cocaine abuse varies widely among the various subgroups within our general population. For example, various studies of students have found the following use rates[15]:

1.2 percent among junior high students

2.6 percent among senior high students

10.4 percent among college students

Sixteen percent of a sample of male high school graduates reported that they had used cocaine at some time during the five years following graduation.[16]

From April 1974 through April 1975 cocaine ranked twentieth in the drugs mentioned in DAWN reports and accounted for 1.1 percent of the DAWN mentions.[17] Of these mentions, 64 percent were for males. Th greatest prevalence of drug use (53 percent of all mentions) was among individuals between the ages of twenty and twenty-nine. More than half of the people recorded using drugs in the DAWN reports were whites.[18]

Cocaine appears at this time to be primarily a party or recreational drug. Of the individuals who came to the attention of the DAWN system, 61 percent stated that their primary reason for taking the drug was to experience its psychic effects. Only 30 percent felt that they were dependent upon it. Cocaine is used on an occasional basis, that is, several times a month or less, usually in the company of others. It is often taken in conjunction with alcohol or another drug such as marijuana.[19]

Heroin and cocaine are sometimes used together in a combination known as a "speedball." This mixture is said to maximize the effects of both drugs. In addition cocaine users will also often resort to depressants such as heroin or barbiturates to soften the effects of the crash which occurs when cocaine's effects wear off. Drug users in methadone maintenance programs have also been known to use cocaine. Its powerful stimulating effects are capable of producing a high even when an individual is under the influence of methadone. When cocaine is not available, amphetamines are often pressed into service as a substitute.

Recognizing the Abuser

As with other drugs, the reaction of one individual to cocaine may vary substantially from that of another. In addition, because its effects wear off so rapidly, it is unlikely that a police officer will encounter many users who are directly under its influence. These factors make it extremely difficult to spot the signs of cocaine abuse with any certainty. However, there are a number of symptoms and behavioral traits that may indicate cocaine abuse, particularly if it is severe. These include:

1. Extreme excitability
2. Hyperactivity
3. Excessive restlessness
4. Anxiety
5. Talkativeness

6. Visual and auditory hallucinations
7. Damage to nasal mucous membranes
8. Dilated pupils
9. Open sores and scabs from picking at imaginary bugs under the skin
10. Paranoid fears
11. Hostile and belligerent behavior (Figure 6-10)

LEGAL CONTROLS

Cocaine is, along with the opiates, designated as a narcotic drug by the Controlled Substances Act, and it is listed under Schedule II. This schedule includes those drugs that, though used in medicine, are subject to severe restrictions. Such drugs have a high potential for abuse, and they may lead to severe psychological or physical dependence. Among the other drugs included in this schedule are methamphetamine, opium, and many of the derivatives of opium.

IN CONCLUSION

Cocaine is a powerful and dangerous drug. At the present its abuse appears to be spreading, and it seems likely that as time goes by it will become even more of a problem than it is today. This, plus the violent behavior that is sometimes associated with its severe abuse, makes cocaine potentially one of the most troublesome drugs available.

NOTES

[1]*The Gourmet Cokebook* (DC Production Enterprise, 1972), p. 14.
[2]Edward M. Brecher and Consumers Union Editors, *Licit and Illicit Drugs* (Boston: Little, Brown, 1972), pp. 272, 274–275.
[3]Arthur Conan Doyle, *Sign of the Four* (New York: Ballantine Books, 1975), pp. 1–2.
[4]Goeffrey Marks and William Beatly, *The Medical Garden* (New York: Scribner, 1971), p. 48.
[5]David F. Musto, *The American Disease: Origins of Narcotic Control* (New Haven, Conn.: Yale, 1973), p. 7.
[6]George Andrews and Simon Vinkenoog (eds.), *The Book of Grass: An Anthology of Indian Hemp* (New York: Grove Press, 1967), p. 53.
[7]David F. Musto, p. 8.
[8]Domestic Council Drug Abuse Task Force, *White Paper on Drug Abuse* (Washington, D.C.: GPO, 1975), p. 24.
[9]Nicholas Gage, "Latins Now Leaders of Hard-Drug Trade," *New York Times*, Apr. 21, 1975, p. 2.
[10]Malcolm X, *The Autobiography of Malcolm X* (New York: Grove Press, 1965), p. 134.
[11]Frederick G. Hofmann, *A Handbook on Drug and Alcohol Abuse: The Biomedical Aspects* (New York: Oxford, 1975), p. 42.

**RECOGNIZING
THE ABUSER: COCAINE**

Damage to cartilage
of nose in cases of
severe abuse

Sores and scars
from picking at
"bugs" in cases
of severe abuse

GENERAL BEHAVIOR

Excitable, restless
behavior

PUPIL APPEARANCE

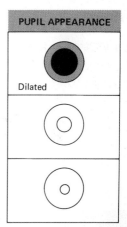

Dilated

PARAPHERNALIA

Mirror or other hard surface

Fluffy, white crystalline powder

Razor blade

Straw made of metal, paper,
ivory, or some similar material

Spoon

FIGURE 6-10
Common signs of cocaine abuse

[12]Louis S. Goodman and Alfred Gilman (eds.), *Pharmacological Basis of Therapeutics* (New York: Macmillan, 1970), p. 295.

[13]Frederick G. Hofmann, p. 242.

[14]Herbert I. Abelson and Ronald B. Atkinson, *Public Experience with Psychoactive Substances* (Rockville, Md.: National Institute on Drug Abuse, August 1975), pp. 9–10.

[15]Domestic Council Drug Abuse Task Force, pp. 24–25.

[16]Domestic Council Drug Abuse Task Force, pp. 24–25.

[17]Frederick G. Hofmann, p. 5.

[18]Frederick G. Hofmann, pp. 78–79.

[19]Domestic Council Drug Abuse Task Force, p. 25.

Chapter 7

MARIJUANA AND RELATED SUBSTANCES

Fact Sheet on Marijuana and Related Substances

Street names
   Grass, pot, Acapulco gold, Mary Jane, weed, hash, hash oil
Appearance
   Greenish brown vegetable matter; brownish cake; brown, viscid oil
How used
   Smoked, swallowed
Source
   Derived from *Cannabis sativa* plant
Medical uses
   None recognized at present
Control schedule
   I
Effects
   Euphoria, relaxed inhibitions, disoriented behavior
Tolerance
   Yes
Physical dependence potential
   Degree unknown
Psychological dependence potential
   Moderate
Duration of effects
   2 to 4 hours
Overdose
   Fatigue, possible paranoia and psychosis

As popularly used, the term "marijuana" refers to the hemp plant, *Cannabis sativa*, as well as the drug that is made by drying its leaves, small stems, and flowering tops. The cannabis plant is widely cultivated throughout tropical and temperate regions as a source of rope fibers, animal fodder, and plant oil as well as for its intoxicating properties.

   Cannabis sativa is usually found in this country in the form of a relatively tall, woody annual plant. (Plants 15 or 16 feet tall are often found in the wild.) Cannabis plants are sexually differentiated; that is, there are both male and female plants (Figure 7-1). The male plant is usually shorter lived, withering quickly after pollination has taken place. The leaves of both male and female are characteristically divided into five to seven leaflets and covered with tiny hairs. They have notches along the edges and are veined. The upper side is a deep green in color, and the underside is light green. The seeds are about the size of a large kernel of wheat, and they are encircled by a prominent ridge. Burning marijuana plants give off a pungent, characteristic burnt-rope smell.

In this country marijuana is usually smoked. It is either rolled into small handmade cigarettes, called "joints," "reefers," or "sticks," or used in a pipe. It can also be eaten—for example, it can be added to the batter for cookies or brownies or to the ingredients of some other dessert-type recipe.

HISTORY

People have known and grown the cannabis plant for thousands of years (Figure 7-2). Both the ancient Chinese and Greeks prescribed it as a medicine. The Spaniards first brought the plant to Chile in 1545, but it was the British who introduced it into North America. The Jamestown settlers had it by 1611, and it was first planted in New England in 1629. From that time until the 1940s it was widely cultivated in many parts of this country. From 1629 to the end of the Civil War cannabis was a major American crop and its hemp a significant factor in our early economy.

Use for Rope

In the days of sailing ships hemp was a vital commodity. The strong fibers found in the woody stem of the cannabis plant were woven into canvas for sails and into rope for rigging. It was also extensively used in weaving cloth.

The South was the early center of cannabis cultivation. In colonial days such gentlemen-farmer-statesmen as Thomas Jefferson and George Washington grew it on their Virginia plantations. Washington's 1765 diary contains entries about aspects of its growth. By the nineteenth century large hemp plantations were to be found in Kentucky, Mississippi, Georgia, California, South Carolina, Nebraska, and elsewhere, including Staten Island, New York. For a period of many years only tobacco and cotton ranked above hemp as America's leading cash crop.

The invention of the cotton gin and machinery for processing

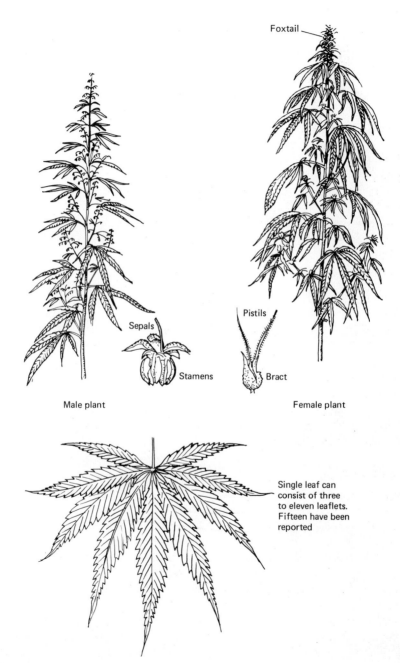

Foxtail

Sepals

Stamens

Male plant

Pistils

Bract

Female plant

Single leaf can
consist of three
to eleven leaflets.
Fifteen have been
reported

FIGURE 7-1
Typical male and female marijuana plants.

FIGURE 7-2
Illustration from fifteenth-century Persian manuscript of a woman
smoking hashish (a powerful marijuana derivative). *(National Library of Medicine)*

wool, together with cheap imported hemp, led to a decline in cannabis cultivation after the Civil War, but it did not end. In 1937 there was still a crop of roughly 10,000 acres, mostly in Kentucky, Illinois, and Wisconsin. In addition 4 million pounds of marijuana seed were used in birdfeed each year.

During World War II an acute shortage of imported hemp developed. To prevent a dangerous scarcity of rope, the Department of Agriculture encouraged the expanded cultivation of cannabis in the national interest. A by-product of this war effort is that decades after all commercial cultivation was ended, cannabis can still be found growing lushly as a weed. The Drug Enforcement Administration estimates that there is as much as 150,000 acres of wild marijuana growing in this country today.

Use as a Medicine

Mythology has it that marijuana was used in China as early as 2700 B.C. as a remedy for gout, constipation, and absentmindedness and as a surgical pain-reliever. The Greek historian Herodotus reports that in 500 B.C. the Scythians used it as a drug. It is less reliably reported that an ancient Moslem leader rewarded his hired killers with a form of marijuana, and that is was from his name, Hashshashin, that the words "assassin" and "hashish" are derived.

Marijuana was used in ancient India, but even then there was a difference of opinion about the value of its use. The Hindu wise men viewed it as a holy plant and necessary to religious life. But the warrior caste despised it and claimed that it led to lazy dreaming and cowardice.

More recently, in the nineteenth century, the respectability of the medical applications of marijuana is evidenced by British practice. Dr. J. Russell Reynolds, Queen Victoria's physician, wrote in the highly regarded medical journal *Lancet* in 1890 that in his opinion marijuana was "one of the most valuable medicines we possess." In 1898 Sir William Osler, who served both in this country and in Great Britain as a professor of medicine at John Hopkins University and at Oxford University, asserted that the drug "is probably the most satisfactory remedy" for migraine headaches.

In this country marijuana was widely used medically from 1850 to 1937. It was listed in the *U.S. Pharmacopeia*, and extracts of marijuana were made by leading drug firms for sale over the counter in pharmacies. It even served as a poultice for corns, and Girmault and Sons sold ready-made marijuana cigarettes as an asthma remedy.

With the progress of medicine the therapeutic applications of marijuana declined, and the passage of the Marijuana Tax Act in 1937, inspired by public fear of its growing use as an intoxicant, effectively put an end to its medical use. However, recent research suggests that marijuana may have a future in medicine. It may prove beneficial in the treatment of pain, anxiety, insomnia, excessive coughing, excessive menstrual bleeding, withdrawal from narcotics and alcohol, appetite stimulation, epilepsy, migraine headaches, and glaucoma.[1] There also have been indications that marijuana may be useful in organ transplant surgery and that it can inhibit the growth of solid tumors.

Use as an Intoxicant

Marijuana as an intoxicant was not viewed as a social problem in the United States until the early 1900s. For generations before that Mexican farm workers in the Southwest had gathered wild marijuana and rolled it into crude cigarettes. Local farmers considered these a poor man's substitute for tobacco and came to refer to all the cheapest grades of Mexican cigarette tobacco as marijuana. In time, the smoking of marijuana itself spread among Americans. Many copied the Mexican workers, and others were introduced to it by the sailors going between Central America and the United States, particularly to the southern ports. New Orleans, the busiest American port on the Gulf of Mexico, became the first United States city to know a marijuana cult. Jazz was being born in New Orleans at roughly the same time that marijuana made its debut there. The two became intertwined, and marijuana became a part of the jazz scene.

About that time a link was made in the popular mind between crime and marijuana. Its use was confined largely to groups in the poorer segments of society—those who traditionally have had the highest incidence of crime. Thus, the inference was drawn that the smoking of marijuana led to the commission of crime. This belief has been challenged since, but for many years the connection remained firmly fixed in the public mind.

There has been a marijuana subculture in the United States for many years, but it was not until the 1960s that there was a virtual explosion in its use.

ACTIVE INGREDIENTS

Several active alkaloid chemicals are found in marijuana. Cannabinol and tetrahydrocannabinols are the predominant ones. The tetrahydrocannabinols—or as they are more commonly known, THC—are the most active and consequently are thought to be responsible for marijuana's mind-altering properties. The potency of marijuana is directly related to the amount of THC present.

The concentration of THC found in different samples of marijuana, and hence its effects, vary greatly. Several factors account for the differences. These include:

1. Where the plant is grown
2. What part of the plant is used
3. How it is prepared
4. How it is stored

The marijuana grown in this country is relatively low in THC, usually containing less than 0.2 percent.[2]

There is a large variation in the amount of THC found in different parts of the plant. Very little is contained in the roots, large stem, and seeds. The small stems and leaves have a higher content and the flowers and resin even more.

The way in which marijuana is handled also has a marked effect on its potency. THC, a relatively fragile chemical, deteriorates rapidly upon exposure to excessive heat or cold. It is only stable within a limited temperature range of about 45 to 60 degrees Fahrenheit.[3]

FORMS AND DERIVATIVES

Many different preparations of the cannabis plant are popular in different parts of the world. In India, for example, *bhang* is a cheap, widely used, and relatively impotent drink that is brewed from the cut tops of the uncultivated female plant. It is about as strong as native American marijuana. *Ganja,* another favorite in India, is a considerably more potent marijuana derivative that is especially used as a smoke. It is made from the leaves and flowering tops of the cultivated female plant.

In the United States marijuana is generally smoked. The cigarette papers, which are usually of doubled thickness, are sometimes printed with colorful designs and patterns. The marijuana "tobacco" is often greener in color than cigarette tobacco and may have bits of stem and small oval-shaped seeds mixed in it. A wide range of paraphernalia is available for marijuana smoking. Pipes, hookahs, scales, sorting trays, and cigarette holders are just a sampling of the many items supplied by the thousands of "head shops" in this country (Figure 7-3).

Bulk marijuana may be sold in lots that range from less than an ounce to several tons. In small quantities it is often packed in such containers as matchboxes, used film canisters, and small plastic bags.

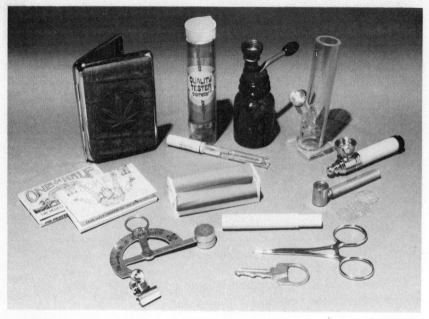

FIGURE 7-3
Paraphernalia used by marijuana smokers. *(Libby Wolfe)*

Larger amounts are often packaged in the form of kilogram bricks (Figure 7-4). These are made by compressing bulk marijuana into a rectangular shape that usually measures 5 by 2½ by 12 inches.

Hashish

Perhaps the best known and most popular in this country of the marijuana derivatives is hashish. Native to those areas bordering the eastern Mediterranean Sea and the Gulf of Arabia, hashish has been both eaten and smoked for thousands of years. Depending on its purity, the THC content of hashish will range from about 4 to 15 percent.

Hashish is made by compressing the crude resin of the cannabis plant into a solid mass. There are several traditional ways of harvesting the resin, and the product of each is graded according to its potency. Scraping the resin from leaves with a piece of leather is traditionally thought to yield the highest-quality hashish. Beating dried marijuana plants in sealed rooms and then collecting powder from walls, floors, and ceilings, as well as the bodies of the beaters, is another favored technique. Still another consists of pressing the marijuana against a coarse cloth and then collecting the resin that clings to the fabric. This produces the lowest-grade product.

FIGURE 7-4
Large quantities of marijuana are often packed in bricks. These
usually weigh about 1 kilo.

The finest-grade hashish is usually a rich dark brown color and
sold in small sticks or lumps. Next in quality is a brownish-green or
gray variety, which is generally stored in cloth bags. Having been
stacked and put under pressure, these bags are flat and foot-shaped.
Known as "pantougles" (the French word for slipper), they were, and
perhaps still are, often smuggled by being slipped into a courier's
shoes.

Hashish Oil

A fairly recently developed and very potent marijuana derivative is
hashish oil. Samples whose THC content ranges from 22 to almost 70
percent have been seized. Drug enforcement agency laboratories have
analyzed hashish oil marketed on the street with 63 percent THC content, and there is reason to believe that even more potent forms are
being developed. Considering that American marijuana usually contains less than 0.2 percent THC and the far more potent hashish usually
only contains from 10 to 12 percent THC, hashish oil can fairly be
called "dynamite." The oil is a dark-colored thick and sticky fluid.

It is a simple matter to produce hashish oil, and only the most
rudimentary equipment is needed. The process is the same as percolat-
ing coffee: ground-up marijuana is the substitute for the coffee beans
and a solvent such as acetone replaces water. The longer the mixture
percolates, the more THC is leached from the marijuana, and the
stronger the hashish oil becomes. Even the most elementary oil-

extracting apparatus can be amazingly effective. One Rube Goldberg contraption was seized that was capable of extracting 2½ quarts of hashish oil from 80 pounds of marijuana in an hour's time.[4]

For law enforcement officers the advent of hashish oil further complicates an already complex problem. Now, instead of searching for often large and bulky packets of marijuana and hashish, officers must hunt out small containers that can be easily concealed.

SOURCES OF SUPPLY

Most of the marijuana used in this country is grown in Mexico, Central America, or South America. At present, Mexico is the principal supplier. It attained this position for very understandable reasons. As our southern neighbor, Mexico shares over 2,000 miles of border with the United States, much of it over desolate, hard-to-patrol countryside. Thus smuggling supplies into this country is made easier. In addition, the volume of travel between the two countries is enormous. In 1974 over 6 million Mexicans entered the United States. During the same period thousands of American tourists crossed into Mexico and returned. Obviously, with such extensive border traffic it becomes extremely difficult to deter smugglers.

The cultivation of marijuana is illegal in Mexico. Thus most of the crop is grown in small, easily concealed plots nestled among the slopes of the wild and rugged Sierra Madre mountains. The inaccessible nature of this countryside provides almost perfect concealment and protection from the authorities.

A major marijuana eradication drive has been initiated by Mexican authorities. To assist in this effort, the United States government has provided technical assistance and equipment, such as communications gear, helicopters, and radar equipment, to track down marijuana farmers and processors. Though this combined effort has resulted in the destruction of a number of marijuana fields, it still remains to be seen if it will have any major, long-term effect on the overall supply.

EXTENT OF USE

The use of different derivatives of the cannabis plant is widespread in many parts of the world. Although any figures pertaining to world usage must at best be considered an educated guess, the United Nations World Health Organization has estimated that between 200 and 250 million people use some form of cannabis preparation.[5]

During the past decade there has been an explosive increase in the use of marijuana in the United States. Arrest statistics, seizures figures, and usage surveys all confirm the upward spiral.

During 1965 there were an estimated 18,915 persons arrested by local and state authorities for the sale or possession of marijuana. By 1974 this figure jumped to a staggering 445,600, accounting for over two-thirds of all state and local drug arrests made in the United States.[6] Between July 1971 and June 1972 federal authorities working at home and abroad seized 218,905 pounds of marijuana. Between June 1974 and July 1975 the figure had risen to over 1 million pounds.[7]

A number of studies have been made to determine the extent and nature of marijuana use in America. A late 1974 survey commissioned by the National Institute of Drug Abuse revealed that some 25 to 30 million Americans have used marijuana at least once. Of the adults interviewed, 19 percent admitted to using marijuana at least once (as compared to 15 percent in 1971). Of the youths interviewed, 23 percent said they had used it at least once (as compared to 14 percent in 1971). Among the 19 percent of the adult population who tried marijuana once, 7 percent used it within the month previous to the interviewing. They were classified as current users. Of the 23 percent of youths who acknowledged using marijuana, more than half (12 percent) had used it within the past year. Virtually all those who said that they had used marijuana within the month previous to the survey stated that they intended to use the drug again.[8]

The rate of use of marijuana is not, however, constant within the entire population, but varies dramatically from group to group. For example, among those interviewed in a 1975 study there was a dramatic generation gap among marijuana users and nonusers. In the eighteen to twenty-five age group 53 percent of those interviewed had used marijuana at least once. However, only 2 percent of those over fifty years of age reported having done so. More males (24 percent for both adults and youths) used marijuana than females (14 percent for adults and 21 percent for youth).[9] More nonwhites (26 percent) used the drug than whites (18 percent). However, current usage is about the same among races.[10]

There is also a strong relationship between education and marijuana use. Only 9 percent of the survey subjects who had not been graduated from high school had tried marijuana. This contrasts with the 27 percent of those who had had some college education and the 61 percent who were college students at the time of the survey.[11]

EFFECTS

Since 1968 the U.S. Department of Health, Education, and Welfare has conducted an intense, high-priority research program aimed at determining the effect of marijuana. The lack of hard scientific data as well as the intense emotionalism that the marijuana issue provoked had for years made it extraordinarily difficult to acquire the kind of authenticated, reliable data that was needed if a workable policy toward marijuana was ever to be promulgated.

Currently, the National Institute on Drug Abuse is supporting, to the sum of nearly $5 million a year, some sixty-five different marijuana research projects. It is from these and similar efforts that we have begun to gain the knowledge that is so vital if we are to accurately gauge the impact of the hazards associated with marijuana use.

Over the last few years we have come to realize that much of the original concern about the drug's effects was based more on myth than on fact. For example, government research has shown that the use of marijuana does not, except in the rarest instances, lead to violent behavior. The classic stereotype of the marijuana dope fiend is simply not substantiated by current research. However, this does not mean that marijuana can by any means be given a completely clean bill of health. Recent studies have raised a number of serious questions, especially regarding the chronic use of the drug.

Marijuana is, of course, not the only drug whose effects and impact have been hotly debated. As Dr. Robert Dupont, Director of the National Institute on Drug Abuse, points out:

> History bears witness to the difficulties of placing drug use, especially of new substances, in realistic perspective. Dangers have sometimes been minimized; at other times potential risk has been exaggerated. When coffee, for example, was introduced into Western Europe from the Near East much controversy arose over the possible dangers associated with its use. Penalties as extreme as death were exacted for its use. Conversely, the hazards of other drugs later proven to be dangerous have not always been obvious on initial introduction. Had cigarettes come into use at a time when their present health implications were well documented, there is little question that public health measures would have been taken to prevent or discourage their adoption and habitual use.
>
> The medical and scientific community have also not been immune from error. Heroin at the time of its first introduction was believed to be non-addictive and was even advocated as a "cure" for morphine addiction. Cocaine was at first thought completely safe and seen as a substance with profound therapeutic implications. More recently, thalidomide was originally believed to be an unusually safe sedative—especially for use by pregnant women—because it was thought to be usually nontoxic and free of hangover effects. Diethylstilbestrol was the drug of choice for various gynecological and obstetrical problems, and only after several decades of use did we realize that when given to pregnant women during certain critical periods of fetal development the drug may lead to cancer development in the female offspring of those pregnancies.

It is against this backdrop of historical error that the present concern over marijuana must be considered. Earlier reports, including that of the National Commission on Marijuana and Drug Abuse, have tried to place the health and social concerns over cannabis use into realistic perspective. Perhaps inevitably, material from these reports, often taken out of context, has been employed in polemics and the reports have sometimes been criticized for being either "too soft" or "too hard" on marijuana.[12]

In the following sections both the immediate and the long-term effects of marijuana use are summarized. It is important to keep in mind that marijuana and the other cannabis derivatives affect individuals differently. People sitting in the same room and smoking marijuana from the same "stash" may well have completely different reactions to the drug. For one person the drug's effects can be so subtle that they are hardly noticeable, while for another they may cause a severe reaction. Three factors in particular influence how a given individual will be affected by marijuana or any other drug: (1) the user's psychological makeup and expectations, (2) the setting in which the drug is consumed, and (3) the potency of the particular cannabis preparation being used. As already noted, the potency can vary widely according to where the plants were grown, the part of the plant used, and how the substance was prepared and stored.

Short-Term Effects

In small amounts marijuana acts in a manner that is similar to many other mild intoxicants. Some of its more commonly observed effects include:

1. Restlessness
2. An increased sense of well-being
3. A dreamy carefree state of relaxation
4. An altered sense of perception
5. A feeling that time and space have expanded

Any or all of these sensations or a combination of them may be experienced in a typical marijuana high.

Larger doses of marijuana may tend to intensify all the reactions just listed. In addition, the user may experience:

1. Rapidly changing moods and emotions
2. Shifting sensory imagery
3. Fragmentary thought with disturbed patterns of association
4. Dulling of attention

5. An altered sense of self-identity
6. A sense of enhanced excitement

Very large doses can produce more severe reactions. These can include:

1. Fantasies
2. Distortion of body image
3. Loss of personal identity
4. Hallucinations[13]

Severe abuse, especially of the more potent cannabis preparations such as hashish and hashish oil, can bring on depression, panic, and in rare instances even a psychotic breakdown.[14]

With even small doses of marijuana, psychomotor performance is impaired. Thus, while an individual is under the drug's intoxicating influence, the ability to drive or to operate any form of machinery is influenced. As more and more people turn to marijuana, there undoubtedly will be an increasing effect in the areas of traffic and industrial safety.

Long-Term Effects

Our information about the long-term, chronic use of marijuana is still too inconclusive to be the basis for much more than broad generalities. The very nature of the problem rules out hasty answers. Obviously, experiments that are designed to discover long-term effects on any drug can be sped up only so much if they are to yield accurate findings. However, though scientists are still groping their way through much uncharted territory, from our current understanding of the matter it seems correct to state that there is at present no convincing scientific evidence that marijuana causes any permanent biological harm to its users.

This is not, however, to say that marijuana use is without its hazards. As already mentioned, marijuana-induced intoxication can definitely affect psychomotor skills, and this can have serious consequences in such areas as traffic and occupational safety. In addition, there is preliminary evidence of a range of other potentially serious consequences to the body itself. These include the disruption of basic cell metabolism, possible effects on the level of the male hormone testosterone, and a lowering of the body's disease defenses. The findings in all these areas are in a preliminary stage. Only with additional research will we be able to assess the true impact of long-term, chronic marijuana use.

Tolerance and Dependence

Current research indicates that users can develop a tolerance to some of the effects of marijuana, especially when there is extensive and long-term abuse.[15] Some users may also develop a moderate psychological dependence upon it.[16] The question of physical dependence is still open to debate. Some authorities feel that a true physical dependence upon marijuana as it is commonly used has as yet not been demonstrated. Others, however, feel that it has.[17] Resolution of these different opinions will have to await the outcome of further research.

Marijuana and Other Drugs

One of the basic tenets of drug abuse is that an individual who uses one drug is likely to use another. This holds true for marijuana. The prior use of alcohol and tobacco by youths has been found to be closely related to the later use of marijuana.[18] Similarly, those who use marijuana are more likely than nonusers to use or have used other licit and illicit psychoactive drugs. As might be expected, the more intense an individual's use of marijuana, the greater the probability that he or she will use other drugs.[19]

An idea of the broad spectrum of drug use associated with many marijuana users can be gathered from the data collected by Erich Goode of the State University of New York at Stony Brook.[20] In a study of 204 marijuana users Goode found that 68 percent of those interviewed said that they had taken other drugs at least once. Those drugs most commonly used in addition to marijuana by Goode's subjects and the percentage of the interviewers using them is shown in Table 7-1.

One of the most controversial areas associated with multidrug use is the relationship of marijuana use to that of heroin. According to the

TABLE 7-1
USE OF OTHER DRUGS BY MARIJUANA USERS

Drug	Users (% of Those Interviewed)
LSD	49
Amphetamines	43
DMT or DET	26
Barbiturate or tranquilizer	24
Opium	20
Cocaine	19
Peyote or mescaline	19
Heroin	13

oft-quoted stepping-stone theory, marijuana users frequently graduate to heroin. This theory is presently being examined in a number of studies. Some of the more important finds were summarized in *The Pharmacists' Drug Abuse Manual* published by the Drug Enforcement Administration:

> The belief that marijuana use almost invariably leads to the use of heroin stems from the observation that most heroin addicts used marijuana prior to the first use of heroin. Until recent years, statisticians did not look first at marijuana smokers as a group to determine how many of them went on to use heroin. Nor did they look for other reasons that might account for the use of both marijuana and heroin. Recent analyses of new data have gone beyond the assumption that there is a simple, direct relation between marijuana and heroin use. They lead to three conclusions: Some marijuana users go on to use heroin, but the incidence varies in different kinds of groups.
>
> Other factors appear to be as important as marijuana in predicting eventual heroin use, including feelings of alienation and teenage delinquency—to mention a few.
>
> If the switch from marijuana to heroin does occur, it may be the result of the person's group life, his contact with drug peddlers, or the particular needs these drugs fill in his life.[21]

Recognizing the Abuser

There are few tell-tale signs that will help identify a person under the influence of marijuana. However, there are some indications for which one should be on the alert:

1. Intoxicated or disturbed behavior. While under the influence of marijuana, users may exhibit many of the symptoms of alcohol intoxication. The odor of alcohol will, however, be missing. Sometimes marijuana use may precipitate panic, hallucinations, and irrational behavior.
2. Inflamed or reddened eyes often accompanies the use of marijuana.
3. The odor of burning marijuana. When marijuana is smoked, it gives off a strong characteristic odor similar to that of burning hemp.
4. The odor of incense or a room deodorant. Users will sometimes burn incense in an attempt to mask the strong marijuana odor. Small ozone spray cans are sold to deodorize rooms in which marijuana has been smoked (Figure 7-5).

Of course, possession of marijuana cigarettes or paraphernalia used by marijuana adherents would indicate a probable user. Marijuana

**RECOGNIZING
THE ABUSER: MARIJUANA AND RELATED SUBSTANCES**

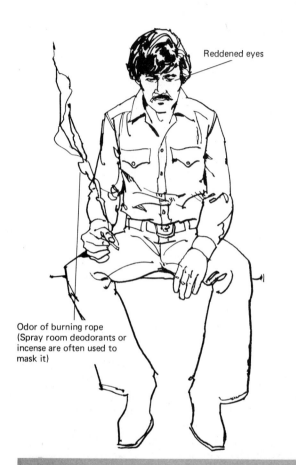

Reddened eyes

Odor of burning rope
(Spray room deodorants or
incense are often used to
mask it)

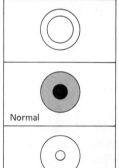

GENERAL BEHAVIOR

Sluggish, intoxicated. In
rare cases, use may pre-
cipitate panic or other
irrational behavior.

PUPIL APPEARANCE

Normal

PARAPHERNALIA

Cigarette papers

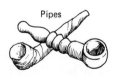

Pipes

Roach clips

FIGURE 7-5
Common signs of marijuana abuse.

in cigarettes differs in color and texture from true cigarette tobacco. As already noted, it is greener in color and may have bits of stem and small oval-shaped seeds mixed in it.

The behavior patterns described in the section on Effects are also indications of marijuana abuse. Many of these are also characteristic of other types of drug abusers; thus, their presence alone cannot be the only standard for identifying a marijuana abuser.

LEGAL CONTROLS

At the present time marijuana is listed in Schedule I of the Controlled Substances Act of 1970. Other drugs in this schedule include the opiates, hallucinogens such as LSD, and the powerful stimulant methamphetamine.

Over the past few years there has been a movement to reevaluate the legal sanctions that are currently directed against the use of marijuana. Two alternatives to the present approach have been proposed. They are legalization and decriminalization. Though these two terms are often used interchangeably, they are, in actuality, very different concepts.

Legalization, in the context of marijuana use, means that the drug could, under government control, be legally sold on the open market. If legalized, *both* the use and sale of it would be permissible.

Decriminalization, on the other hand, pertains only to the user. The acts of smoking marijuana in private and possessing small amounts of the drug for personal use would be reduced from a crime to a civil infraction similar to a parking violation. If caught, violators would be subject to a small fine, but they would not be given criminal records. Some versions of this approach go even further. The private use and transfer of small amounts would be considered legal. Under the concept of decriminalization, trafficking in marijuana would still be against the law and no legal market would be permitted.

The trend toward reduced legal sanctions against marijuana has had a pronounced effect since the early 1970s. By 1974 every state in the nation had reduced first-offense possession of small amounts from a felony to a misdemeanor. Currently half of the state legislatures are considering bills designed to decriminalize marijuana. Oregon was the first state to do so, in October 1974. There it is a civil offense to possess an ounce or less of the drug. The maximum penalty that can be imposed under the new Oregon law is a $100 fine. In May 1975 Alaska became the first state to make legal the possession of marijuana for private use in the home. In a 5 to 0 decision the Alaskan Supreme Court said that mere scientific doubts about the effects of the drug were not justification for governmental invasions of the privacy of the home.

IN CONCLUSION

The use of marijuana is by far the most widespread form of drug abuse in this country today. There is little doubt that during the next decade or so we will see a major reevaluation of the legal status of marijuana in this country. Decriminalization and perhaps even complete legalization are not far away. Until that time, however, marijuana will continue to be a large, costly, and time-consuming enforcement problem.

NOTES

[1]Fred Leavitt, Drugs and Behavior (Philadelphia: Saunders, 1974), pp. 74–75.

[2]National Commission on Marijuana and Drug Abuse, Marijuana: A Signal of Misunderstanding (Washington, D.C.: GPO, 1972), p. 50.

[3]John T. Mayer, Cannabis Sativa, lecture in 1976. Reprint provided by the U.S. Department of Justice, Drug Enforcement Administration, Washington, D.C.

[4]Robert M. Stutman, The Marijuana Controversy (Washington, D.C.: U.S. Bureau of Narcotics and Dangerous Drugs, n.d.), pp. 24–25.

[5]Marijuana (Washington, D.C.: U.S. Bureau of Narcotics and Dangerous Drugs, 1972), p. 11.

[6]Federal Bureau of Investigation, Crime in the United States, 1974, Uniform Crime Reports (Washington, D.C.: GPO, 1975), p. 79.

[7]DEA Drug Enforcement Statistical Report (Washington, D.C.: Drug Enforcement Administration, 1975), p. 304.

[8]Herbert I. Adelson and Ronald B. Atkinson, Public Experience with Psychoactive Substances (Rockville, Md.: National Institute on Drug Abuse, August 1975), p. 7.

[9]Herbert I. Adelson and Ronald B. Atkinson, p. 7.

[10]Herbert I. Adelson and Ronald B. Atkinson, pp. 39–40.

[11]Herbert I. Adelson and Ronald B. Atkinson, p. 35.

[12]National Institute on Drug Abuse, Marijuana and Health, Fourth Report to the U.S. Congress (Washington, D.C.: GPO, 1974), pp. 1–2.

[13]Drug Enforcement Administration, Drugs of Abuse, vol. 2, no. 2, pp. 26–27, Spring 1975 (Washington, D.C.: GPO, 1975).

[14]Dealing with Drug Abuse: A Report to the Ford Foundation (New York: Praeger, 1972), p. 101.

[15]National Commission on Marijuana and Drug Abuse, p. 21.

[16]Drug Enforcement Administration, p. 21.

[17]Drug Enforcement Administration, pp. 26-27. National Institute on Drug Abuse, pp. 79-80.

[18]National Commission on Marijuana and Drug Abuse, Drug Use in America: Problem in Perspective (Washington, D.C.: GPO, 1973), p. 92.

[19]National Institute on Drug Abuse, p. 92.

[20]Erich Goode, "Multiple Drug Use among Marijuana Smokers," Special Problems, vol. 17, no. 1, pp. 48–64, Summer 1969.

[21]Drug Enforcement Administration, The Pharmacist's Drug Abuse Manual (Washington, D.C.: GPO, 1973), p. 15.

Chapter 8
HALLUCINOGENS

Fact Sheet on Hallucinogens

Street names
Acid, big D, businessman's special, mesc, button, peace pills
Appearance
Liquid, powder, capsules, tablets, plant material
How used
Swallowed, sniffed
Source
Clandestine laboratories, plants
Medical uses
None recognized at present
Control schedule
Most in Schedule I
Effects
Illusions and hallucinations
Tolerance
Yes
Physical dependence potential
None
Psychological dependence potential
Degree unknown
Duration of effects
Variable
Overdose
Longer, more intense episodes, psychosis
Special notes
Under influence of these drugs, users may indulge in irrational acts such as attempting to "fly" from high buildings.

The hallucinogens are a diverse group of substances capable of inducing bizarre changes in the manner in which individuals perceive the world about them. A wide range of substances derived from both plants and the chemical laboratory possess hallucinogenic properties. Peyote, nightshade, ragroot, donana cactus, yopo, Hawaiian wood rose, henbane, juniper, Madagascar periwinkle, mandrake, maraba, coleus, morning glory, thorn apple, jimson weed, syrian rue, nutmeg, and assorted mushrooms are but a small sampling of the many plants that can produce hallucinations when consumed.

Since earliest times humans have sought the aid of the natural hallucinogens in their eternal quest for a means by which to communicate with the gods. From the barren Arctic wastes of Siberia to the steaming jungles of equatorial Africa, numerous hallucinogenic plants have been an integral part of the religious and mystical lives of countless primitive peoples.

To this natural hallucinogenic salad we must add the products of the chemist's labors. LSD, STP, PCP, and MDA are just a few of the many different synthetic and semisynthetic hallucinogens that are currently available.

EXTENT AND PATTERNS OF ABUSE

Many who work in the field of drug abuse feel that the use of hallucinogens has declined in recent years. In the case of adults, the survey data seems to support this notion. For example, in 1972 4.6 percent of the adults questioned by the National Commission on Marijuana and Drug Abuse said that they had used LSD or some other hallucinogen.[1] In 1974 a comparable study found that 4.5 percent of the adults interviewed had used hallucinogens at least once. However, in the case of youth there has been a noticeable increase in their use. In 1972, 4.8 percent of the youth surveyed reported having used hallucinogens; by 1974 this had increased to 6 percent.[2]

In the DAWN III reports for April 1974 through April 1975, LSD, one of the most widely used hallucinogens, was mentioned more than 8,700 times, placing sixth among the frequently mentioned drugs in the DAWN III survey.[3]

Most of those who use LSD and other hallucinogens do so rarely. Of the 4.5 percent of adults and 6 percent of youth who admitted to using them, only 0.6 percent and 1.3 percent, respectively, said that they had used hallucinogens in the month preceding the 1974 survey. Only 0.1 percent of both groups reported using them five days or more a month.[4] Other surveys have found once a month to be the average rate of use.[5]

Tolerance, Dependence, and Withdrawal

The body is capable of developing a tolerance to many of the effects of hallucinogens. They do not, however, appear to produce a true physical dependence. Consequently, withdrawal symptoms do not seem to occur when an individual stops taking them. As yet, the degree of psychological dependence upon hallucinogens is not completely understood.[6]

Recognizing the Abuser

There is no one sign or mode of behavior that will definitely indicate that a person is under the influence of a hallucinogenic drug. The associated physical and behavioral signs vary widely. The following, however, are sometimes observed:

1. Dilated pupils
2. Rambling, incoherent speech
3. Increased sweating
4. Distortion and changes in the senses of time, smell, sight, hearing, and touch
5. Nausea, chills, flushes, trembling hands
6. Euphoria
7. Trancelike behavior
8. Anxiety, panic, and terror
9. Complaints of visual and auditory hallucinations, which can range from the pleasant to the terrifying (Figure 8-1)

LEGAL CONTROLS

LSD, mescaline, MDA, and most of the more commonly available hallucinogenic substances are listed in Schedule I of the Controlled Substances Act of 1970. This schedule includes those drugs or other substances that have a high potential for abuse and have no currently accepted use in treatment in the United States and for which there is a lack of accepted safety for use under medical supervision.

LSD

In all probability, when asked to name any hallucinogenic drug, the average citizen would reply, "LSD." Lysergic acid diethylamide, the most powerful hallucinogen commonly available, has received by far the greatest publicity. It is a semisynthetic compound produced from lysergic acid, a substance produced in nature by a fungus disease that attacks rye plants.

Drs. Alfred Hoffman and W. A. Stoll, research chemists for the Sandoz Pharmaceutical Company in Switzerland, discovered LSD in 1938. Its hallucinogenic qualities were not realized until Dr. Hoffman accidentally swallowed some of the drug. He recorded the results in his diary:

> Last Friday . . . I had to interrupt my laboratory work in the middle of the afternoon and go home because I was seized with a feeling of great rest-

**RECOGNIZING
THE ABUSER: HALLUCINOGENS**

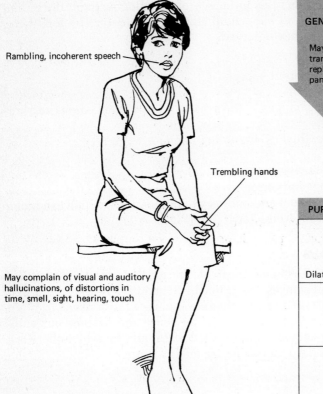

Rambling, incoherent speech

Trembling hands

May complain of visual and auditory
hallucinations, of distortions in
time, smell, sight, hearing, touch

GENERAL BEHAVIOR

May appear to be in a
trancelike state; can be
replaced by a state of
panic

PUPIL APPEARANCE

Dilated

PARAPHERNALIA

Sugar cubes

Peyote button

"Windowpane"

Capsules   Pills

FIGURE 8-1
Common signs of hallucinogen abuse.

lessness and mild dizziness. At home, I lay down and sank into a not unpleasant delirium, which was characterized by extremely excited fantasies. In a semi-conscious state (with my eyes closed I felt the daylight to be unpleasantly dazzling) fantastic visions of extraordinary realness and with an intense kaleidoscopic play of colors assaulted me. After about two hours the condition disappeared.[7]

Forms

LSD is found on the street in three forms—a tablet, white powder, or a clear, odorless, and tasteless liquid. Users have pressed everyday items into service to be their LSD carriers. They have dabbed it on such diverse things as paper, gelatin squares, animal crackers, sugar cubes, candies, cake, the back of stamps, fingernails, and beads.

An extraordinarily potent drug, LSD has been known to produce effects when as little as 20 micrograms (a microgram equals one-millionth of a gram) have been swallowed. Such a minute dose equals one seven-hundred millionth of an average man's weight. A dose of only 100 to 200 micrograms is usually all that is needed to produce a full-fledged hallucinatory experience—or as it is called in the drug culture, a "trip." One ounce of LSD is enough to produce over a quarter of a million doses.

Effects

Most individuals who take LSD do so in order to experience its psychic effects. Rarely do they give dependence and self-destruction as reasons for its use. This motivation pattern is similar to that of marijuana and markedly different from that of heroin and the barbiturates.

LSD has profound effects upon the human mind that are far from fully understood. The effects vary greatly from individual to individual. Some users contend that LSD allows them to reach new insights about themselves and the world in which they live. They are certain that it spurs their creative selves, that it leads them to a fundamental understanding of themselves and their place in the world. They tend to view the LSD experience as one that is shrouded in deep mystical and/or religious significance. There are others with the same personality and talent makeup who deny that LSD stimulates creativity.

However, there are other users for whom the LSD experience is fraught with the most devastating of terrors. For example, one user during a bad trip said that he was being chased, stabbed by a sword, run over by a horse, and frightened by a hippopotamus. Imaginings such as this, bizarre as they may seem, are not uncommon.[8]

As is true for all drugs, the effects that LSD produces are, to a large extent, determined by both the expectations of the user and the setting in which the drug is taken. If the user is actively looking forward to the experience, it probably will turn out to be a pleasant one. By the same token, if he or she is apprehensive when the drug is taken, there is an excellent chance that the experience will turn into a bad trip. The user's chance of a pleasurable experience is increased if the drug is taken in a setting in which the user feels secure and at ease.

Although there is no such thing as the typical LSD reaction, the following outline paints a broad picture of the sequence that often follows after the drug is taken. For the first half hour or so the user usually experiences nothing out of the ordinary. Within forty-five minutes or so, however, visual changes start to become noticeable. Colors often appear to intensify, and brilliant symmetrical designs appear. Sensory crossover in which the user "hears" colors and "sees" sounds may occur. Stationary objects may begin to move and spin, or they may change shape and size. Some users report strikingly vivid hallucinations during which they "see" and "hear" any number of unreal and often extraordinary bizarre and complex sights and sounds.

Under the influence of LSD, all the user's senses may be affected. Hearing may be intensified, as may be the senses of touch and smell. Time may appear to slow down or speed up. Users may or may not be aware of and in touch with their surroundings, and they may or may not be able to communicate with those around them. Rapid changes in mood may occur. LSD may produce a complete and utter panic in some users. Typically, these individuals feel that they are being engulfed and totally overwhelmed by the LSD experience. They may be plagued by terrors so devastating that they suffer complete psychological disintegration.

In some instances LSD users become convinced that they can accomplish impossible tasks—that they are invincible. The unfortunate record of those individuals who have died while attempting to "fly" from high buildings points up the dangers associated with such grandiose feelings.

The immediate effects of LSD usually wear off within six to eight hours. Then users experience a feeling of overall letdown similar to that following any other intensely emotional experience. It is not uncommon for people who no longer take the drug to experience flashbacks, or unexpected reoccurrences of LSD effects. This has been reported by some individuals weeks or even months after the drug was last taken.

During the late 1960s and early 1970s a great deal of publicity was given to the dangers that were said to accompany the use of LSD. Chromosomal and brain tissue damage were among the most publicized effects. Subsequent research failed to substantiate these fears. To date there have been no deaths that are directly attributable to LSD. However, instances of attempted suicide as well as deaths attributable to confusion, delusions of grandeur, and panic caused by the drug have been reported. LSD users have been known to suffer from convulsions.[9]

At times, even the most experienced LSD users may suffer adverse consequences from the drug. During these bad trips users may be overwhelmed by panic. In its grips they may become convinced that they are going completely mad. It has already been noted that some users may also suffer spontaneous reoccurrences of the LSD experience long after the drug's original effects have worn off. Usually such flashbacks only last for a few minutes. However, in severe cases they may go on for several hours.

Treatment

Treatment consists primarily in providing an atmosphere in which the user's anxiety can be relieved. To this end, the user is placed in a warm, comfortable room away from noise and other disturbing stimuli. The user's fears and fantasies are discussed in a friendly, confident, and reassuring manner. During this talk-down period users should not be left by themselves. Though physical restraints are usually not needed, care must be taken to make sure that they do nothing to injure themselves or others. Hospitalization is usually not required, though it may be needed in particularly severe cases.[10]

User Profile

There is no typical LSD user—no particular social, economic, age, educational, or occupation classification. However, there are broad generalizations that can be made. For example, experience has shown that the bulk of LSD users are from eighteen to thirty years old. Many are either students or recent dropouts from middle- or upper-middle-class homes. From DAWN data it appears that LSD is used predominantly (64 percent) by males. It also appears to be used primarily by whites; 70 percent of both the male and female LSD users reported by DAWN were white.[11] A study of 114 LSD users conducted by Dr. Donald B. Louria of Cornell University Medical College supports these findings as indicated in Table 8-1.[12]

TABLE 8-1
LSD USER PROFILE

Male	68.4 percent
White	88.4 percent
Used LSD one to three times only	72.8 percent
Suffered from underlying overt mental disease	34.2 percent
Average age	23 years

LSD users frequently take other drugs as well. Typically these include amphetamines, barbiturates, marijuana, and other hallucinogens such as mescaline, PCP, STP, and DOM.

Sources of Supply

Since the federal government rigorously controls all licit supplies of LSD, clandestine labs are its only street source. There the drug is produced with relative ease by underground chemists, or "cooks." These labs are located both in the United States and abroad in such countries as Canada, Switzerland, and Israel.[13]

A number of extremely volatile and potentially explosive chemicals are used in the manufacture of LSD and many other hallucinogens. In all too many cases illicit laboratories have been blown apart with an explosive force equal to many sticks of TNT. With that in mind, it is absolutely imperative that an experienced chemist be called to the scene immediately whenever a suspected laboratory is discovered. Only such an expert, thoroughly familiar with the ins and outs of organic chemistry, will know how to shut down such an operation in a safe manner.

Medical Uses

For the past three decades, LSD and similar mind-altering substances have been studied intensely in an attempt to find ways in which they can be used therapeutically. To date LSD is still classified as an experimental drug with no demonstrable medical use. However, there are several areas in which it may someday prove medically useful. For example, LSD is being tried in a number of experiments that are designed to unlock the secrets of how the brain functions. It is also being tested for use in treating patients with several forms of severe mental illness, and it is being considered in the treatment of heroin addicts and alcoholics.[14]

Research is also being conducted on ways in which LSD can be used to ease the agonies of those suffering from incurable cancer. In a study conducted by Dr. Eric Kast of Cooke County Hospital, Chicago, it was found to be about as effective as the opiates in relieving pain. LSD has an added benefit in that its effects last considerably longer. Dr. Kast also noted that patients treated with it were able to cope with the pain more successfully when it returned.[15]

MESCALINE

There grows across the barren desert wastelands of northeastern Mexico and parts of the southwestern United States a small, nondescript, spineless cactus with the imposing botanical name of *Lophophora williamsii*—more commonly known as peyote (Figure 8-2). This cactus, called "the fruit of the gods" by the Mexicans, is the natural source of the powerful hallucinogenic drug mescaline.

FIGURE 8-2
Peyote, the cactus *Lophophora williamsii*, is the natural source of the strong hallucinogenic drug mescaline. Most mescaline now found on the street is manufactured synthetically.

History

The vision-inducing properties of peyote have been known since the days of the Aztecs. During the latter part of the nineteenth century Indians of the American Southwest began to use mescaline in their religious and healing rituals. Eventually several religious cults developed whose faith centered on the consumption of the peyote. As a response to efforts of the U.S. Bureau of Indian Affairs to have Congress outlaw the use of peyote in their religion, several cults banded together and incorporated in 1918 as the Native American Church in Oklahoma. In 1944 the church changed its name to the Native American Church of North America. Members of this sect are the only individuals who may legally use mescaline in the United States, and they must do so only within the confines of their established religious ritual.

Medical Uses

Medical investigators have experimented with a number of possible uses for mescaline. It has been suggested for the treatment of angina pectoris (a sudden, severe pain of the heart), as a depressant, as a respiratory stimulant, and as a cardiac tonic. Mescaline was one of the first hallucinogens to be tried in the treatment of alcoholism, neurosis, and other mental disorders. The outcome of many of these research efforts is still unresolved.[16]

Forms

On the street mescaline is found either as a white crystalline powder in its purified form or as dried pieces of the peyote cactus, called "buttons." The pure drug is now produced synthetically, and it is either swallowed or injected. Bits of the cactus may be eaten fresh or may be dried and then later chewed or boiled into a tealike beverage. Much of the so-called mescaline available on the street is actually LSD, PCP, or some other, more common hallucinogen.

Effects

Though far weaker than LSD, mescaline taken in sufficient quantities has about the same effects.[17] These vary considerably for each individual. Some users, especially novices, suffer from severe intestinal cramps, nausea, and vomiting. These may go on for several hours, and they are often accompanied by profuse sweating, increased blood pressure, muscle twitches, and dilated pupils.

The passing of these symptoms is followed generally by a period of intense hallucinogenic activity that lasts from four to twelve hours.

There have been people, however, for whom hallucinations continued for a day or more.[18]

Users may experience frequent changes in mood and temperament. They may also suffer terrifying reactions such as those in the description that follows:

> Suddenly I found myself at the bottom of a black pit, clawing at the sides, attempting to escape. Leering into the pit was Satan, an evil-looking creature with the head of a spider. He was sneering at me and uttering words, "Alone! Alone! Alone!" The words echoed throughout the pit like a curse, an affliction from which I could not escape. . . . There was no one with whom to share my plight; I was alone in the pit.[19]

Tolerance, Dependence, and Withdrawal

After repeated doses, users can develop a marked tolerance to the effects of mescaline. There is a distinct cross-tolerance between mescaline, LSD, and psilocybin, the active ingredient of many hallucinogenic mushrooms. Someone who is tolerant to mescaline will also be tolerant to the other two. The body does not develop a physical dependence upon mescaline; hence, withdrawal symptoms do not develop when its use is stopped. The degree to which a psychological dependence may develop is not known.[20]

There are no cases known in which death can be attributed to the direct effects of mescaline. However, certain drugs such as insulin and barbiturates are known to increase its toxicity. Consequently, it is not impossible that, under some circumstances, the increased sensitivity to other drugs created by mescaline has indirectly caused fatal overdoses.

PCP

Phencyclidine is a hallucinogenic drug that is becoming increasingly popular. Developed during the 1950s, PCP was widely experimented with as a surgical anesthetic. At first it was also prescribed as a painkiller and to treat mental disorders. However, its use with humans was discontinued because of unwanted side effects. At the present time it is marketed under the trademark of Sernylan as a veterinary anesthetic and tranquilizer.

Form

PCP, sometimes called "angel dust," is merchandised as a tablet, capsule, or powder. The drug is taken orally (frequently in combination with other drugs) or smoked after it has been sprinkled on some carrier such as marijuana, parsley, or tobacco. PCP is often passed off on un-suspecting customers as LSD, mescaline, THC, or some other hallu-cinogen.

Though there is evidence that some legitimately manufactured Sernylan is diverted into the black market, most of the PCP on the street originates in clandestine laboratories (Figure 8-3). All too often this homemade PCP is contaminated with dangerous impurities.

Effects

As with all hallucinogenic substances, the effects of PCP vary widely. Many users report relatively nondescript and somewhat unpleasant experiences under its influence. Some of the effects specifically noted include perceptual distortions, feelings of depersonalization, visual and auditory hallucinations, apathy, and estrangement. In addition, some users report drowsiness, an inability to concentrate, and a preoc-cupation with death. In rare instances, users suffer severe psychotic episodes.[21] PCP may also produce profuse sweating, dizziness, nausea, vomiting, and a lack of muscular coordination.[22]

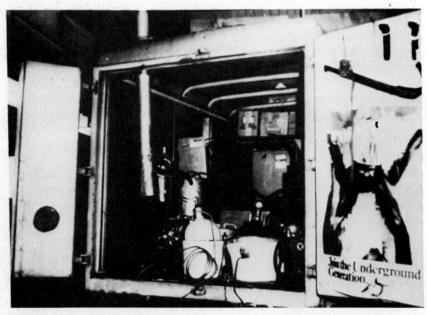

FIGURE 8-3
Most of the hallucinogens found in this country are manufactured in clandestine laboratories. This particular lab was located in a van. (*Drug Enforcement Administration*)

Tolerance, Dependence, and Withdrawal

With repeated use the body develops a tolerance to PCP. It does not develop a physical dependence upon it. Consequently, withdrawal symptoms do not materialize when its use is stopped. The extent to which psychological dependence develops is not known.[23]

MAGIC MUSHROOMS

Psilocybin and its derivative psilocin are two hallucinogens whose chemical structures closely resemble each other as well as those of LSD and DMT. They are obtained from several different genera of "magic" mushrooms, most notably the *Psilocybe* (Figure 8-4).

Known as "teonnacatl," or "flesh of the gods," these mushrooms are mentioned in ancient Mexican records dating back to 1500 B.C. For centuries Indians throughout Mexico and Central America invoked their magical power in religious ceremonies. One chronicler tells of them being served at the coronation feast of the last of the mighty Aztec god-kings, Montezuma II, in 1502. Today they are still used in a number of Mexican Indian religious rituals.

FIGURE 8-4
Several species of mushrooms found in this country are hallucinogenic.

Psilocybin and psilocin are usually swallowed, though they also can be smoked or sniffed. Their results are similar to those of LSD, but far less severe and shorter lived. Because of the natural toxins of many of the mushrooms that serve as the base for these drugs, users from time to time may experience nausea and vomiting. The body builds up a tolerance to their effects, but physical dependence does not develop. The extent to which a psychological dependence upon them may develop is not known.

Recently there has been a marked increase in interest in and use of the magic mushrooms. Magazine articles and pamphlets have appeared that detail techniques for growing them. As might be expected, the result has been a steep climb in their street price.

DOM

DOM (4-methyl-2,5-dimethoxyamphetamine), commonly referred to on the street as "STP," was first synthesized in 1964. Chemically it is related to both mescaline and the amphetamines. It is estimated to be from 30 to 50 times less potent than LSD and 100 times more powerful than mescaline.[24] The effects of DOM appear to be quite similar to those produced by LSD, though they may be longer lasting.

MDA

MDA (methylenedioxyamphetamine) is a drug that is chemically similar to the amphetamines and mescaline. It is capable of producing a mildly hallucinogenic state. Synthesized in clandestine labs, MDA is available on the street in powder, liquid, or tablet form. Though usually swallowed, it also may be snorted or injected intravenously. MDA is said to produce a feeling of general stimulation as well as a sense of well-being. It does not produce the vivid visual or auditory distortions that accompany the use of LSD or mescaline. There is little information available on its long-term effects.

DMT AND DET

For centuries the natives of Haiti have used the pulverized seeds of certain plants as snuff. They believe that the snuff enables them to communicate with the gods. We now know that the seeds from which this snuff is made contain the hallucinogens DMT (dimethyltryptamine) and DET (diethyltryptamine).

Both DMT and DET are usually injected into a muscle or mixed with plant material such as parsley or marijuana and smoked. They produce intense but short-lived hallucinogenic effects. Users can become tolerant to the effects of these drugs, but physical dependence does not develop. The extent to which a psychological dependence can develop is not known.

MORNING GLORY SEEDS

For centuries the Indians of Mexico and South and Central America have known of the ability of the seeds of certain tropical morning glories to produce mild intoxicating and hallucinogenic effects (Figure 8-5). They call these plants "ololiuqui"—"the green serpent"[25]—and that is what the hallucinogenic drug based on these seeds is known as today. The hallucinogenic agent in the seeds is about one-tenth as active as LSD.

The seeds of numerous morning glory varieties currently available in this country can produce hallucinogenic reactions. The strongest varieties are said to be Heavenly Blue, Pearly Gates, Flying Saucers, Wedding Bells, Blue Stars, and Summer Skies.[26]

Morning glory seeds may be chewed and swallowed, or they may be soaked and the resulting liquid swallowed.

FIGURE 8-5
The seeds of a number of commonly grown morning glories have hallucinogenic properties.

IN CONCLUSION

Both nature and humanity's fertile imagination have provided a wide variety of mind-expanding drugs. While their abuse is somewhat less potentially dangerous to users and society than is the abuse of drugs such as heroin and the depressants, it can still present a serious problem. The faddish popularity of drugs such as LSD may lessen, but the abuse of hallucinogens will probably continue as long as people attempt to follow the chemical path to enlightenment.

NOTES

[1] National Commission on Marijuana and Drug Abuse, *Drug Use in America: Problem in Perspective* (Washington, D.C.: GPO, 1973), p. 68.

[2] Herbert I. Abelson and Ronald B. Atkinson, *Public Experience with Psychoactive Substances* (Rockville, Md.: National Institute of Drug Abuse, August 1975), pp. 11–12.

[3] Drug Enforcement Administration and National Institute on Drug Abuse, *Drug Abuse Warning Network, Phase III Report* (Washington, D.C.: GPO, 1976), p. 4.

[4] Herbert I. Abelson and Ronald B. Atkinson, pp. 11–12, 49.

[5] Domestic Council Drug Abuse Task Force, *White Paper on Drug Abuse* (Washington, D.C.: GPO, 1975), p. 28.

[6] Drug Enforcement Administration, *Drugs of Abuse,* vol. 2, no. 2, pp. 20–21, Spring 1975 (Washington, D.C.: GPO, 1975).

[7] Edward M. Brecher and Consumers Union Editors, *Licit and Illicit Drugs* (Boston: Little, Brown, 1972), p. 346.

[8] Edward M Brecher et al., p. 352.

[9] Louis S. Goodman and Alfred Gilman (eds.), *Pharmacological Basis of Therapeutics* (New York: Macmillan, 1970), p. 197.

[10] *A Treatment Manual for Acute Drug Abuse Emergencies* (Rockville, Md.: National Institute on Drug Abuse, 1975), pp. 73–75.

[11] Drug Enforcement Administration and National Institute on Drug Abuse, p. 4.

[12] As reported in Louis P. Lasher, *LSD: The False Illusion* (Washington, D.C.: U.S. Department of Health, Education, and Welfare, September 1967), part 2, p. 2.

[13] Richard R. Lingeman, *Drugs from A to Z: A Dictionary* (New York: McGraw-Hill, 1969), pp. 129–130.

[14] Sidney Cohen, *The Drug Dilemma* (New York: McGraw-Hill, 1969), pp. 25–26.

[15] Edward M. Brecher et al., p. 353.

[16] National Clearinghouse for Drug Abuse Information, *Mescaline,* U.S. Department of Health, Education, and Welfare Report Series 15, no. 1, p. 3 (Rockville, Md.: The Clearinghouse, 1973).

[17] Thomas S. Szasz, *The Stoned Age* (New York: Putnam, 1974), p. 152.

[18] Kenneth L. Jones, Louis W. Shainber, and Curtis O. Byer, *Drugs and Alcohol* (New York: Harper & Row, 1969), pp. 62–63.

[19] National Clearinghouse for Drug Abuse Information, p. 8.

[20] Louis S. Goodman and Alfred Gilman, p. 195.

[21] Drug Enforcement Administration, p. 25.

[22]National Clearinghouse for Drug Abuse Information, *Phencyclidine,* U.S. Department of Health, Education, and Welfare, Series 14, no. 1, p. 6 (Rockville, Md.: The Clearinghouse, 1973).

[23]Drug Enforcement Administration, pp. 20–21.

[24]Drug Enforcement Administration, p. 25.

[25]Sidney Cohen, p. 45.

[26]*Legal Highs* (New York: High Times Press, 1973). p. 21.

Chapter 9
INHALANTS

Fact Sheet on Inhalants

Street names
 Glue, fluid, gas
Drug family
 Glues, solvents, and fuels
Appearance
 Clear liquid or glue
How used
 Inhaled
Source
 Volatile solvents, anesthetics, aerosol propellants
Medical uses
 None, except for some gases such as nitrous oxide that are used as
 anesthetics
Control schedule
 Not included in CSA
Effects
 Intoxication
Tolerance
 Probably develops to some
Physical dependence potential
 Degree unknown
Psychological dependence potential
 Yes
Duration of effects
 Short—15 to 30 minutes
Special notes
 Death can occur from suffocation.

The inhalants—also called "deliriants"—are volatile chemicals whose fumes produce intoxication when inhaled. A great variety are readily available in the home, in schools, in stores, in offices, and in factories. Inhalants can be divided into three major groups:

1. *Volatile solvents*, such as those found in glue, nail polish, and paint remover
2. *Aerosol propellants*, which include a wide range of consumer products currently packaged in aerosol spray cans
3. *Anesthetics*, such as nitrous oxide (laughing gas), ether, chloroform, and related gases (Figure 9-1)

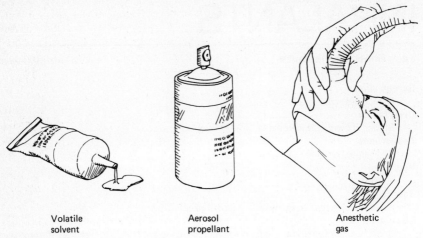

Volatile
solvent

Aerosol
propellant

Anesthetic
gas

FIGURE 9-1
The principle types of inhalants that are abused are aerosol propellants, anesthetic gases, and volatile solvents such as those
found in glue or cleaning fluids.

VOLATILE SOLVENTS

A wide range of preparations, many of which are commonly found
around the house, contain volatile solvents. Some of the more common
ones are model cement, paint thinner, lighter fluid, fingernail polish
remover, gasoline, cleaning fluid, rubber cement, paint and lacquer
remover, and brush cleaner. Solvents that are commonly used in these
preparations include toluol (toluene), benzene, naphtha, ketone,
acetone, methylene chloride, and carbon tetrachloride.

By far the most widely publicized inhalant abuse involves the solvents found in various kinds of glues and plastic cements.

AEROSOL PROPELLANTS

Innumerable household and commercial products are packaged in
pressurized aerosol containers. Everything from paint to deodorants is
currently available in these convenient spray cans. The propellants
used in most aerosols are gases containing chlorinated or fluorinated
hydrocarbons. When inhaled, these substances can produce intoxication. Some aerosol products also contain volatile hydrocarbon solvents
that are also capable of producing intoxication when inhaled.[1]

The problem of aerosol abuse seems to have become more serious
since 1967. It was then that aerosol cocktail-glass chillers were first
marketed. Youngsters soon found that when they inhaled the chilling

substance, they experienced a pronounced and supposedly safe high. Also, the relatively recent practice adopted by some glue manufacturers of adding a noxious substance to their products to prevent sniffing has, it appears, succeeded in forcing some former glue abusers to switch to aerosols.[2]

ANESTHETICS

Nitrous oxide, ether, and chloroform have long histories of use as intoxicants both here and abroad. Ether was first used as an anesthetic by Crawford Long of Georgia as early as 1842, but its use and effectiveness was not publicized until a Boston dentist, William T. G. Morton, published his results of using ether for a tooth extraction 1846. By the 1860s ether was being recommended as a general tonic, and as early as the 1890s it had become extremely popular as an intoxicant on both sides of the Atlantic Ocean.

Nitrous oxide was discovered by Sir Joseph Priestly in 1776. It was first synthesized in that same year by Sir Humphrey Davy, who observed that the initial effect of nitrous oxide is a feeling of gay boisterousness. This information quickly made the rounds of the social set, and laughing gas became the rage. Chloroform was introduced in 1831, and its intoxicating properties were immediately noted.

At present the abuse of anesthetic gases does not appear to be particularly widespread in this country. Both ether and chloroform are relatively hard for laypeople to obtain. Nitrous oxide, on the other hand, can be purchased easily. It is available commercially in several preparations, including gas-leak tracers, the propellants used in canned whipped-cream toppings, and preignition suppressors for racing cars.

EXTENT AND PATTERNS OF ABUSE

It is difficult to estimate how widespread the abuse of inhalants is in the United States. This is largely due to the fact that inhalants are not covered by the provisions of the Controlled Substances Act of 1970. Therefore, figures are not collected systematically on a national basis. However, from data we do have, it appears that during recent years there has been a gradual increase in inhalant abuse. This is especially true among youths. In 1972 a national survey conducted by the National Commission on Marijuana and Drug Abuse found that 2.1 percent of the adults and 6.4 percent of the youths questioned had used glue or some other inhalant at least once. In a similar survey conducted in 1974, 2.8 percent of the adults and 8.5 percent of the youths questioned acknowledged its use.[3]

Hard data on inhalant-abuse patterns are relatively limited. It appears that there are two distinct groups of inhalant abusers. At one end of the spectrum there are the classic glue and aerosol sniffers. Typically, these are young, male adolescents.[4] In the early 1960s when authorities first became aware of the problem of inhalant abuse, the typical abuser came from an impoverished, deprived family—more often than not, a broken, fatherless home. However, as time went by, more and more youngsters from "normal" middle-class homes became involved.

At the other end of the inhalant-abuse scale are those individuals who prefer anesthetic gases, such as nitrous oxide, ether, and chloroform. These substances are not as readily available as volatile solvents and aerosols. Though verifiable information on the subject is scant, it is the opinion of many of those working in the field that, with the exception of nitrous oxide, which is currently enjoying renewed popularity among the general population, most of the abuse of these gases is carried out by individuals who have ready access to them. This includes such professionals and paraprofessionals as doctors, nurses, psychologists, medical technicians, and therapists.

HOW USED

Glue sniffers utilize a variety of different techniques in order to achieve the desired high. Some prefer to squeeze the contents of one or more tubes of glue into a paper or plastic bag. They then hold the bag over their mouth or nose and inhale deeply until the fumes take effect. Others squeeze the contents of a glue tube on a handkerchief or rag. This can then be rolled into a tube or folded over itself and placed over the mouth and nose much like a medical mask.

The use of plastic bags for sniffing is particularly dangerous. They form an airtight seal around the sniffers face. If, as frequently happens, the sniffer loses consciousness and the bag continues to cling to his or her face, the user is almost certain to die of suffocation.

Gasoline, paint remover, and other liquids are inhaled directly from the container or are used to saturate a cloth that is then placed in a paper or plastic bag for sniffing.

Aerosol sniffers usually try to separate the propellant from the contents of the spray can. Favorite methods of doing this are to filter the spray through a gauze or cloth or to turn the can upside down so that only the propellant escapes when the valve is depressed.

EFFECTS

Inhalants have a generally depressing effect upon the central nervous system. In this way they are similar to barbiturates and narcotics.

Though the effects vary according to the user's own particular psychological makeup and expectations as well as the setting in which they are used, in many ways they are similar to those produced by alcohol. Inhalant users may experience feelings of euphoria and excitement and the release of inhibitions. They may experience dizziness and bizarre thoughts as well as visual and auditory hallucinations. At times these sensations may be accompanied by feelings of recklessness and omnipotence. This state of mind may lead to impulsive and/or disturbed behavior.

The following quotation by a young gasoline sniffer is a good description of the effects produced by inhalants:

At first, I felt nauseated, real stuporous, light, like floating away. We were swinging our arms. Some of the boys were getting on the top of the garage and jumping off. Then I started to hear a constant buzzing as if someone was talking real fast. It sounded like echoes pretty far away. When talking to each other, I could understand and I could see, but seeing a little bit more than usual. Then everything went back to normal, I guess I didn't take too much. The second time I tried it . . . I felt like getting drunk. I was getting pretty high, higher than from drinking whiskey. I felt this kind of lightheadedness every time I inhaled the fumes. I started seeing little ants like crawling all over the ground real fast. There were billions. I felt like I was in a dream, like in another world. It does not seem like you're in reality. It gets to the point that you don't want to go back to reality. Then I saw walls change colors. One of the boys looked like a sailor with a blue suit, tie, and hat all in colors. Then I felt I was floating again in the air; everything and everyone was smaller than normal size and in color. . . . The next morning I had a headache, but I felt like doing it again.[5]

The immediate effects of inhalants are quite short-lived, most lasting for only fifteen minutes or at most a half an hour. The users may, however, experience a general drowsiness and stupor for an hour or so after sniffing while the effects completely wear off.[6]

A number of deaths from sniffing have been reported. In many of these the immediate cause of death was suffocation. Plastic bags, as mentioned earlier, present a particular threat.

The extent to which many of the more commonly encountered inhalants harm the various organs of the body has not been fully determined and is subject to a good deal of disagreement among authorities. However, with the exception of trichloroethylene and trichloroethane (found in many cleaning fluids) and the fluorinated hydrocarbons that are sometimes used as aerosol propellants, most of the commonly abused inhalants appear to have only a minimal risk of permanent damage to the organs of the body.[7]

Tolerance, Dependence, and Withdrawal

It has been demonstrated that the body develops a tolerance to the solvents contained in glue and many other compounds. Children who use inhalants on a weekly basis have been observed to develop tolerance in only three weeks. In one case an inhalant abuser required eight tubes of glue to obtain the same effects that one tube produced three years earlier. The development of tolerance to nitrous oxide has not yet been documented.

Some abusers develop a strong psychological dependence upon inhalants. One case was reported in which a youngster needed more than twenty-five tubes of glue a day to satisfy his compulsive need for the effects of the glue. The body does not appear to develop a physical dependence upon inhalants. Classic withdrawal symptoms have not been observed; however, some individuals have experienced such discomforts as tremors, irritability, insomnia, and anxiety when they stopped sniffing.[8]

Recognizing the Abuser

As is true for most drugs, there is no foolproof way of recognizing inhalant abusers. However, the following are indicators:

1. A pungent chemical odor on the person's breath or clothes
2. Excessive nasal excretions
3. Red, watering eyes
4. Dilated pupils
5. Rapid, involuntary eye movements
6. Complaints of double vision, ringing in the ears, vivid dreams, hallucinations
7. An overall intoxicated appearance
8. Drowsiness, stupor, and in extreme cases unconsciousness
9. Slobbering from the mouth
10. A white, powdery ring of dried glue around the nose and mouth
11. Paraphernalia such as glue tubes, balloons, aerosol cans, and rags and paper and plastic bags with traces of glue on them (Figure 9-2)

TREATMENT

Most of the effects of inhalants are so short-lived that emergency medical treatment is seldom necessary. However, in cases of particularly severe abuse, psychosis has been known to develop. In such instances abusers are usually treated in the same manner as those suffering from a

RECOGNIZING
THE ABUSER: INHALANTS

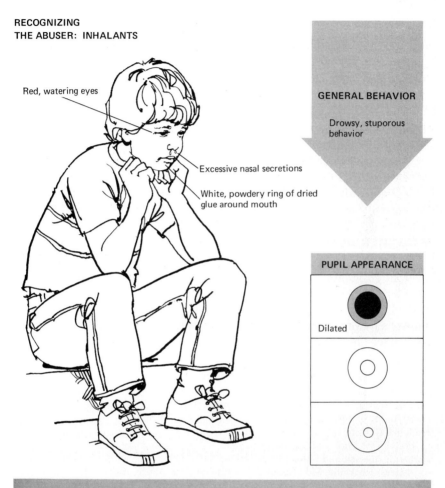

Red, watering eyes

GENERAL BEHAVIOR

Drowsy, stuporous
behavior

Excessive nasal secretions

White, powdery ring of dried
glue around mouth

PUPIL APPEARANCE

Dilated

PARAPHERNALIA

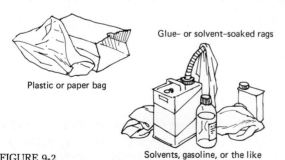

Plastic or paper bag

Glue- or solvent-soaked rags

Solvents, gasoline, or the like

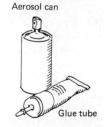

Aerosol can

Glue tube

FIGURE 9-2
Common signs of inhalant abuse.

severe reaction to hallucinogens. They are placed in a calm, non-threatening environment that is free from such external stimuli as bright lights or loud noises. They are then "talked down" in a calm and reassuring manner until they regain their self-control.[9]

LEGAL CONTROLS

At the present time aerosol products, organic solvents, plastic glues, and related substances are not covered by the Controlled Substances Act of 1970. Many states and municipalities have, however, enacted legislation to control their distribution, particularly to minors. Most states regard nitrous oxide and other anesthetic gases as prescription drugs.

IN CONCLUSION

Were it not for the fact that each year a number of youngsters needlessly die from suffocation related to glue sniffing, inhalant abuse could be considered a relatively minor drug problem. However, because of its potentially lethal consequences, it must be included as among this country's more dangerous drug-abuse practices, particularly in relation to younger children.

NOTES

[1]National Clearinghouse for Drug Abuse Information, *The Deliberate Inhalation of Volatile Substances*, U.S. Department of Health, Education, and Welfare Report Series 30, no. 1, p. 4 (Rockville, Md.: The Clearinghouse, 1974).

[2]Frederick G. Hofmann, *A Handbook on Drug and Alcohol Abuse: The Biomedical Aspects* (New York: Oxford, 1975), p. 130.

[3]Herbert I. Abelson and Ronald B. Atkinson, *Public Experience with Psychoactive Substances* (Rockville, Md.: National Institute on Drug Abuse, August 1975), p. 16.

[4]National Clearinghouse for Drug Abuse Information, p. 3.

[5]National Clearinghouse for Drug Abuse Information, p. 11.

[6]Frederick G. Hofmann, p. 136.

[7]Frederick G. Hofmann, p. 137.

[8]Frederick G. Hofmann, pp. 136–138; National Clearinghouse for Drug Abuse Information, p. 2.

[9]National Clearinghouse for Drug Abuse Information, p. 889.

Part 2
INVESTIGATION

Chapter 10

INFORMANTS

In police usage the term "informant" means anyone who, for a variety of reasons, supplies information to the authorities on the understanding that his or her identity will not be revealed. In many cases informants are themselves at least marginally involved in illegal or questionable activities. They usually provide information in order to secure a benefit for themselves, such as money or official leniency.

Informants are helpful in the investigation of many types of crimes. In drug enforcement they are indispensable. The types and kinds of information and services that they can provide a drug investigation are many. The most common ones follow:

1. Investigative leads relating to such matters as (a) the location of a dealer's stash, (b) the time and the place that drug shipments are expected, (c) the names of a dealer's suppliers, customers, and associates, and (d) the location of a dealer's base of operations
2. The introduction of undercover officers into drug dealing organizations
3. The supply of information that will enable the authorities to obtain search warrants
4. Tactical help, such as leaving a strategic door or window unlocked in a building that is about to be raided

TYPES OF INFORMANTS

People from all walks of life and all occupations become informants. It is not possible to stereotype informants, but for purposes of discussion we can separate them into several (sometimes overlapping) categories.

Those Who Operate Outside the Law

Bootleggers, numbers writers, gamblers, addicts, prostitutes, and others who operate outside the law will often provide valuable leads or information about drug activities. For the most part these individuals are small-time operators who function on the fringes of the criminal world. This gives them the opportunity to hear and see things that can be of value.

Some investigators tend to dismiss the information that these petty criminals can provide—a feeling that since they are not in the "big time," they cannot know anything of real importance. A case involving an informant who was a shoeshine boy and a small-time (very small) numbers writer points up the folly of this attitude. One day two rather shady-looking individuals stopped off at this informant's stand for a shine. The informant listened to their conversation in detail. In the course of it he heard reference to the planned elimination of a local drug pusher of rather substantial worth. Thinking that the authorities might be interested in hearing about this (and, no doubt, that they might pay for it), he made a note of the strangers' license plate number as they drove away and passed on the information.

The drug enforcement authorities followed up his tip and were soon able to identify the two strangers as imported killers who were hired by the local dealer's wholesaler to get rid of him. When told that he was about to be murdered, the dealer readily agreed to turn states evidence. As the result of his testimony, a number of substantial convictions and seizures were made.

This case shows that no lead from an informant should ever be dismissed as worthless without some follow-up. Though it is true that many may turn out to be a waste of time and energy, those that result in a conviction more than make up for the others.

Occupational Listeners

Many people have a compulsion to talk about themselves. They will go on for hours about their various problems, involvements, and triumphs. Bartenders, barbers and beauticians, people who work in restaurants, and others in such service occupations are frequently the recipients of such conversation. They can, from time to time, provide useful bits and pieces of information.

Invisible People

Workers in some occupations are taken so much for granted that to many people they might as well not exist. This category includes taxi drivers, bellhops, waiters and waitresses, maids and janitors, poolroom operators, and the like. Because they are so often ignored, these people are in a perfect position to overhear conversations of others. Many an important drug case has been made as the result of a tip from one of these "invisible" informants.

Curious People

Many people have an insatiable curiosity about the affairs of others. Frequently the same individuals have an equally insatiable desire to pass on what they learn. Some of the best informants fit into this category. An example is a man who ran a small hardware store and possessed an unquenchable thirst for information about everyone else in the neighborhood. The moment that he found out about anything of which he did not approve, he was on the phone to the authorities. For the most part his information was worthless. However, every now and then he did pass on something that proved useful.

Those with Special Opportunities

Some people have jobs that place them in a position to observe things that law enforcement people would like to know. If they are observant and their cooperation can be cultivated, they can prove to be invaluable sources of information. Individuals in this category include building superintendents, desk clerks in hotels and motels, cleaning people, guards, repair people, and others.

MOTIVES

Individuals become informants for a variety of reasons. For many people no one motive can be singled out. A number of factors are involved. In any drug investigation, it always pays to consider an informant's motives carefully. Before you take any action based on an informant's information, ask yourself, "Why is this person telling me this? What will be gained from telling me?" Sometimes the answer will be obvious. Other times it may not be so clear. When that is so, proceed with caution in your dealings with the informant. Such caution may well allow you to get a far better understanding of the case.

For example, in one case a local hoodlum, who up to that time would have nothing to do with the authorities, suddenly started to supply information. Probing into the new-found informant's affairs, one drug enforcement officer was able to uncover the reason for this sudden change of heart. The informant was taking over a small piece of the local vice action, and by feeding the authorities information he hoped to use them to put some of his competition out of the way.

What moves people to inform can be a fascinating psychological study. However, here only the most common and basic motives will be noted.

Money

The number of people who would "sell their own mothers up the river" for a few dollars is amazing. There will always be those individuals who regard informing as a convenient way of making money. In some ways they are the easiest informants to understand and, consequently, to handle. You always know what is foremost in their minds. However, in other ways they can be a problem.

For example, they may embellish or greatly inflate the worth of the information that they are providing in an attempt to get more money. The small-time pusher may well be presented as a medium-sized dealer; the medium-sized dealer as the kilo-lot wholesaler. Thus, it is always wise to heed the ageless warning, "Let the buyer beware."

Fear

Fear motivates many people to become informants. Some informants provide information because they fear that their associates are out to get them, others because they fear prosecution. The world of drug dealing is a particularly savage one. And in the jungle in which drug dealers and users make their day-to-day existence, violence is the rule rather than the exception. Consequently, there will always be those individuals who have incurred the wrath of their associates and who are on the run. One place they sometimes run is to the authorities. Such individuals can, if properly handled, prove very useful.

Most informants who are motivated by fear, however, are afraid not of their associates but rather of the law. These are the individuals who become informants in an attempt to save their own skins. More often than not such an informant is a small-time operator who is facing a charge and who hopes either to get it dismissed or to get off with a suspended or light sentence in return for cooperation.

Revenge

One of the most powerful motives is revenge. More than one drug dealer is behind bars today as the result of an informant who came to the authorities in order to get even for some actual or imagined wrong. Most quarrels have developed over such things as the refusal to provide drugs when a user was short of cash, holding out on profits, failure to pay for services rendered, and romantic entanglements.

A word of caution is due at this point. Whenever you feel that an informant is giving you information for the purpose of getting even with someone, it is wise to proceed with utmost caution. All too often such informants will go to any lengths, including feeding you totally fictitious information, in order to achieve their ends. In such cases it is a surprisingly easy matter to find yourself working for the informant rather than the other way around.

Elimination of Competition

Some informants, as in the example mentioned earlier, supply information in an effort to eliminate the competition. It is not at all uncommon for one dealer to supply information about another for this reason. It saves the informant the trouble and expense of having to do the job personally, and it keeps everything perfectly "legal."

Intelligence Gathering

Drugs are big business. The stakes are enormous. The million-dollar deal is not uncommon. Under these circumstances it is not hard to understand why drug dealers, especially the big ones, are keenly interested in what the authorities are up to. If they are to survive in the big league, they have to know what the authorities are doing.

One of the many ways in which dealers try to gather this kind of information is by planting bogus informants in law enforcement agencies. For this reason it is imperative always to be on guard when dealing with an informant. Be sure that you do not let slip any information about the cases on which you or others are working or mention other informants who may be working on cases.

Setups

Finally, keep in mind that an informant may appear to cooperate in order to set you or another investigator up for a robbery or attack. The files of every law enforcement agency contain cases in which informants provided "information" that was designed to lure officers into a position where an attempt could be made to assault or rob them.

One officer who was the victim of just such a setup had arranged with an informant for a buy of several thousand dollars worth of heroin by the officer in a deserted part of the city. When the officer arrived on the scene, he was jumped from behind and severely beaten and the buy money was stolen.

HANDLING INFORMANTS

There are no magic secrets that will enable anyone always to be successful in dealings with informants. Like all other forms of human contact and interchange, the relationship between informants and investigators is subject to the pressures and influences of many factors. However, successful drug investigators have found that there are a number of dos and don'ts that should generally be observed when dealing with any informant.

Be Flexible

Remember that there is no such person as a typical informant. The truth of the matter is that informants are recruited from the human race and as such are subject to all the human frailties and faults. Each informant presents a unique combination of strengths and weaknesses with which you must deal if he or she is going to be useful to an investigation. Techniques that work with one informant may have no effect on another. A jilted lover cannot be handled in the same way as a small-time dealer who is trying to stay out of jail. Do not be afraid to experiment, to try different approaches. Just because an approach did not work with one informant does not mean that it will not with another.

Be Careful

Never trust an informant. Always keep your guard up. Try never to act on the unsubstantiated word of a single informant. Always try to verify by some other means whatever an informant tells you. Make your informants prove their reliability. For example, if an informant tells you that he or she was in a particular dealer's house, ask for a detailed description. Ask, for example, "What color is the living room? What kind of furniture is in it? Where is the bathroom?" Then try to find out the answers to these questions from another source. If the answers your informant gives turn out to be correct, it is a point in his or her favor. If they are wrong, you know to be on your guard. (See also Checking the Informant's Reliability in Chapter 13.)

Keep Your Word

Never make a promise that you cannot keep. This is a cardinal rule when dealing with informants. The relationship that you will establish with them will, at best, be difficult. The very nature of the situation plus the fact that the prospect of violence is ever present will tend to keep informants on edge. Theirs is a trick world, and most of them have a desperate need to feel that even if they cannot trust anybody else, at least they can trust you. To a large extent it is this sense of trust in the officers with whom they deal that keeps many informants providing information year after year.

One of the areas where promises can cause the greatest problems is that involving the dropping or reducing of criminal charges. In drug enforcement the situation often arises when suspects decide to inform against their associates in order to save their own skins. These individuals offer to supply information in exchange for a better deal for themselves. This usually involves reducing the charge against them or dropping it all together.

As a general rule, no such promise should ever be made. For one thing, there is a very good chance that you will not be able to keep your word. The informant is then liable to try to do something to damage your case in retaliation. For another, when you get into court you can be sure that if the informant takes the witness stand, the defense will bear down hard on his or her testimony. Experience has shown that the testimony of informants is notoriously unreliable. Often it is a relatively easy matter for an astute defense attorney to completely shatter an informant's testimony under cross-examination. In addition, since most informants in the drug business have unseemly backgrounds, attorneys will attempt to degrade their testimony by demonstrating their poor character and lack of trustworthiness. One of the questions that is sure to be brought up in the process is that of whether or not a promise of leniency was made in return for the informant's testimony. If the defense can show that this is indeed what happened, the case may be lost.

Protect the Informant's Identity

Once an informant's name is known to the underworld, he or she is of no value to you. Consequently, it is absolutely vital to take every precaution possible to keep an informant's identity secret. If you do not, it will not be long before your informant is murdered and the word spreads on the street that you do not look after your people. When this happens, it will be next to impossible to find anybody who will pass the time of day with you, much less pass on the kind of information that you need in order to make cases.

Many agencies have very strict guidelines spelling out the manner in which informants are to be handled and how their identity is to be protected. You should, of course, follow those laid down by your agency. If, however, your agency does not have such guidelines, be sure to abide by at least three rules for safeguarding an informant's identity:

1. *Avoid meeting with informants in your office.* They may be seen coming or going, or another suspect who is in the building may recognize them. Try instead to arrange meetings in out-of-the-way locations where you will not be observed.
2. *Do not refer to informants by name.* If you must refer to them in a report, it is safer to do so by a code name or number. Then, if the document falls into the wrong hands, your informant's identity will not be exposed.
3. *Keep informants' files under tight security.* Many agencies make it a policy to keep a master file that lists all their informants and the code names or numbers by which they are identified. The access to such files should be closely guarded at all times.

Be Sure of an Informant's Identity

It may seem ridiculous to emphasize that you make certain of a known informant's identity, but in the underworld identities have a way of changing. Joe Smith may find that it is much more convenient to suddenly become Tom Jones. When it gets too hot for a criminal, one of the first things he or she will do is switch names and move somewhere else.

Not knowing the true identity of an informant can cause untold trouble and embarrassment. In one case, the investigators had been dealing with an informant regularly for two years in connection with several low-level drug cases before they found out that he was not a petty street hood. In actuality, he was a felon with a lengthy record and was wanted in another jurisdiction for the murder of a police undercover officer.

For reasons such as this, many agencies require as a routine precaution that all informants be fingerprinted and photographed and that a complete criminal record check be made on them. It is also advisable to find out as much general background information as possible, including such facts as where the informant was born, the names of friends and relatives, and the type of job skills possessed. Then, if in the middle of an investigation the informant decides to disappear, at least you will have an idea of where to start looking.

Establish Alternate Contacts

There is a tendency for some investigators to regard their informants as their own personal property. Though this is understandable, it can cause serious problems. If you are not available and your informant has valuable information, there must be another channel of communication. One of the best ways is to establish an alternate contact with whom your informant can deal in your absence.

Some informants will resist such a plan. As they see it, they are in enough danger by just talking to one officer, and two can only make things worse. For that reason it is important to impress upon informants from the moment that you come in contact with them that they are responsible to your agency (after all it is agency money that is paying them) and not just you.

Keep Control of the Informants

Control your informants. That is another cardinal rule of survival in the world of drug enforcement. Drug enforcement is, at the very best, a difficult and dangerous business. Once you start investigating the drug trade, you are marked. Too many mistakes on your part and you will not survive for long. If you are to survive and remain effective in such a world for any length of time, you have to see that things are done your way—that you "call the shots."

Because informants have to rely on their wits to stay alive, they often try to do things their way, the way that they think is best for them. From the moment of your first encounter with an informant, make sure that he or she understands that *you* are the *boss*: you are the one who is giving the orders and you are the one who decides what is done, when it is done, and how it is done.

That there be no doubt who is boss and makes the decisions is particularly important when informants are used to make drug buys. In order for a buy case to prove successful, it must be meticulously planned and executed. If it is not, there is every chance that the case will be thrown out of court and, more importantly, that one of the officers involved will be injured or worse. Under such circumstances you cannot have informants making changes in the game plan because they want to do things their way.

In Conclusion

It cannot be repeated too strongly that caution should dominate all dealings with informants. If the suggestions made in this chapter are followed, your dealings with informants can prove to be most successful and your investigations helped tremendously.

Chapter 11
UNDERCOVER OPERATIONS

As the term is most frequently used, "undercover operations" refers to the use of investigators whose identities are carefully concealed in order to penetrate criminal organizations and gain the confidence of their members. Once in place, undercover officers become the eyes and ears of the law enforcement authorities within the underworld. They are in a perfect position to find out a wealth of information about the nature and extent of any criminal activities that the group has been involved in or is planning for the future. Undercover investigators can provide vital information for drug enforcement authorities, such as:

The names of suspected drug dealers as well as those of their customers, associates, and suppliers

The location of suspects' hangouts

Information on where drugs are stored

Advice on the best time to conduct raids

When, where, and how shipments and deliveries are made

Undercover officers, either by themselves or in conjunction with informants, are frequently delegated to make purchases of drugs from suspected dealers. As discussed in Chapter 13, these buy cases are one of the most fruitful of the enforcement techniques in combating the drug trade.

QUALIFICATIONS FOR UNDERCOVER AGENTS

Undercover work is an art, not a science. There is no ideal set of qualifications that, if met, assures that any given investigator will be able to function effectively in an undercover assignment. However, past experience has shown that certain characteristics and qualifications are important.

Desire

To be effective, the undercover officer must want the assignment. Undercover work is not the sort of task to which investigators can be assigned against their will. Unless their whole heart is in it, they will never prove effective. Moreover, they may get themselves or someone else hurt or killed.

Self-confidence

Investigators who want to work undercover have to be sure of themselves. They have to be able to draw from that inner strength that comes from knowing that they can do the job—that they are up to the task, no matter how difficult it may turn out to be. They must be confident that once they have made a decision, it will be followed—unless, of course, circumstances show that it must be altered.

Resourcefulness

Undercover operators must be able to think "on their feet." They have to be able to sense problems before they occur and be able to deal with them once they do occur. In other words, they must be able to survey a situation and take appropriate action immediately.

Courage

Undercover operatives live in a world fraught with danger. From the moment that they assume their false identities and submerge themselves in the underworld, they are marked. They are targets. If they are to be effective, they must be able to deal in their own minds with these occupational hazards and act positively when faced with the inherent dangers of the work.

Adaptability

To function effectively, undercover agents must possess the ability to adapt to new circumstances and surroundings. They must be chameleons: blend unobtrusively into their new surroundings, no matter how different these are from the settings and lifestyles to which they are accustomed.

Incorruptibility

Officers assigned to undercover activities must be completely incorruptible. They must have strong ethical convictions. They are bound to be confronted with numerous temptations. If they succumb to them, they not only jeopardize the investigation but also place others who may be involved in grave danger.

Special Talents or Backgrounds

In some investigations undercover officers must possess certain specific talents or backgrounds. For example, an undercover investigator posing as a rabbinical student had better be able to speak Hebrew. An investigator posing as a musician must be able to play an instrument.

ASSUMING A NEW IDENTITY

After investigators have been selected for undercover activities, they must be provided with complete new identities. They must be "born again." The first step of this rebirth involves the complete abandoning of their official identities. Anything that might link them to their law enforcement roles must be removed or concealed. Many agencies require that when investigators go undercover, they turn in anything that could possibly identify them as law enforcement officers. This includes badges, identification cards, notebooks, official papers, uniforms, and other official equipment that they possess. Even the most seemingly trivial items must be disposed of. In one case, an undercover officer was exposed when the suspect searched the officer's wallet and found a Blue Cross hospitalization identification card. Another officer was exposed (and nearly killed as the result) when the suspect's henchmen searched the officer's apartment and found a picture that had been taken of the recruit's class upon graduation from the police training academy.

Many agencies also go to the trouble of purging their files of any reference to investigators who are given undercover assignments. That may seem like an unnecessary precaution. However, in a number of cases undercover officers have been exposed when the underworld was able to gain access to official files. For example, in one case a civilian file clerk was bribed to steal the identification photo of an officer who had been assigned to set up undercover drug buys.

Once the investigator's official identity has been concealed, he or she must be given a new one that is appropriate to the investigation in question. The guidelines discussed in the following paragraphs will prove helpful in establishing a new identity for the agent.

Credentials

Undercover investigators should be provided with a complete set of bogus credentials. This often includes such items as credit cards, a driver's license, a Social Security card, membership cards for social or fraternal organizations, and military discharge papers. In particularly important cases some agencies go to such lengths as developing fictitious criminal records. All these items should bear the fictitious cover name and address the investigator has assumed.

Clothing

Undercover investigators should also be provided with items of clothing that are appropriate to the role that they are assuming. Care should be taken to see that the labels and laundry marks in them either are removed or match the assumed identity. Such precautions may seem excessive, but they may mean the difference between success and failure. For example, in one case an undercover officer was exposed when it was discovered that though she said she had recently lived and worked in one city, her clothes bore labels indicating that they had been purchased in another.

Cover Story

Investigators who are going to work undercover must also develop a comprehensive cover story that is appropriate to and substantiates their fictitious role. As a general rule, it is wise to keep the story as simple and direct as possible. If it is made too involved or complex, it may prove difficult to remember. When constructing the part of the cover story dealing with the undercover officer's origin, it is helpful, if possible, to pick an area with which the agent is familiar and the suspect is not. If this is not feasible, the officer must be thoroughly briefed on the area in question before beginning the undercover assignment. The same is true of occupations. If possible, any assumed occupation should be one with which the undercover operator is familiar. Again, if this is not possible, the officer should be briefed as thoroughly as possible before beginning the undercover assignment.

CONTACTING THE SUSPECT

At times informants can be used to introduce undercover investigators to suspects and to vouch for them. However, the danger is always present that the informant will decide to play both ends against the middle and warn the suspect of the officer's true identity.

In some instances you may be able to use neighborhood bartenders, waiters, hotel clerks, prostitutes, poolroom clerks, and others in similar positions whom you trust and whom past experience has shown to be reliable to introduce and vouch for undercover officers. Again, however, the danger exists that they may decide that it is in their best interests to tip off the suspect rather than to assist you.

Because of the risks involved in employing informants and other outsiders to help penetrate criminal organizations, many undercover officers attempt, at least initially, to do it on their own. Though this is often difficult, many times with a little ingenuity and luck it can be done. If this course of action is selected, the key rule is, *do not rush things*. Most drug dealers are deeply suspicious of everyone—and of strangers in particular. Many are outright paranoid on the subject. The moment that a stranger approaches them they become suspicious and assume the worst. Therefore; for the undercover officer the best tactic may be to adopt an indirect approach that will, in time, allow the officer and the suspect to meet under seemingly casual circumstances. One way of establishing this seemingly chance acquaintance is for the undercover officer to move into the area where the suspect lives and/or operates. The agent then is in a position to start hanging out where he or she can come in contact with the suspect and the suspect's associates without arousing too much suspicion.

A good procedure to generally follow is to attempt to get to know the target suspect's associates before trying to get to know the suspect. When trying to set up drug buys, make it a point to become acquainted with as many of a dealer's customers as possible before trying to meet the dealer. In this way you can build up a bank of references who can vouch for you to the dealer you want to meet.

There are times when an undercover officer can contrive a set of circumstances that will force a dealer to take the initiative and make the first move. In one such case a pair of undercover officers arrived in town dressed in expensive clothes and driving an expensive sports car. Their first move was to start buying small quantities of heroin at a premium price. Their first contact was a small dealer. Gradually they worked their way up the ladder to larger and larger dealers, each time ordering larger quantities and paying more than the drugs were worth. Finally, they put the word out that they wanted to make a big buy and they were ready to pay well for it. This last bait was too much for their target to ignore. Even though the dealer in question had never dealt with the officers before, their reputation for being easy marks was too much of an inducement. The buy was arranged, and the dealer being sought from the outset was apprehended.

DEVELOPING THE CONTACT

It is one thing to set up a false identity and to make contact with a target suspect. It is another to make a buy or get the desired information from the suspect. Though there are no hard and fast rules for dealing with and obtaining information from suspects, the following techniques are often useful:

1. *Be a good listener.* Try to get the suspect talking about anything. Appear interested in whatever is said. Drug dealers are like most people in that they appreciate a good audience.
2. *Do not talk about yourself more than you have to.* The less you say about yourself, the less your opportunity of saying something that will expose your true identity.
3. *Avoid asking too many questions.* Asking specific questions is a sure way of arousing suspicion.
4. *Be careful about drinking.* It is hard enough to remember a cover story when you are sober. In addition, under the influence of a few drinks, details of your true identity may inadvertently slip out. Stomach ulcers can be given as an excuse for limiting your drinking to moderate amounts.
5. *Always bargain about price.* In the rough-and-tumble world of drug dealing, haggling about price is a way of life. If you agree to buy drugs at the first price at which they are offered, you may well arouse the dealer's suspicion.
6. *Avoid any member of the opposite sex with whom the suspect is involved.* The last thing that you need is to end up in the middle of a lovers' quarrel.
7. *Do not rush things.* Haste produces nothing but waste when it comes to drug investigations. One of the easiest ways to arouse suspicion is to appear to be in too much of a hurry.
8. *Do not use drugs.* Never use drugs while undercover. You may not be able to maintain your cover while under their influence. You will also be much more vulnerable and unable to defend yourself from attack. In addition, your testimony in court will be far less credible if the defense can show that you ever used drugs.
9. *Never make notes in public.* If you do, you will be immediately suspected. Train yourself to remember important facts without writing them down. If you absolutely must make a note of something, do it where you will not be observed—for example, in a stall in a restroom. Write the note where it will not be easily found if you are searched. Such places as the inside of a cigarette pack or matchbook can be useful for this purpose.
10. *Do not be afraid to say no.* If you are working in an undercover assignment and you do not like the way a deal is shaping up, do not be afraid to back out. Your excessive caution may save your life. In addition, it will not necessarily blow your cover. Many

individuals in the drug business, as the result of years of experience, are very cautious. Your own caution may be taken as a sign of street savvy.

MAINTAINING CONTROL

In any undercover operation a means must be established by which undercover officers can contact and be contacted by their supervisors, or as they are frequently called, their "controls." It is usually best to set up regular times at which the officers are expected to check in. In most instances this can be done conveniently by telephone. Because of the danger of taps, the calls should be made from a different pay phone each time. In addition, many agencies recommend that the control officer be called at home rather than at work.

Undercover officers should also be provided with an emergency phone number that is always monitored and a series of prearranged signals. In that way urgent messages can be passed on at any time and in relative security.

If undercover officers are expected to mail written reports, it is usually best to address them to a fictitious individual or organization at either a post office box or general delivery address. Again, a series of prearranged code signals is useful in maintaining security. Such reports should always be mailed promptly so that they do not fall into the wrong hands. Additionally, it is safer to mail them from a post office than to deposit them in a street collection box.

Financial Controls

It is not unusual for undercover officers who are involved in drug investigations to handle and be responsible for large sums of money. The illicit drug trade, like everything else, has been affected by inflation. In 1976 heroin often brought $20,000 to $25,000 per kilogram in wholesale lots. Cocaine was being bought for over $2,000 per ounce—more than ten times the price of an equal amount of gold! The $50,000 or $100,000 drug buy is routine in many areas and the $1 million deal not uncommon.

Because of the size of the sums involved and the nature of the assignment, careful financial controls are absolutely necessary. Detailed records must be kept that account in full for the disposition of all undercover funds, or as they are often called, "confidential" funds. The exact manner in which these funds are accounted for will vary somewhat from agency to agency. However, to be meaningful, any financial control system should, as a minimum, record the following information:

1. The amount of cash dispensed to each undercover officer.
2. By whom, when, where, and the date on which it was dispensed.
3. A detailed, transaction-by-transaction accounting of how the funds were used. This accounting should include the name of the person to whom the funds were paid; the date, the time, and the place where the transaction took place; and what was received in return.

Obviously, such detailed records can pose a serious threat to the security of an investigation. Consequently, they must be as closely guarded as any of the other working files that relate to it. Some agencies take the precaution of referring to both the undercover investigator and suspects only by code names and numbers.

Surveillance

Sometimes a drug investigation may be deemed by those in authority to be so dangerous that the undercover officers involved must be kept under constant surveillance. In these cases the undercover officers must be alert to do everything they can to make the job of the surveillance officers as easy as possible. If they do not, they may well be putting their own lives as well as the lives of the officers assigned to protect them in jeopardy.

Challenges

At times even the best undercover officers are challenged and accused of being "the law." There is no perfect way of handling such a challenge. In some instances the old adage "A good offense is the best defense" works. You may be able to divert suspicion from yourself by accusing your accuser of being a police officer. At other times you may be able to defuse the situation by calling your accuser "crazy" and falling back on your cover story. On still other occasions you may want to rely on a combination of physical force and indignation. In one such case an investigator, after being accused of being an undercover officer, flattened his accuser and then demanded an apology for his "ruined reputation."

However, in some cases it may be pointless to deny a challenge. Your accuser may have evidence of your law enforcement involvement that is beyond refutation. What to do in such situations will depend, of course, on the particular circumstances. It may be that the proper move is to draw a gun and make a hasty exit. If you are not carrying a firearm at the moment, you may want to consider diving out the nearest window or breaking a handy bottle and using it as a weapon.

Or you may want to try to bluff your way out, as one officer successfully did. He was unarmed at the time and hopelessly outnumbered. So, instead of denying the accusation that he was a police officer or making a run for it, he took a completely different approach. He acknowledged that he was, indeed, a police officer, and he went on to warn his accusers that if they harmed him in any way whatsoever, they would be guilty of assaulting an officer. Furthermore, he continued, the entire resources of the department would be brought to bear on their apprehension if they touched him. By the time this dragnet finished its work, he said, there would be only the faintest possibility that they, his attackers, would be alive to stand trial. The bluff worked, and the officer walked away unscratched from an encounter which well could have been his last.

EMPLOYMENT OF WOMEN

As more and more women enter the law enforcement profession, their employment in undercover assignments is sure to increase. This is bound to be beneficial. Skillful, well-trained female undercover officers will undoubtedly arouse less suspicion with many suspects than their male counterparts. However, at least for the foreseeable future, female agents are likely to present some serious problems for the agencies employing them, and there are serious problems for the female investigators themselves.

It is a fact of life that a certain percentage of undercover officers will be exposed. Some of these individuals will be injured. Others will be killed. If any of these unfortunates should happen to be women and the public finds out about it, the agencies involved may well be subjected to severe criticism for assigning women to such obviously dangerous tasks. Similarly, some agencies who employ female undercover operators have found that male supervisors tend to adopt an overly protective attitude toward them. As a result, they are hesitant to assign women to cases in which they feel there is a substantial element of danger.

Female investigators who are given undercover assignments are faced with all the problems that confront their male counterparts as well as a few that are particular to themselves. Most of the latter revolve around physical violence and sex. The world of drug dealing is a violent one. Murder and mayhem are everyday occurrences. Undercover investigators must make themselves a part of this scene. As a result, they may at any time be called upon to defend themselves from attack. For this reason, any woman who works as an undercover agent must be thoroughly trained in unarmed combat. Only with such training does

FIGURE 11-1
Female officers are often useful in undercover operations. However, because of the nature of the drug trade, they can face some
unique and dangerous problems.

the average woman stand a chance with the hoodlums she will be up
against (Figure 11-1).

In addition, every woman who submerges herself in the underworld becomes the target of all forms of sexual advances and attacks.
For example, in one case, the dealer under investigation would not sell
drugs to a woman until he had sex with her. In another situation, the
dealer would not have anything to do with a woman unless she provided sexual favors for his major supplier—an individual with two
rape and three felonious assault convictions on his record. Obviously,
before any woman can be expected to go undercover, she must resolve
in her own mind how and if she can deal with such situations.

IN CONCLUSION

Undercover techniques are a vital part of many drug enforcement programs. They often provide information that would be impossible to
gather by any other means. As with any other investigative approach, the
yield that you receive from your undercover operations will directly
reflect the time and trouble that you take to plan and administer them.

Chapter 12
SEARCH AND SEIZURE

This author's introduction to the complexities of search and seizure as it relates to drug enforcement came on a clear and crisp fall
afternoon some years ago. On that day a judge ruled as inadmissible
the evidence seized in the biggest case the author had handled up
to that time. The search of the defendant's apartment—a search
that had netted a sizable stash of heroin—was based on a faulty
warrant. It was not specific enough!

As the author left the courthouse in a rage, he encountered the
defendant's lawyer. Known around town by such nicknames as
"Mr. Crafty" and the "Silver Fox," this veteran of thousands of
courtroom clashes, sensing the author's animosity, said, "Look kid.
Don't blame me because you blew your case. If you are going to
play in this league, you damn well have to know the rules."

Right he was, and right he is. Unless one has a thorough understanding of the constitutional underpinnings and day-to-day mechanics of the rules and requirements governing search and seizure,
one is almost sure to lose cases that might otherwise have been
won.

This chapter presents an overview of the field of search and
seizure as it relates to drug enforcement. Since the discussion here
must be confined to general principles, it is strongly recommended
that readers familiarize themselves with any local legal requirements and peculiarities that pertain to the manner in which
searches and seizures must be conducted in their jurisdiction.

HISTORICAL PERSPECTIVE

Constitutional prohibitions against unreasonable searches and seizures exist for the purpose of protecting one of the most comprehensive and highly valued rights that we enjoy—the right to privacy. British disregard for this important right was one of the significant causes of the American Revolution. General search warrants
known as "writs of assistance" empowered British officials with
authority to conduct searches anywhere and at any time for illegal
goods. Hatred of these often indiscriminate searches was so intense
and so widespread that the federal Constitution was not ratified

until it was amended to include a Bill of Rights that protected the rights of each individual. The Fourth Amendment of the Bill of Rights is of primary concern to law enforcement officers engaged in the search for and seizure of drugs. It reads: "The right of the people to be secure in their persons, houses, papers and effects, against unreasonable searches and seizures, shall not be violated, and no warrants shall issue but upon probable cause, supported by oath or affirmation, and particularly describing the place to be searched, and the persons or things to be seized."

Similar provisions are found in the state constitutions. All reflect the fundamental American respect for the importance of the individual and each person's home and possessions. Searches are an invasion of privacy and as such must be governed by strictly enforced legal guidelines if we are to remain a free society.

THE EXCLUSIONARY RULE

In order to discourage illegal searches and seizures, federal, state, and local courts utilize the exclusionary rule. This is a basic rule of evidence which holds that evidence against an accused person must be obtained legally or it cannot be used against the defendant in court. Thus it is readily apparent that the narcotics officer must be thoroughly familiar with the laws concerning search and seizure if he or she is to be successful in collecting admissible evidence for purposes of prosecuting drug-law violators.

LEGAL SEARCHES NOT CONSTITUTIONALLY PROTECTED

Certain searches for the seizures of evidence are not, however, constitutionally protected. Thus any discussion of the law of search and seizure must begin by differentiating between searches that are constitutionally protected and those that are not.

Plain-View Doctrine

If a police officer, acting in a lawful manner, makes observations from a place where he or she has a right to be, such observations are not classified as searches for Fourth Amendment purposes. Police seizure of evidence discovered in open view is permitted under what has come to be known as the "plain-view doctrine." In the Supreme Court case *Coolidge v. New Hampshire*,[1] Justice Stewart laid down three basic requirements for a search to come under the scope of this doctrine: (1) A valid intrusion; (2) an inadvertent discovery; and (3) immediate recognition that the subsequently discovered evidence relates to wrongdoing.

The first element, *a valid intrusion*, means that the plain-view doctrine cannot be used to justify what would otherwise be an unlawful entry. Justice Stewart cited four examples of intrusions that are permissible for the doctrine to apply:

1. "The situation in which the police have a warrant to search a given area for specified objects, and in the course of the search come across some other article of incriminating character."
2. "Where the initial intrusion that brings the police within plain view of such an article is supported, not by a warrant, but by one of the recognized exceptions to the warrant requirements"—for example, during an occasion when "the police may inadvertently come across evidence while in hot pursuit of a fleeing suspect."
3. When "an object comes into view during a search incident to arrest that is appropriately limited in scope under existing law."
4. "Where a police officer is not searching for evidence against the accused, but, nonetheless, inadvertently comes across an incriminating object." An example of this would be when a police officer, while securing the evidence in a car in preparation for impounding the vehicle, observes contraband in it.

The second necessary element is that the discovery of the evidence must be *inadvertent*. Thus, seizures that occur in instances where the officer knew of the evidence prior to the search and failed to get a warrant for the particular evidence in question are illegal—even where the initial intrusion is a valid one.

The final element, *immediate recognition*, has been subject to differing criteria by different courts. These conflicts are of special importance to drug enforcement officers since the conflicts have centered mainly in the area of identification of controlled substances.

Some courts interpret this element in a very strict sense. For example, in a 1966 Kentucky case,[2] the court held that recognition was not immediate because the contents of a sack could be positively identified as marijuana only after the officer had removed some of the substance and examined it closely. Therefore, the evidence was not admissible under the plain-view doctrine.

Such a stringent interpretation, however, is the exception rather than the rule. Today a majority of the courts hold the more reasonable view that this element is satisfied if the officer has probable cause at the time of the discovery to believe that the substance in question is evidence of criminal activity. Thus the court in the *State v. Reed* case[3] found in favor of immediate recognition when police seized a bottle of pills from the dashboard of a car, even though it was not determined until later laboratory tests that it contained illegal drugs.

An important factor in such probable-cause approaches of the immediate-recognition element is the expertise of the particular officer. What might qualify as probable cause for immediate recognition by a veteran drug enforcement officer may not suffice for an officer unfamiliar with substances and customs prevalent in the drug trade.

At this point it should be stressed that plain view alone is never enough to justify the warrantless seizure of evidence. The seizure must at all times be reasonable. In most instances this presents no problem. However, there are cases that do necessitate a warrant before objects in plain view can be seized. If, for example, an officer observes marijuana plants growing on the balcony of an apartment in a high-rise complex, it would seem that it would be more reasonable to obtain a warrant before entering the apartment.

Abandonment

At present there is only one other area of infringement generally not considered covered by the Fourth Amendment. Property to which a person has said to have voluntarily and intentionally relinquished any claim of ownership is considered to be abandoned and not within the scope of the Fourth Amendment safeguards.

Thus, when criminals check out of hotels, apartments, or similar living places, they are said to have abandoned the premises. Therefore, they have waived any claims over the premises that would have entitled them to Fourth Amendment protection concerning searches of the dwellings. However, even in such cases it is usually desirable, although not absolutely necessary, to obtain permission of the owner of a building before conducting a search.

The concept of abandonment comes up most frequently for drug enforcement officers in the so-called "dropsy" cases. These are instances in which the suspect drops or throws away narcotics upon seeing police officers. While some courts hold that under the circumstance such abandonment is not really voluntary, a majority of courts hold that "dropsy" cases fall under the abondonment doctrine.

CONSTITUTIONALLY PROTECTED SITUATIONS

In general, there are only four situations in which a search and subsequent seizure of evidence are legally permitted:

1. Incident to a lawful arrest
2. With consent
3. With a warrant based on probable cause
4. Without a warrant in certain limited instances where probable cause exists but circumstances preclude obtaining a warrant

Searches Incident to a Lawful Arrest

The first requirement of a permissible search is that the arrest must be lawful. Searches incident to an unlawful arrest are unlawful. The scope of the search following a lawful arrest is strictly limited to those areas over which the subject has immediate control. Such restrictions still, of course, make a complete search of the arrestee's person legal. Courts differ as to what other areas may be searched, but a safe rule is the "arm's-reach" doctrine. Under this rule anything within arm's reach is said to be under potential control of the suspect and thus subject to search.

The intent here is to limit the authority to search for weapons and for evidence that the arrestee could destroy or conceal. In most situations further search requires a warrant. If it is not possible to obtain one prior to the arrest, one officer can be left to guard the premises while another obtains a warrant. This procedure may seem inefficient, but it is a necessary one if legally obtained evidence is to be secured.

Searches Based on Consent

In instances where legally effective consent to search is obtained, a search may lawfully be conducted without a warrant and without probable cause. Thus it can be seen that the citizen who consents to a search is voluntarily waiving Fourth Amendment protections. Such a waiver will be evaluated carefully by the courts, and for this reason it is very important that the officer be able to show that consent was clearly voluntary.

From a tactical point of view consent searches are risky. If the consent is not obtained, the suspect must be informed that an investigation is being conducted. This advance notice could give the suspect enough time to escape or dispose of incriminating evidence. Therefore, it would seem wise to limit such searches to situations where there is insufficient probable cause to obtain a warrant.

WHO MAY CONSENT.   Since a consent search involves a waiver of constitutional rights that are personal in nature, only the person whose rights are being waived may consent to the search. Thus, a landlord cannot consent to a search of a tenant's dwelling, and an employer cannot usually consent to search of areas under an employee's exclusive control, such as the individual's desk or locker.

Cases have been mixed as to whether a parent can consent to a police search of the room or property of a child living at home. The parents, however, are free to conduct such a search personally. Search consent to property that is jointly owned, such as the family home or automobile, is also unresolved. Since there is conflict in the courts in these areas, the safest course of action would seem to be to obtain the consent of the occupant of the premises against whom the search is directed.

CONSENT MUST BE VOLUNTARY. The courts are careful to evaluate each consent to determine if it was given voluntarily. In a high percentage of cases submission to police authority is found not to be consent because it is not voluntary. For example, courts within the District of Columbia have held that consent while under arrest is invalid. Other courts have said that any consent to a police search is implicity coercive. While most courts are not quite that strict, voluntariness is an important factor in a consent search, and the searching officer must take care to be prepared to show that this factor was present.

Besides being given voluntarily, that is, without coercion or duress, the consent must be given with full knowledge of the right to refuse consent. Therefore, the officer must explain fully to the person whose consent is sought that he or she has a constitutional right to refuse a search of person or property without a warrant. Some states require that full "Miranda-type" warnings be given.

In addition, the consent to search must be clear and explicit. For this reason a written consent is preferable wherever possible.

CAPACITY TO CONSENT. The drug enforcement officer may frequently have occasion to have contact with persons who are permanently or temporarily (usually due to the influence of drugs) incapable of making a valid consent. If a question is raised concerning an individual's capacity to consent, at the time consent was given, it is up to the prosecution to show that the consenting person was in fact competent at the time.

SCOPE OF CONSENT. Officers cannot use deception or false pretenses to obtain consent. That is, they cannot say that they intend to look for specific evidence and then use consent as a justification for a general exploratory search.

Searches Based on a Warrant

THE FOUR QUALIFICATIONS OF A VALID WARRANT. The Fourth Amendment stipulates four basic elements for a valid search warrant.

1. The warrant must describe, with particularity, the place to be searched.

   This requirement is designed to prohibit general searches. If there is more than one building at a particular address (for example, a house and garage), each particular building to be searched must be specified. In multiunit buildings, such as apartments or rooming houses, each particular apartment or room to be searched must be specified in the warrant. If there is no number available for the premises to be searched, the occupant's name must be given. It is good practice to include this information even in cases where the exact address is available. If separate units with different occupants are to be searched, separate affidavits should be prepared.

2. The warrant must describe, with particularity, the things to be seized.

   As in the first qualification noted, this requirement is designed to prohibit general searches. Consequently, the complaint must describe in detail the objects to be seized. General and broad descriptions, such as "various controlled substances," are not adequate. Instead the warrant should spell out in detail the various drugs sought.

3. The warrant must be based on probable cause.

   The general test for probable cause is the existence of facts and circumstances sufficient to justify a person of reasonable prudence to believe that an offense has been committed and that the particular property to be seized is located at the particular place named. If the officer obtained these facts on the basis of personal observation, they must be set out in detail, including the dates, times, and places where the observations were made and exactly what was observed. Because of this requirement, it is vital that officers involved in surveillance activities maintain careful notes covering everything that they observe.

   If the information comes from another source—for example, an informant—the complaint must note where the facts were related to the officer, when and where personal observation by the third party was made, what exactly the third party observed, and an explanation of why the officer believes the information supplied to be valid.

   For purposes of a search warrant it is not necessary to disclose the identity of a confidential informant, but such cases do require proof of the informant's credibility. Credibility can be evidenced by (a) an informant's past history for accuracy, (b) prior arrests and/or convictions based on past information from the informant, and (c) all corroborating or supporting evidence that the officer may have that tends to show the informant's information to be true and accurate. Proof of credibility is of particular importance at the trial stage. Defense attorneys routinely attempt to break cases by attempting to show insufficiency of probable cause based on information supplied by anonymous informants.

4. The warrant must be supported by a sworn affidavit.

This element is self-explanatory and should present no problem since most jurisdictions have a standard form for use by police officers in applying for a search warrant.

EXECUTION OF WARRANTS.   Warrants must be executed within a reasonable time after they are issued. Reasonableness is determined on the basis of the particular facts in each situation. However, in most cases a warrant should be executed within three to four days. Sometimes even less time is allowed if the execution is to be reasonable under the circumstances.

The general rule concerning time for execution is that search warrants be executed during the day. If there is strong indication that the evidence sought is better obtained at night, it is safe practice to have this information specified in the warrant and to obtain a special "nighttime warrant."

Generally, the officers executing a warrant must knock, announce their identity and purpose, and wait a reasonable time for the occupant to respond. If the occupant refuses entry or fails to answer, officers may use reasonable force to gain entry. If the destruction of evidence or unreasonable risk of physical harm is anticipated, and therefore an unannounced entry is contemplated, the circumstances must be explained to the magistrate issuing the warrant, for special judicial permission is necessary before an officer can legally make an unannounced entry to execute a warrant.

While executing a warrant, police officers may detain and search anyone discovered at the premises for the purpose of protecting themselves from attack or preventing the destruction of evidence.

Searches without a Warrant in Certain Limited Instances

Of primary concern in situations where probable cause exists but circumstances preclude obtaining a warrant is the warrantless search of movable objects, especially vehicles, although planes and boats may also qualify. Note that probable cause is still necessary. The exception applies to movable objects only when there is danger of the vehicle being moved. There the exception requires that the vehicle actually be moving when stopped for a search or that it be parked where it could easily be moved before a warrant could be obtained.

REASONABLE BEHAVIOR

All rules concerning police conduct during search and seizure require that police act in a reasonable manner. Evidence can be suppressed, even when obtained on the basis of probable cause, if in the judgment of the court the police behaved unreasonably. The most familiar case involving unreasonable police behavior is *Rochin v. California*,[4] in which the defendant, surprised by sheriff's deputies in his bedroom, swallowed two capsules that deputies had spotted on his bedstand. The deputies attempted to force the defendant to cough out the capsules. After an unsuccessful struggle they handcuffed the defendant and took him to a hospital to have his stomach pumped out. The court in this case held that police conduct was so excessive as to "shock the conscience."

IN CONCLUSION

It is vital for anyone involved in drug enforcement to have a clear understanding of the rules of search and seizure under which they operate. A chapter such as this can, at best, only touch on the high points. Therefore it is important that you thoroughly familiarize yourself with and keep abreast of the particular rules and guidelines that apply to your own jurisdiction and agency.

NOTES

[1]*Coolidge v. New Hampshire*, 403 U.S. 443 (1971).
[2]*Nichols v. Commonwealth*, 408 S.W. 2d 189 (Ky. 1966).
[3]*State v. Reed*, 208 S.E. 2d 699 (N.C. App. 1974).
[4]*Rochin v. California*, 342 U.S. 165 (1952), 72 S. Ct. 205 (1952), 96 L. Ed. 183 (1952).

Chapter 13
BUYS

Enforcement activities aimed at suppressing drug traffic are hampered by all the problems that are inherent in dealing with the so-called victimless crimes. Usually drug sales are carried out (1)among willing participants and (2) in a secretive manner. There is no "victim" in the usual sense of the word as it is applied to such crimes as burglary and rape. Instead, the victim is a willing participant in the crime. As a result there is no complainant. And in most cases the only witnesses to a drug buy are the participants themselves.

Because of these characteristics, the traditional police methods of apprehension and detection are almost worthless against drug sellers. Other methods must be used. One of the most common techniques is the buy. A buy is an attempt by authorities to maneuver the suspected dealer into selling drugs to either an undercover officer or an informant. If this can be done, the authorities can then either arrest the seller on the spot or use the buy as a basis for obtaining a search warrant for the seller's home or other base of operations.

At best, setting up and making a buy are both difficult and dangerous. The investigators and informants involved will be required to exhibit ingenuity, patience, and stamina. Throughout the proceedings they must be constantly on their guard; otherwise they may endanger their own lives and those of their associates. Although the exact particulars in conducting a buy case vary from jurisdiction to jurisdiction and case to case, there are certain underlying principles that are universally important, and these are outlined in this chapter.

For the sake of clarity, the activities involved in making a successful buy have been arbitrarily placed under three time periods: (1) before the buy; (2) during the buy; and (3) after the buy.

BEFORE THE BUY

Preparation is the key to a successful buy case. A case that has been carefully planned and, as a result, proceeds in an orderly, tightly managed fashion is the case that is most likely to succeed. The buy that is put together on the spur of the moment and managed as the action occurs will almost invariably end up a waste of time, money, and energy. It is also the kind of investigation that can get someone hurt or even killed.

Obviously, the specific preparation that is required depends on the nature of each case. However, there are certain steps necessary in the preparation of most drug buy cases. These include:

1. Checking the informant's reliability
2. Planning the operation
3. Instructing the participants
4. Preparing the buy money
5. Searching the informant

Checking the Informant's Reliability

Informants are essential to the success of many buy cases. They can be used to make buys by themselves, to gather advance intelligence on the seller and his or her associates, to introduce an undercover officer to the seller, and to help establish the credibility of the officer. They can also serve as witnesses to buys that are made by an undercover officer.

Though informants can be very useful, they can also be notoriously unreliable. Put yourself in the informant's place. Try to figure out his or her motive for providing you with information. Ask yourself such questions as: What is the individual up to? Why is this person giving me information? What does he or she want in return? What will he or she gain if I arrest the seller being fingered? (The types and motives of informants are described in Chapter 10.)

Never make the mistake of taking anything that an informant tells you at face value. Try to verify everything. This policy demands time and effort, but in the long run it will more than pay off in cases made and problems avoided. It may also prevent someone from being killed.

Checking the reliability of informants is not only important in terms of the personal safety of others who will be involved in the case but also necessary if there is to be a search warrant based on information provided by the informant. Unless a record of past reliability can be established and demonstrated to the court, there is little chance that the informant's information will prove sufficient for the issuance of a search warrant.

There are several ways to check on an informant's reliability. None of them are foolproof. No matter how much time and effort are invested in checking, deception is possible. The questions suggested in the next paragraph will usually give a fairly accurate picture of the kind of a person that the informant is and how much faith can be put in the information that he or she provides. The answers will also provide an inkling of how much attention the court will give to the informant's testimony—if and when it is needed.

One of the best ways to begin checking on the reliability of informants is to check their past records. When doing this, look for the answers to five basic questions:

1. How many arrests have been made in the past as a result of information they supplied?
2. How many of these arrests resulted in convictions?
3. What are their reputations with other investigators who have dealt with them in the past?
4. Have they provided information in the past about other kinds of criminal activity? Has it proved to be reliable?
5. Do the past criminal records and known criminal activities indicate that they can provide the kind of information that they say they can?

A must in the close questioning of the informants themselves is to see how familiar they appear to be with the local drug scene. Try to ask a number of questions to which you know the answers. Correct answers indicate some degree of reliability. Wrong ones should serve to put you on your guard.

If an informant claims to know the suspected seller well, question him or her closely about facts that can be readily verified. For example, ask about the seller's phone number, hangouts, known associates, address, the make of the seller's car and its license plate number.

Finally, you may want to ask the informant to provide you with a sample of drugs purchased from the suspect. Of course, if the informant does produce drugs, it does not necessarily mean that they came from the seller in question. Nevertheless, it does indicate that the informant is sufficiently streetwise to obtain drugs. That may be a favorable sign.

Document each step taken in checking on the reliability of the informant. Keep a written record of the questions asked and the answers received. Note all information that is unfavorable toward the informant as well as that which is favorable. Some agencies maintain centralized intelligence files in which investigators can record information provided by informants. If your agency does, include your findings in it.

This complete and careful documentation is vital for two reasons: (1) If you decide to apply for a search warrant, the court will require you to substantiate the reliability of your informant. (2) It will greatly assist other investigators to evaluate the reliability of the informant should he or she become involved in a subsequent case.

Planning the Operation

Once you are satisfied with the reliability of your informant, your next step is to plan the case in detail. The importance of *careful planning* cannot be overemphasized. The success of the case and the lives of the officers and informants involved depend on it. Needless to say, some buy cases are relatively simple affairs. For these proper planning is neither particularly difficult or time-consuming. Other cases, however, are complex, and a great deal more time must be spent in getting ready for them.

Though the complexity of buy cases varies widely, there are a number of basic similarities between a buy that results in a million-dollar seizure and the simple "bust" of a neighborhood pusher. No matter how simple or involved the case may be, the officers in charge of planning must devote their attention to certain areas in all cases:

1. Gathering intelligence about the seller and his or her operation
2. Gathering intelligence about the neighborhood or area in which the buy is planned
3. Developing a cover story for the undercover officer if one is to be used
4. Arranging for signals
5. Anticipating problems and developing alternative plans
6. Warning participants about problems of entrapment
7. Maintaining security

INTELLIGENCE ON THE SUSPECTED SELLER.   The success of any buy case is greatly influenced by how much information you can gather on the suspected drug dealer. To make a good case, it is essential to know as much about the seller and his or her operation as possible. As one veteran narcotics officer commented:

> When I go to work on a buy, I make it my business to learn all I can about the dealer. I want to know everything I can about him. Hell, I want to know him better than he does himself. When I get through with him, nobody— except maybe his mother—knows him better than I do. I know what the hell he does when he gets up in the morning and what he does when he goes to bed in the evening—and every hour in between.

Facts to learn about the suspected dealer include:

1. Past criminal record, including arrests, convictions, and time served

2. Friends and associates, including family, suppliers, lovers, employees, and partners
3. Business fronts or legitimate cover operations
4. Vehicles used, including make, model, color, license plate number
5. Residence, including address, floor plan, possible escape routes and hiding places
6. Hiding place or stash where drugs are kept before being sold
7. Favorite location for selling drugs

The more of the listed information known about the suspect, the better your chances are. A good deal of it may be obtained from criminal record and intelligence files (Figure 13-1). Informants may be able to furnish still more, and surveillance and undercover operations may be able to fill in the blanks.

THE NEIGHBORHOOD.   It is also important to find out as much as possible about the general neighborhood in which the suspect lives and deals. Study maps of the area and plans of any buildings that may be involved. If possible, reconnoiter the area in person so that you have a firsthand feel for it. It is often helpful to photograph the area. In more important cases it is sometimes worth the trouble of taking aerial photos. If it is anticipated that the buy will be made in the dealer's home or business or some other area that you cannot visit in person, get an informant or undercover officer to provide as detailed a description as possible.

As you familiarize yourself with the area, make a note of the following things:

1. Locations that will provide surveillance officers with as good a view of the buy as possible.
2. Escape routes that the dealer may use. These routes may also prove useful to either an informant or an undercover officer if something goes wrong during the buy.
3. Danger spots where the undercover officer or informant could be ambushed, hijacked, or robbed.
4. Approach routes that officers may use to sneak up on the buy scene without being spotted.
5. Lookout points where the dealer's accomplices are posted.
6. Location of the dealer's stash. Does the dealer always go into a particular room, apartment, vehicle, alley, or building and then return with the drugs?

INFORMATION REPORT

Date _____ 10/3/xx _____ Number: I – 91-521 _____

Subject: _____ Mary Brown _____
                        (person) business, organization)

Alias: _____ Bigtooth _____

Address: _____ 1905 "K" St. N.W. _____

Description: sex _/_ race _W_ age _23_ height _5'7"_ weight _150_ eyes _Brown_ hair _Br_

Vehicle _72_ _Ford_ _DC 2103_   Occupation: _Prostitute_
    (year) (make) (license)

Associates: _Carlos Mantia_   Criminal Activity: _Drug Dealer_
        (persons & places)   (known or suspected)

Lupo Wolleman   _Drug Dealer_

FBI # _52-514-2993_ State ID # _DC-39-29-5221_ Other ID # _—_

Places Frequented: _The California Lounge 21st & "K" st N.W._

Additional Information: _She is a frequent source of information._
She has supplied information leading to arrests # 91-4221
_# 99-296 / # 107-6592._
She is a small scale dealer & prostitute.
Her favorite place to hide drugs is in back of the
record cabinet in her bedroom.

Received by: _Det. Sgt. Simpson_ Date Received: _12/5/xx_

Received from: _actual records_
              (Address)

Actual Names: _yes_   Assumed Name: _____

Reliability of Source: Reliable ___✓___ Unknown _____ Doubtful _____

FIGURE 13-1
A form such as this one is useful for summarizing information on
persons involved in buys.

veillance equipment make such recording practical even in such dimly lit areas as alleys, hallways, and basements.

If both an undercover officer and an informant are participating, the officer should be the one to turn over the money and receive the drugs from the dealer.

At each step in the transaction the buyer should be sure to give the appropriate prearranged signal. This is vital if the surveillance officers are to keep abreast of what is going on.

During the buy every effort should be made to find out where the dealer's supply or stash of drugs is hidden. At times this can prove to be difficult, particularly when the dealer is not a user. As might be expected, user dealers often keep their supply of drugs close at hand. They do not want to be running around the neighborhood whenever they need a fix. For such individuals the convenience of having their drugs easily available is more important than the risks involved by so doing.

In contrast, nonuser dealers are likely to be far more cautious about where their supplies are kept. Security is foremost in their minds. These dealers generally hide their drugs in a place away from where they live. Small-time dealers, the street peddlers, often conceal their meager supplies in such locations as nearby abandoned buildings, warehouses, basements, or lofts. Another favorite location is the house or apartment of a nonuser friend. Larger dealers frequently go to the trouble and expense of renting a separate room or apartment, or as it is called on the street, "stash pad," in which they can safely store their drugs.

The actual delivery of the drugs to the buyer depends on the dealer's style of operation. Sometimes the dealer will hand over the drugs directly to the buyer. From a law enforcement point of view, this is the ideal situation. There can be no question about it later in court. However, such a procedure is rare. Many dealers are more cautious.

A far more common procedure is for the customer to pay the dealer "up front" before the drugs are turned over. The dealer then goes to where the drugs are hidden, takes the quantity paid for, and goes to a hiding spot near where the customer is waiting. After concealing the drugs there, the dealer returns to the customer and informs the customer where the drugs can be found. Less cautious dealers do not seclude the drugs. Upon their return to the customer from their stash, they simply drop the packet of drugs on the floor or street, and the customer picks them up.

The surveillance officers who have been assigned to observe and record the sale can play a major role in helping and locating the dealer's cache. They may be able to follow the dealer and locate where the drugs are being kept. This, however, can be very difficult if the dealer is particularly cautious. It is not unusual for dealers to post confederates to observe if they are being followed and to use every evasive trick in the book to shake a tail. When dealing with such an operator it may take several buys before the surveillance officers are able to locate the stash.

As mentioned earlier, fluorescent powder sometimes can be a great help in a buy. If the dealer handles money that has been dusted with it, some of the powder will rub off on his or her hands. It will then be transferred to anything that the dealer touches. The surveillance officers may be able to trace the dealer's route with the aid of a small, portable ultraviolet light.

A word of caution is due on the use of this technique. At least one case has been lost because the investigator acted too hastily. Following a dealer into an apartment house and shining an ultraviolet light on every doorknob until finding one that glowed with the fluorescent powder that had rubbed off on the suspect's hands, the investigator rushed out and obtained a search warrant for the apartment in question. Sure enough, when the apartment was raided, a sizable supply of drugs was found. However, the defendant's lawyer had the case dismissed because the investigator had stopped examining doorknobs after finding the first one that glowed. The judge ruled that every doorknob in the building should have been examined. Testimony should have shown that one, and only one, doorknob had the powder on it. This would have indicated with the required legal certainty that the dealer entered the right apartment. With this story in mind, then, if you use this technique always make sure that you follow through with it.

If the dealer uses a car to go to the place where the drugs are hidden, it may be possible to use an electronic tailing beeper to assist in the surveillance. This device is small and is easily attached with a strong magnet to the frame or body of a car. It is a simple matter for an officer posing as a passerby to place one on a suspect's car. Chase units can then follow by tuning in on the distinctive radio signal broadcast by the beeper. However, in many jurisdictions there are legal restrictions on the use of such tailing devices. Do not employ them unless you are thoroughly familiar with the legal restrictions that apply in your district and the policies and procedures that are dictated by your agency.

If the decision has been made not to arrest the seller immediately after the buy is made, the purchaser should make a detailed report about the location or probable location of the drug stash. If the buyer actually saw where the dealer's drug supply was kept, the exact location should be noted in the report. If this is not the case, the buyer should note all that he or she witnessed that might indicate where the drugs were kept. For example, a typical entry might read, "After I paid John Smith $20, he went into the bathroom. I heard what sounded like the top of the toilet tank being removed. He returned a minute later with a small red balloon that was wet. He said it contained two capsules of heroin."

Surveillance officers should be equally specific in their reports. The more exact such reports are as to the probable location of the dealer's drug stash, the better is the chance of obtaining a search warrant and the less likely it is that the case will be thrown out of court because a defense lawyer is able to convince a judge that your search was based on a warrant that should not have been issued.

A final word of caution is appropriate. Drug buys are *always* dangerous. You can never afford to let your guard down for a moment. The list of officers who have been injured and killed while attempting to make a buy is a long and sad one.

Stay alert and stay alive!

AFTER THE BUY

As soon as practical after the buy is completed, it is essential to (1) take possession of the drugs and any unused buy money, (2) process the evidence, and (3) debrief the buyer.

Taking Possession of the Drugs and Unused Funds

To repeat, as soon after the buy as it is safe to do so, the officer in charge of the buy should take possession of the drugs. If an informant made the buy, any unused buy money should also be recovered. If the seller is arrested immediately after the sale, the buy money that is seized should be treated in the same way as any other evidence.

It is advisable, if possible, to have another officer present to act as a witness when the drugs are turned over to the officer in charge. This second officer should remain to witness the entire handling procedure until all evidence is turned over to either the laboratory or the property custodian.

When informants transact the buy, they should be taken as soon as possible to a place where they can be thoroughly searched. They frequently try to "sweeten the deal" by holding out some of the drugs or buy money. This search should be witnessed by another officer and a notation made of it in the case report.

Many agencies require that a detailed financial report be made after each buy (Figure 13-2). A typical report contains the following information:

1. The date, time, and place of the buy
2. The type and quantity of drugs purchased
3. The amount of money spent
4. The name of the seller from whom the drugs were bought
5. The name of the person who made the buy

Undercover officers and informants are frequently identified in such reports by code names or confidential identification numbers instead of their real names. When this is done, the name of the control officer or case supervisor is also sometimes given.

Processing the Evidence

During the past several years the law enforcement community has been rocked by a number of unfortunate scandals involving drug evidence. In several instances large quantities of drugs worth millions of dollars have been stolen while under the control of the police. Needless to say, such incidents are hardly conducive to generating public confidence and support.

Such happenings cannot be tolerated by any dedicated, professional law enforcement agency. If cases are to be made and if public support and confidence are to be maintained, it is essential that the integrity of all drug evidence be kept inviolate. A standardized and closely supervised evidence-handling sequence is vital to ensure this. Each and every item of evidence must be completely accounted for from the moment that it first comes into the hands of the authorities until it is finally disposed of.

There is no single set of procedures that can be adopted by all law enforcement agencies to assure the integrity of the drug evidence in their possession. Local conditions, needs, and requirements vary too much. However, a study by the Drug Enforcement Administration and the International Association of Chiefs of Police[3] noted some of the hallmarks of a poor system:

Failing to weigh the evidence or, at best, accomplishing this function in a perfunctory manner

Failing to photograph the evidence

Allowing a single, unobserved individual, aside from the evidence custodian, to be in close proximity to or in possession of the evidence

BUY EXPENDITURE—CONFIDENTIAL FUNDS

Case No. _76-2103_   Expenditure No. _235_

Date of expenditure _12/9/xx_   Amount _$25.00_

Subject _Mary Brown AKA "Bigtooth"_

Description of Material _1 capsule containing aproximately 500 milligrams of white powder suspected to be heroin. Place of buy in kitchen of 1905 "K" St. SW._

Agent _J.C. Custer_   Date _12/9/xx_

Approved by Unit Commander:

William Sirius, Capt.   Date _12/10/xx_

CONFIDENTIAL FUND EXPENDITURES LEDGER

Date	Expenditure	Purchase of Evidence	Payment of Informant	Expenses	Running Total
12/3/xx	$25	1 capsule of heroin	—		$25.00
12/4/xx	$50	—	$50.00	—	$75.00
12/5/xx	$50	1 gram of heroin	—	—	$125.00
12/9/xx	$25	1 capsule of heroin	—	—	$150.00

FIGURE 13-2
It is vital to maintain absolute control of the funds used to make narcotics buys. Records such as these will help to ensure that every dollar is accounted for.

Permitting unaccompanied forensic chemists to withdraw narcotic and dangerous-drug evidence from storage for purpose of analysis

Disregarding or deviating from written directives or standing orders which outline approved procedures for evidence handling

Failing to institute active and frequent measures or requests in an effort to gain permission to dispose of (destroy) evidence which is old or has no further evidentiary value

Failing to install intrusion detection devices on apertures which afford access to narcotic and dangerous-drug evidence storage areas

Utilizing makeshift containers, bins, and cabinets for evidence storage

Failing to provide a secure, adequate, readily available, temporary repository for evidence which is seized during other than normal duty hours or which cannot be processed further due to the absence of the regularly appointed custodial or technical personnel

Permitting narcotic and dangerous-drug evidence to be stored indiscriminately with other types of evidence

In contrast, an effective evidence-processing system is one in which:

1. All items of evidence are properly identified and marked (Figure 13-3).
2. Records are kept that describe the evidence in detail and note what is done with it.
3. Receipts are generated every time that the evidence changes hands for any reason.
4. The procedure that is to be followed in handling drug evidence is clearly spelled out in official department orders.
5. All evidence is locked in a secure vault when it is not actually being used or examined.
6. The evidence-handling system is closely supervised, and periodic checks are made to see that there is compliance with all the orders pertaining to it.

It is impossible to outline in detail a processing procedure for drug evidence that will work equally well in every enforcement agency. Local conditions and requirements vary far too widely. However, certain basic procedures, if adapted to fit individual circumstances, will go a long way toward ensuring the integrity of drug evidence.

The following evidence-processing sequence is presented as a

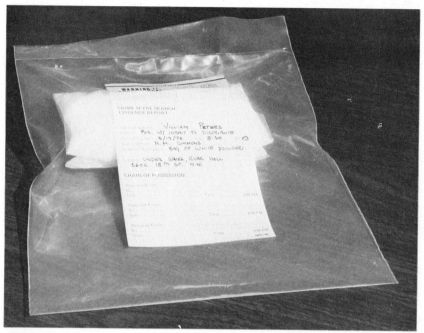

FIGURE 13-3
All evidence should be packaged in some form of tamperproof
container as soon as possible.

skeleton upon which any agency can build its own system. Although
the procedures deal specifically with drugs obtained through a buy,
with very minor modifications and additions they could be employed
with drug evidence obtained under any circumstances.

STEP 1.   The suspected drugs are given by the purchaser to the officer
who is designated to receive them as soon as possible after the buy is
made. Another officer should be present to act as a witness for the
turnover. (If the purchaser is a law enforcement officer, he or she
should have previously marked the drugs as in Step 2.)

STEP 2.   The officer who receives the drugs marks them with either
his or her initials or badge number, the time, the place, and the date.
The officer also notes this information and a description of the drugs in
his or her notes along with the name of the individual from whom the
drugs were received and the name of the witnessing officer. When the
evidence itself cannot be marked, it is placed in a suitable container
which is then marked.

STEP 3.   Some agencies find it convenient to make a field test immediately after the buy in order to determine if the susbstance they have purchased is indeed a drug. Such tests may be conducted while still on the street or in headquarters. If such a test is made, its results should be included in the receiving officer's notes.

STEP 4.   The officer who has taken custody of the drugs and the witnessing officer should return to headquarters as soon as practical.

STEP 5.   At headquarters a supervisory official should be immediately notified of the buy. If possible, the succeeding steps should be witnessed by this official.

STEP 6.   A complete inventory of the drugs should be made at once. Some agencies recommend that along with being accurately weighed and/or counted, the evidence should also be photographed.

STEP 7.   A complete and accurate description of the drugs should be entered immediately in a permanent evidence-control or inventory log. This record should, at the minimum, provide a complete history or audit trail of the evidence from the moment it comes into police custody until it is finally disposed of. Everytime the evidence changes hands there should be a written receipt signed by the giver and the recipient.

STEP 8.   After all the evidence has been marked and the necessary forms completed, the evidence should be sealed in a tamperproof container. Many agencies have found special evidence envelopes to be useful for this purpose. Both paper envelopes with tamperproof seals and polyethylene envelopes that may be heat-sealed are available.

STEP 9.   Finally, when the processing is completed, the drugs should be taken in the presence of a witness to a designated secure area where they can be stored until needed.

Debriefing the Buyer

The buyer should be thoroughly debriefed after the buy is made so that there is as complete a record of the transaction as possible (Figure 13-4). This record is important for two reasons. First, it may provide investigative leads. For example, during the course of the buy the dealer may have mentioned his or her source of supply or mentioned

FIGURE 13-4
The buyer should be thoroughly debriefed as soon as practical
after the purchase is completed.

when a big shipment of drugs was due to arrive. Second, the documentation will allow detailed and specific testimony when the case gets to court or when there is an application for a warrant.

The informant or undercover officer who made the buy should record the transaction in as much detail as possible. Later, when applying for a warrant or testifying at the seller's trial, one's ability to answer questions about the smallest details of the transaction may prove to be the difference between success and failure. The report should begin by describing the events that led up to the buy. It should then describe the buy itself in detail and close with a description of what took place after the buy was completed. It is essential to include all pertinent names, times, dates, and places in this report as well as a description of the drugs purchased and the amounts paid for them.

If you follow the procedures outlined in this chapter, you will have an excellent chance of putting drug dealers where they belong—behind bars.

IN CONCLUSION

Drug buys are an integral part of many drug enforcement efforts. The guidelines covered in this chapter are designed to be of help before, during, and after the buy. If followed carefully, they will go a long way toward assuring that each buy you make will provide the kind of solid evidence today's courts require.

NOTES

[1]*Sorrels v. United States*, 356 U.S. 372, 78 S. Ct. 821.
[2]*People v. Estrada*, 211 Calif. App. 2d 722 (1962).
[3]Drug Enforcement Administration and Field Operations Division, International Association of Chiefs of Police, *Guidelines for Narcotic and Dangerous Drug Evidence Handling and Security Procedures* (Washington, D.C.: GPO, 1974), pp. 33–34.

Chapter 14
RAIDS

Raids are an important part of many drug enforcement programs. In essence a drug raid is a sudden and surprise invasion of a suspected drug trafficker's base of operation by law officers aimed at arresting the trafficker and seizing the illicit supplies. Raids vary in size, scope, and complexity. In their simplest form they may be directed at a neighborhood street pusher and involve only two or three officers. On the other hand, raids targeted against major drug trafficking networks may involve hundreds of law enforcement officers who simultaneously strike a dozen or more different locations and seize millions of dollars worth of drugs. Obviously, there is a great difference in the problems of and complexity associated with such situations. However, no matter how large or small the raid situation may be, there are certain basic procedures and techniques that are vital to its success.

Regardless of the nature of the raid, it can never be approached in a careless or offhand manner. Far too many things can (and probably will) go wrong. Even the simplest raid can blossom into a full-fledged nightmare if it is not properly handled. Suspects can escape; evidence can be destroyed or whisked away before it can be seized; participants and/or bystanders can be hurt or killed if the operation is not under perfect control. And, even if the enforcement officers are successful in getting in the door and seizing the target evidence, a judge may dismiss the case if a minor detail has been overlooked pertaining to the warrant or the handling of the evidence. In addition, evidence seized at raids can be lost, stolen, or misappropriated. Poor publicity relating to the raid can subject the agency responsible to an avalanche of unfavorable criticism. With so much at stake and the potential for serious problems so enormous, every effort must be taken to ensure that each raid is conducted in as professional a manner as possible. A successful raid has three essential characteristics:

1. THOROUGH PREPARATION. This involves gathering all the necessary intelligence, selecting experienced personnel to command and staff the operation, and planning it in meticulous detail.

2. COORDINATION AND TEAMWORK.   In a well-run raid all those participating know what they are supposed to do and when and how they are supposed to do it. They act as a team with a single common objective.
3. STRONG COMMAND PRESENCE.   There is no substitute for an experienced, able, and decisive commander.

This chapter will examine procedures that are necessary in order to plan and execute a raid in the most advantageous manner. For the sake of clarity, as in the preceding chapter on the buy, these are discussed under the three time periods during which they are executed: (1) before the raid; (2) during the raid; and (3) after the raid.

BEFORE THE RAID

To a large extent, the success of any raid depends upon the preparation for it. If you are to achieve your objectives, you must be prepared to invest time and effort in proper preparation. The well-prepared raid is the raid that apprehends the target suspects, seizes the necessary evidence, and puts the trafficker behind bars. The ill-prepared raid, directed and carried out with the hope for lucky breaks, is the one that at best is unsuccessful and at worst gets someone hurt or killed.

The preparation for any raid includes three basic tasks:

1. The raid commander and other personnel must be selected.
2. Intelligence must be gathered on the target individuals or buildings.
3. Detailed plans must be made.

Personnel Selection

The importance of selecting the right personnel to direct and participate in raids cannot be emphasized enough. The problems associated with a raid and the things that can go wrong during one are so numerous and so grave that placing the operation under the direction of anyone but the best is pure folly. No one but an experienced and competent individual should ever be selected. Once the commander is designated, he or she should have the freedom to pick an equally well-qualified deputy commander. And if simultaneous raids are to be conducted at different locations, it will be necessary to appoint qualified team leaders to be in charge of the activities at each site.

Again, the same care must be exercised in selecting each member of the raiding party. It is vital to pick only mature, experienced officers who can work well in stress situations. All officers should be people who will behave in a professional, businesslike manner. Unfortunately some individuals seem to feel that a raid is a perfect excuse "to throw their weight around." Such an attitude is sure to cause problems sooner or later for all concerned.

Intelligence on the Suspect

If there is one golden rule in the business of conducting raids, it is that a successful raid cannot be conducted without knowing what the raiding party is up against. Find out as much as possible about the individuals and buildings involved in the raid. Before the plans for the raid are formalized, a series of questions must be answered:

1. Who are the suspects?
2. Who are their accomplices?
3. How are they armed?
4. How prone are they to violence?
5. Are others, such as family members, neighbors, or friends, likely to be present?
6. What type of building is involved?
7. What is its layout?
8. Where are the doors, windows, ventilation shafts, and other entrances and exits located?
9. Is the target building fortified in any way?
10. What kind of locks are used?
11. How are the doors constructed?
12. Do the windows have bars, mesh, or other protective material over them?
13. Are there peepholes or alarms?
14. Does the suspect have a dog?
15. Does the suspect have lookouts posted? If so, where?
16. How much of the surrounding area can the suspect see from the inside of the building?
17. What devices are available for destroying or disposing of evidence? Toilets? Furnaces? Disposals?
18. Are there any hidden escape routes, such as concealed doors, tunnels, or trapdoors to the roof?
19. Is there a fire escape?

Obviously, the circumstances surrounding each case are different, and so is the exact information needed for each raid. However, the list given exemplifies the type of intelligence that must be compiled if the raid is to prove a success.

There are numerous ways that the necessary facts can be gathered. Surveillance operations may fill in such information as the people who come and go from the building, their schedules, and the vehicles that they use (Figure 14-1). Informants and undercover officers will be able

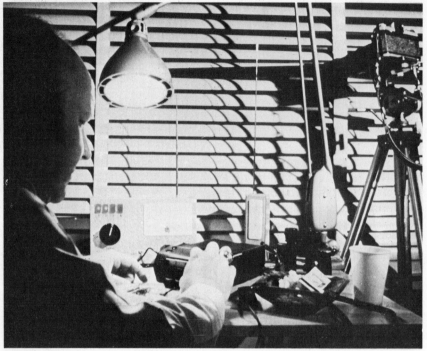

FIGURE 14-1
Careful surveillance may reveal much valuable information about
the raid target.

to provide even more information about the suspects and building involved. A word of caution about the use of informants: Never be so
naïve as to accept information at its face value that is provided by an
informant. Whenever possible, try to verify all data furnished by an
informant. There are too many reasons for an informant to give false or
outdated information. The success of the raid and the lives of the officers involved cannot be risked on the unquestioned acceptance of any
source as notoriously unreliable as an informant's word.

Criminal record and intelligence files may furnish more information. Such sources often contain invaluable notes about the suspect's
known associates, habits, tendency to violence, and past behavior.
They may also reveal the names of other officers who have had contact
with the suspect and who may be able to supply valuable information.

Plans of the target building, which are generally available from the
county assessor or the architect's office, can be invaluable when planning a raid. They can also be useful when searching the building be-

cause they show its original layout. This will help in detecting any alterations or changes that the suspect may have made for the purpose of concealing drugs or other contraband. Street maps and aerial photos can also be useful planning aids. They allow you to familiarize your team with the layout of the area and to decide on the most advantageous places to employ your forces. They may also reveal likely escape routes.

It is advisable for the officer in charge of the entire operation to scout the target area in person. In this way he or she will be able to become familiar on a firsthand basis with the obstacles likely to be encountered. As a matter of fact, all those to take part in the actual raid should become familiar with the area so that the operation can be carried out efficiently and as quickly as possible. These reconnaissance efforts should be done in a discreet manner. The last thing that is wanted is to tip off the suspects of the impending raid.

Planning the Raid

Under the very best of circumstances raids tend to be complex and dangerous undertakings. If they are to succeed, it is essential that they be properly planned. As the familiar army adage asserts, "Prior planning prevents poor performance." No matter how trite this may sound, it could not be truer. Unless a raid is properly planned and carefully thought out beforehand, there is an excellent possibility that its objectives will not be realized and that someone will be hurt.

Quite obviously, the planning phase will not be the same for every raid. A relatively simple raid may require only an hour or so to plan. On the other hand, a complex operation may be preceded by days or even weeks of intense planning. Despite the enormous variation in scope and complexity, all raid situations have certain basic planning considerations:

1. Decide on the strategy for the operation.
2. Select the necessary equipment.
3. Consider all the legal ramifications.
4. Select specialized support units.
5. Brief participants.

In light of the intelligence information, you have to evolve a plan that seems reasonable. This plan should include the tactics to be used when approaching the scene, entering the building, stabilizing the situation, conducting the search, making any arrests, leaving the scene, processing the evidence, and debriefing any suspects. In addition to the main plan, you should have alternative plans that can be put into effect should it become impractical or impossible to utilize the first.

The plan should also cover the selection of the necessary equipment to carry out the raid, such as battering rams, axes, crowbars, gas equipment, weaponry, and communications gear. Everyone should be familiar with how to use each item of equipment, and all the equipment must be in working order.

As part of the planning process, you must make sure that all the legal aspects of the raid have been considered. Go over the case and raid plan with your agency's legal adviser. Make sure that all affidavits and warrants are in order. Prevention is always the best course. Try to anticipate any legal problems that may develop as a result of the raid. Nothing is more discouraging to those involved than to have a successful raid dismissed from court over a legal technicality that could have been avoided with a little forethought.

In some raid situations it is advisable to have specialized units on standby during the operation. For example, if the plan is for a raid on a clandestine narcotics lab, a chemist should be available to examine the scene as soon as it is secure. It also is a wise precaution to have a fire truck on standby.

Thorough briefings are an important and often overlooked part of the planning phase. It is an undeniable fact that people cannot perform at their best unless they understand exactly what is expected of them (Figure 14-2). Be sure that everyone knows exactly what he or she is to do and when it is to be done. In complex raid situations involving many individuals, it is sometimes advisable to prepare information packets for each participant. Thus officers will have in writing, in clear terms, exactly what is expected of them during the entire raid. Give participants an opportunity to ask questions. Never take it for granted that the plan is understood. *Make sure* it is.

Quite obviously, if the suspect finds out about the planned raid before it takes place, all the efforts and care taken will be wasted. For that reason the importance of maintaining strict security cannot be stressed too much. During the planning stage every precaution should be taken to see that as few people as possible know what is going on. Follow the need-to-know rule: tell *only* those people who absolutely need to know about the plan—no one else! It is also advisable to have an office for planning that can be securely protected. At the end of each planning session, all maps, plans, charts, and the like should be locked in a sturdy safe. Both office and safe should be protected by an alarm system. If there is to be a large number of support personnel whose integrity cannot be verified during the raid, it may be wise to delay

FIGURE 14-2
It is important that all those who are going to be involved in a raid
understand exactly what they are expected to do.

briefing them until the last minutes before the raid. Such a policy will
help to prevent an unauthorized leak.

DURING THE RAID

Once the necessary intelligence has been gathered and the plans formu-
lated, the next step is the raid itself. Again, the wide variety of raid
situations makes it impossible to prescribe any one set of rules of conduct that is applicable in all situations. However, there are certain
procedural guidelines that, if followed, will go a long way to assuring
the success of a raid. Normally five tasks must be completed during any
raid:

1. Approaching and surrounding the target building
2. Gaining entry to the building and the suspect's base of operations
3. Stabilizing the situation inside
4. Searching the premises systematically
5. Withdrawing from the raid scene

Sometimes it is impossible to draw a hard-and-fast line between each of these steps. However, they do provide a useful framework against which steps involved in a raid can be examined.

Approaching and Surrounding the Target Building

In all raids the element of *surprise* is the most important weapon. Suspects who know that a raiding team is on the way will destroy evidence or flee. Therefore, it is important to approach the target building as stealthily as possible. Avoid making noise or doing anything that will warn the suspects of your approach. If using a car in an evening raid, turn the lights off. Do not screech brakes or slam car doors on arrival at the scene. If possible, use unmarked cars. Avoid loud talking.

The decision as to the time of day to execute the raid will depend on the circumstances of the case and any legal requirements or restrictions under which you function. Many authorities have found that the early morning hours—for example, around 4 A.M.—are the ideal time for a raid. Suspects and accomplices are usually asleep at that time and will not notice the raiding party's approach. By the time that they are awake enough to realize that it is the law coming through the door, you may have them under control.

However, it may be advantageous to time the raid to coincide with a specific event, such as the delivery of a shipment of drugs or the maximum number of suspects on the scene. In these cases a different time period may be best for the operation. Additionally, in many jurisdictions there are legal prohibitions that dictate the hours of the day when particular types of warrants may be served. This is something to be checked with your agency's legal adviser.

Raiding parties generally consist of two teams. The outside or cover team is responsible for securing the target and preventing the suspects' escape. It also protects police vehicles and controls any crowds that may gather. These functions can be particularly important in areas where there is a good deal of hostility toward the police. The inside team carries out the actual raid.

Gaining Entry

THE BUILDING.   Once the raid commander has checked to see that the cover team has all the exits blocked, the inside team can enter the target building. The usual procedure is to knock on the door, identify yourselves as law enforcement officers, and demand entry. If entry is denied, the team is then free to force its way into the premises. Some jurisdictions under certain circumstances allow breaking into a building without previously announcing the identity of the officers or purpose. These "no-knock" raids are designed primarily for use in recovering easily disposed-of evidence such as narcotics. Though such raids can at times give an edge in terms of time, they are extremely dangerous. The drug business is a violent one. It is filled with endless robberies, rip-offs, and shoot-outs. Since drug traffickers live with this ever-present threat of violence, it is not difficult to understand why most of them have developed a shoot-first-and-ask-questions-later approach to life. Consequently, it does not take much imagination to understand how quickly a no-knock situation can degenerate into a shoot-out if in the confusion of the situation the suspect mistakes you for robbers or rip-off artists. That is why it is preferable whenever conducting a raid—especially if it is a no-knock one—to have a clearly identified uniformed officer at the front of the raiding party. The presence of such an officer can often prevent unnecessary and needless violence.

If all the participants in the raid are not familiar with each other, there is also the danger that they will mistake one another for suspects. The results can be tragic. One way to avoid this type of confusion is to issue plainclothes officers some clearly identifying item of clothing. Some agencies use distinctly marked caps for this purpose. Others use armbands or vests. Still others rely on holders that display the officers' badges or credentials on the outside of their clothes. Whichever method you adopt, make certain that all the members of the raiding party are familiar with it.

THE SUSPECT'S BASE OF OPERATIONS.   As was said earlier, once you have knocked, identified yourself, and demanded entry, if the door is not opened, you are free to force your way in. Sometimes the suspect has gone to great lengths to make sure that entry is no easy matter. This is especially true when dealers fear being ripped off by other drug traffickers or when they hope to gain enough time to dispose of the evidence successfully before the police can get through the door. It is not uncommon to find metal-reinforced doors with strong crossbars to thwart forced entry. In addition, more than one door may have to be breached before gaining entry. The entry may be further complicated by alarms or steep stairways. Windows may be protected by bars, mesh, or shutters. If the intelligence has been accurate, the officers should have advance knowledge of what will be encountered and have the necessary breaching tools.

Some of the more useful tools are fire axes, wrecking bars, picks, sledgehammers, and short, easily maneuverable battering rams. One of the more recent and useful additions to the range of tools available to raiding parties is the hydraulic door-frame spreader. This device can spread apart a door frame so that the door can be pushed open. Lock-picking equipment may also come in handy. Some of the available units make it a relatively easy matter to open all but the most sophisticated locks. Bolt cutters and acetylene torches are also useful from time to time.

A word of caution is due at this point: In the wonderful world of television raids it is all too common to see police officers rush up to a door and shoot the lock open. Such an attack may look great on the screen, but it has no place in the real world of policing. The chance of injuring yourself, a colleague, or an innocent bystander is far too great to ever consider using a firearm in this manner.

Sometimes it is possible to enter the target building by some route other than the door, and it may be a better strategy. For example, one raiding party had as a target a fairly large-scale heroin cutting mill. The particular mill scheduled to be hit was on the second floor of a large cement-block warehouse. Its only entrance was a heavy wooden door at the top of a long flight of stairs. The door was reinforced with double-thickness sheet metal. It was further reinforced by steel crossbars. From the information supplied by the informant about the setup, it became apparent that it would be almost impossible to gain speedy access to the mill itself. It was decided to investigate other possible means of entry.

Reconnaissance of the building revealed that two large skylights led directly into the target area. Though the suspect had done everything possible to reinforce the door, nothing had been done to protect the skylights. At the appointed hour the raid team members simply slipped down onto the roof from another building, smashed in the skylights, and quite literally dropped in on the cutting party.

At other times it may be possible to gain entry by ruse or trick. For example, in one raid the lieutenant in charge walked up to a heavily barricaded door while his team hid around the corner. He knocked sharply and, when asked what he wanted, told the suspect—a woman—that someone had run into her car, which was parked outside. The moment that she opened the door to view the damage to her car, he gave a shove and the team ran inside.

Sometimes informants or undercover officers will be able to help gain entry. If, once the raid is completed, their cover is no longer needed, they may simply open the door at a prearranged time. In other instances they may be able, surreptitiously, to leave key windows or doors open, thus allowing the raiding party rapid entry.

Stabilizing the Situation Inside

As soon as entry is gained to the base of operations, the next step is to stabilize the situation as rapidly as possible. Once inside, teams of officers should proceed to secure every room in the target area. Special attention should be taken to see that officers immediately secure areas in which evidence can be destroyed or disposed of, such as toilets, furnace rooms, and incinerators.

All the occupants of the area being raided should be searched and brought to a central location where they can be watched and kept under control while the building is being searched. The raiding party will be in the greatest physical danger during the stabilization phase of the raid. One never knows who will be found from one minute to the next. Therefore, it is necessary to be on the alert constantly and ready for any type of action. For example, in a seemingly routine raid of a petty bootlegger's headquarters, shooting started the moment the raiding party broke through the door. One of the customers on the scene, a fugitive wanted for assaulting a police officer, naturally assumed that the team was after him. The raiding party had no idea that he was anywhere in the vicinity. The result could have been, and nearly was, tragic.

Once all the people on the premises have been rounded up and brought to a central location, they should not be allowed to move about until the area in which they are going to be detained is searched thoroughly. It is not uncommon to find weapons hidden in such places as under chair and sofa cushions, in drawers, behind TVs and radios, and under piles of magazines and newspapers.

After the search has been made and it is certain that no weapons are accessible, the owner or person in charge should be allowed to examine the warrant. Ask that person if he or she can read. If the answer is yes, have that person read the warrant in its entirety. If the answer is no, read the warrant aloud.

You should then ask if any valuables, money, or weapons are present. If the answer is yes, have the subject point out where they are kept. Retrieve them yourself in the presence of a witness, and give the owner a receipt. At the end of the search—if you can, according to your agency's policy—either return them or instruct the owner to pick them up at the property office. By following this procedure, you can prevent accusations of theft as well as take control of any weapon that might be used against you or your team during the search.

Searching the Premises Systematically

Only after the raid situation has been stabilized can the search for evidence begin. There is no easy way to conduct an effective search. A thorough search takes time and effort. If the attitude is "Let's search this place as quickly as we can and get out of here," you are almost certain to miss the drugs that you are after. On the other hand, if a systematic, methodical approach is followed, you have a good chance of finding the drugs for which you came, no matter how carefully they are hidden.

The key to an effective search is organization. Though there is no one right way to conduct a systematic search, the following approach has proved useful in many instances:

1. Start at a given point and move in an orderly manner through the entire premises until each room has been searched. When an entire building is involved, some investigators prefer to begin in the basement and work upward through the structure, whereas others like to start at the attic or the roof and move down. It does not matter which pattern is followed as long as you establish a routine and stick to it.
2. Search each room in an orderly manner. One of the most effective ways is first to search along the walls and then move into the center of the room. In searching the wall area, it may be useful to divide it into three areas or zones. The first zone includes everything from the floor to the height of your waist; the next zone, everything from the waist to shoulder height; and the third zone, everything from shoulder height to and including the ceiling (Figure 14-3).
3. If you have enough people, have at least two search teams scour each room. Often the second team will find something that the first one overlooked.

Some agencies have found that specially trained dogs are helpful in searches. It is almost impossible to conceal drugs so that these keen-nosed searchers will not find them. In addition to being useful in searching buildings, dogs are also valuable in searching vehicles.

It is impossible to list all the different places that drugs can be concealed. There are literally thousands of places in the average building in which they can be hidden. The only limit is a suspect's ingenuity

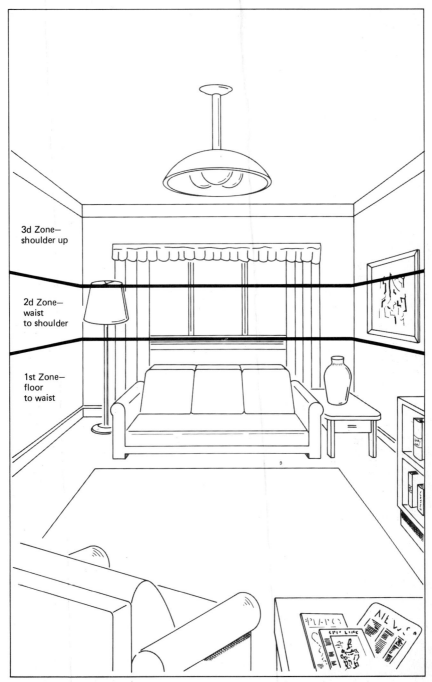

FIGURE 14-3
If a search is to be successful, it must be methodical. The technique shown here is easy to control on the scene and results in a thorough search of the suspect area.

and inventiveness. The only rule of thumb is *check everything*. The following is a list of places that are commonly used to conceal drugs in and around a home or apartment.

INSIDE

Cigarette packages
Telephone hoses and handles
Lamp bases
Mattresses
Hollow doors
Curtain and closet poles
Door chimes
Stairway posts
Rolled-up window shades
Mailboxes
Knife handles
Sink traps
Bedposts
Musical instruments and cases
Books
Magazines
Food boxes and containers
Radio and television sets
Religious sculptures
False aerosol cans
Cameras
Toys and stuffed animals
Clocks
Trophies

Doghouses
Hot-water bags
Film cans
Sanitary napkins
Candlesticks
Fuse boxes
Clothes hampers
Hollow soap cakes
Hollow fruits and vegetables
Salt and pepper shakers
Double boilers
Christmas decorations
Overstuffed furniture
Toolboxes
Hair driers
Tea bags
Surfboards
Toilets
Typewriters
Flashlights
Medicine bottles
Spice jars
Cookie jars
Clothespin bags

BEHIND

Switch plates
Lamp fixtures
Bookcases
Baseboards
Furniture
False walls
Mirrors
Posters

Pictures
Wall phones
Intercoms
Plumbing fixtures
Medicine cabinets
Heating conduits
Air-conditioning conduits

Drug field-test kits are useful in a search situation. If a kit is available while the search is being conducted, it is an easy matter to quickly check any suspicious substance that you discover. Though such tests are not foolproof, in general they are reliable (Figure 14-4).

When a substance that appears to be a drug is found, all those present on the premises can be arrested and charged with possession. However, agency policies vary on this. Some agencies prefer only to arrest principal suspects. For example, if drugs are found in an apart-

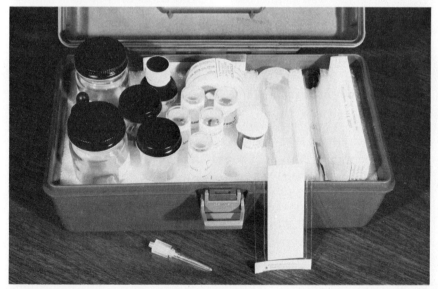

FIGURE 14-4
Simple-to-use and inexpensive field-test devices can indicate with a high degree of accuracy whether or not a suspect substance is, in fact, a drug.

ment in which the occupant and several friends are present, under such a policy only the occupant will be arrested. Other agencies arrest everyone present. Follow procedures and guidelines established by your agency.

It is also the agency's procedures and guidelines that determine the handling and processing of any drug evidence that is located. In the event that your agency has not spelled out procedures for drug evidence handling, the following guidelines will prove useful:

1. One member of the raiding party is designated as the evidence-collection officer. This officer, and only this officer, is responsible for collecting all the evidence found.
2. Another officer is designated to serve as a witness. This officer's primary function during the search is to observe everything that the collection officer does.
3. When a member of the search team uncovers what is suspected to be drugs, the evidence-collection officer should photograph it in place before it is disturbed.
4. The suspected material is then field-tested, placed into a container for safekeeping, and marked with the date, time, and location of discovery as well as the collection and witnessing officers' initials and/or badge numbers.
5. The exact location of its discovery is also noted in the collection officer's field notes. Some officers also find it helpful to mark the location on a sketch of the room, building, or vehicle being searched.
6. This entire process should be observed by the witnessing officer.

The importance of properly processing and specifying all aspects of evidence at the scene cannot be overstressed. Too many cases have been lost because this was not done. For example, this author once lost a case because he became confused about where each item of evidence was found during a search. He was unable to state positively whether a particular item of evidence was found in the top or middle drawer of a bureau. The defense attorney capitalized upon his uncertainty to such an extent that the case was dismissed, and a drug dealer was needlessly set free.

Sometimes clandestine drug-manufacturing laboratories are discovered during searches. These operations are particularly dangerous. Many of the chemicals used in the manufacture of illicit drugs are extremely poisonous or explosive. For example, strychnine and other violent poisons are frequently used to give illicit drugs that little extra "kick" that the consumers demand. Small quantities of these chemicals can cause death. Ether, acetone, and other solvents may also be involved in the manufacturing process. They are highly volatile and, when vaporized, extremely explosive. Another dangerous chemical that sometimes is found is lithium aluminum hydride. It is a particularly difficult compound to handle; the slightest moisture, even damp air, can cause it to explode.

In addition, many of the chemical reactions and manufacturing processes that are a part of drug manufacture are of a highly unstable nature. If they are interrupted at the wrong moment, the whole operation will, quite literally, blow the roof off.

With these problems in mind, if you expect to encounter a clandestine lab, it is vital to take along an experienced chemist as a member of the raiding party. Only such an individual will have the expertise to handle safely the chemicals and processes that are part of the lab (Figure 14-5).

It is important when dealing with a clandestine lab to seize absolutely all chemicals and processes found. In addition, seize all the apparatus. What may appear to be the smallest and most insignificant item of apparatus or test tube of chemicals may make the difference between convictions or dismissal of your case.

Withdrawing from the Raid Scene

When the search is completed, there are several precautions to take before withdrawing from the premises. First and foremost, the safety of all members of the raid team must be assured. Make sure that everyone is accounted for. This includes members of both the outside and inside parties. After one raid it was not until the team returned to the station house that anyone noticed that one of the members was missing. The officer in question had been posted in the alley in back of the building to be searched. The team hastily returned to the scene and found the officer unconscious in a garage nearby, his gun and radio stolen.

Many jurisdictions require that the occupant of the premises that has been searched receive a copy of the warrant upon which is noted every item that has been seized. Other agencies require that if anything is taken during the raid, a formal property receipt be issued. If no one is present during the search, leave a copy of the warrant where the owner can find it upon returning. Finally, in many jurisdictions it is the responsibility of the officers when they leave the raid scene to secure it so that unauthorized persons cannot enter.

FIGURE 14-5
Always proceed with the utmost caution if you discover a clandestine laboratory. Only a trained chemist should ever attempt to
shut down or dismantle one. Otherwise a violent and potentially
lethal explosion may occur. (*Drug Enforcement Administration*)

AFTER THE RAID

Any prisoners taken or evidence seized must be processed as soon as practical after the raid is completed. It is also a good idea to conduct a critique of the raid; during this review any problems that developed can be brought up and discussed.

Debriefing Prisoners

It is important to debrief the prisoners as soon as possible after the raid. Some suspects, of course, will refuse to talk. They understand that one of their constitutional rights is to remain silent—and that is exactly what they do. Other individuals, however, are only too willing to talk. This is particularly true if suspects think that they may be able to gain better treatment at the hands of the law by cooperating. Such individuals frequently decide to serve as informants.

If the suspect is talkative, take the time to conduct a thorough debriefing. The following are suggested questions to ask; the list, of course, is not complete, and the particular circumstances of the raid most certainly lead to other pertinent questions.

1. From whom do you get the drugs?
2. When are they delivered?
3. Does your contact use a car? If so, what color is it? What kind and make? What is the license plate number?
4. Who are your contact's associates and/or employees?
5. Where do they deal?
6. Where do they live?
7. What are their phone numbers?
8. How long have you been dealing with them?

Continue this sort of detailed questioning until you have found out everything that you can from the suspect. Remember, even the smallest detail may prove to be vital at some later stage of the investigation. And do not limit the questioning to only facts about the drug trade. Find out all that you can about any criminal activities of which the suspect has knowledge. Even if this information proves to be of no use in your investigation, it may well prove invaluable to one of your colleagues.

In most instances it is advisable to have another officer present during the debriefing. This officer can act as a witness. If at a later date the suspect accuses you of improperly promising preferential treatment or of making threats, you will be in a much better position to defend yourself. Some agencies also recommend that a tape recording be made of the debriefing session for similar reasons.

Processing the Evidence

In order to see that the chain of custody is maintained and that the integrity of the evidence is assured, you should process the evidence as soon as practical after the raid. Any delay can allow very serious problems to develop. Many agencies have extremely rigorous procedures for processing evidence. You should always adhere strictly to the guidelines laid down by your agency. Review the procedures suggested in Chapter 13 for processing evidence. The same suggestions apply here.

Critiquing the Raid

We have already mentioned the advisability of conducting a critique after each raid. During this session participants should be given a chance to discuss any problems that they encountered and make suggestions as to how they could be avoided in the future. Often valuable suggestions are made for procedures to be followed in future raids based on the experiences of the members of the raid being reviewed. In addition, these sessions give the raid commander an opportunity to point out any areas in which improvement is needed.

IN CONCLUSION

At best, drug raids are dangerous and demanding. The smallest error can have serious if not fatal consequences. The procedures outlined in this chapter are the result of the collective experience of many agencies. If followed carefully they will go a long way toward reducing the danger involved and maximizing the evidence obtained in any raid.

Chapter 15
ORGANIZED CRIME

No book on drug abuse would be complete without at least a brief discussion of organized crime. The two go hand in hand. Since the final quarter of the nineteenth century when the roots of the organized crime networks that we know today first spread among America's burgeoning immigrant populations, drugs, especially heroin, have been a source of enormous profit to the lords of the organized underworld.

The drug trade is ideally suited for exploitation by organized crime—the market is boundless and the profits are great. The President's Commission on Organized Crime in 1967 estimated the gross annual heroin trade in this country at $350 million. Of this $21 million was gauged to be the profits for the importers and distributors. Most of this sum is assumed to flow into the coffers of organized crime.[1] Large-scale drug trafficking requires both the enormous amounts of cash and well-disciplined, tightly controlled organizations that only organized crime can provide.

It is important to understand at this point that the drug trade does not stand alone or separate from the many other activities of organized crime. Rather, it is but one part of the large matrix of activities in which organized crime is currently engaged; it is but one strand of the web. Other strands involving the same or other allied mobsters may include such activities as gambling and loan sharking, with profits going to finance drug purchases; political corruption, which produces an atmosphere in which drug dealers can operate without fear of interference from the authorities; and collusion with unethical attorneys, who provide the best legal services money can buy when drug dealers run afoul of the law. Because of this intertwining of the various different tentacles of the underworld, this chapter will not be solely limited to a discussion of organized crime's drug-related activities. Rather, it will be in the form of an overview of the many different ways in which organized crime operates in this country today.

DEFINING ORGANIZED CRIME

At first it may seem a simple matter to define the term "organized crime." This, however, is not the case. It is a term that is extraordinarily hard to pin down with any exactitude. It means different things to different people. To the lords of television and the movies it means a group of swarthy, dark-haired gangsters who ride around in big black limousines with machine guns and who shoot each other at Umberto's clam house. To the legislators in the state of Mississippi who adopted the following definition, it exists whenever "two or more persons conspire together to commit crimes on a continuing basis." As the U.S. Department of Justice views it, "Organized crime includes any group of individuals whose primary activity involves violating criminal laws to seek illegal profits and power by engaging in racketeering activities and, when appropriate, engaging in intricate financial manipulations."[2] The state of California is even more explicit in its delineation of organized crime activities into five categories.

Organized crime consists of two or more persons who, with continuity of purpose, engage in one or more of the following activities: (1) the supplying of illegal goods and services, i.e., vice, loan sharking, etc.; (2) predatory crime, i.e., theft, assault, etc.

Several distinct types of criminal activity fall within this definition of organized crime. The types may be grouped into five general categories[3]:

1. RACKETEERING. Groups of individuals which organize more than one of the following types of criminal activities for their combined profit.
2. VICE OPERATIONS. Individuals operating a continuing business of providing illegal goods or services, such as narcotics, prostitution, loan sharking, gambling, etc.
3. THEFT-FENCE RINGS. Groups of individuals who engage in a particular kind of theft on a continuing basis, such as fraud and bunco schemes, fraudulent-document passers, burglary rings, car thieves, truck hijackers, and associated individuals engaged in the business of purchasing stolen merchandise for resale and profit.
4. GANGS. Groups of individuals with common interests or background who band together and collectively engage in unlawful activity to enhance their group identity and influence, such as youth gangs, outlaw motorcycle gangs, and prison gangs.
5. TERRORISTS. Groups of individuals who combine to commit spectacular criminal acts, such as assassination and kidnapping of public figures to undermine public confidence in established government either for political reasons or to avenge some grievance.

Though each of these definitions may be useful for a particular purpose, none of them is wholly accurate or complete. However, all of them do provide a useful glimpse at both how people perceive organized crime and what it is in reality.

A further understanding of the definition and nature of organized crime can be obtained by attempting to delineate its characteristics. This was recently done by the Task Force on Organized Crime. In their report[4] they note that organized crime is characterized in the following manner:

1. Organized crime is a type of conspiratorial crime, sometimes involving the hierarchical coordination of a number of persons in the planning and execution of illegal acts, or in the pursuit of a legitimate objective by unlawful means. Organized crime involves continuous commitment by key members, although some individuals with specialized skills may participate only briefly in the ongoing conspiracies.

The President's Commission on Law Enforcement and Administration of Justice remarked that the actions of organized criminals "are not impulsive but rather the result of intricate conspiracies." Prohibitions against conspiracy are the only tools available under existing law to prosecute organized crime participants who have not been implicated in a specific crime. Thus the approach to the crime of conspiracy adopted by the Model Penal Code—increasing the penalty for conspiracy where it is continuing in nature and contemplates numerous as yet unspecified crimes—is valuable in the fight against organized crime. In terms of hierarchical coordination, organized crime members may be part of a set structure where each participant's role is well-defined. This kind of hierarchy, with all the components of a stratified, formal organization, is especially true of La Cosa Nostra (LCN), which is responsible for many, but by no means all, of the activities characteristic of organzied crime.

2. Organized crime has economic gain as its primary goal, though some of the participants in the conspiracy may have achievement of power or status as their objective.

Economic gain is achieved through supplying illegal goods and services, including drugs, loan sharking, and gambling. As many organized crime studies point out, achieving a monopoly or near-monopoly in providing these goods and services guarantees high profits and is thus a primary goal. These illegally acquired funds are frequently used to infiltrate legitimate business.

3. Organized crime is not limited to patently illegal enterprises or unlawful services such as gambling, prostitution, drugs, loan sharking, or racketeering. It also includes such sophisticated activities as "laundering" of illegal money through a legitimate business, land fraud, and computer manipulation.

Organized crime often seeks to secure partial or complete control over many kinds of profitable, legal endeavors. Organized crime attempts to infiltrate wherever there is a potential for profit.

4. Organized crime employs predatory tactics such as intimidation, violence, and corruption, and it appeals to greed to accomplish its objectives and preserve its gains.

These tactics may be sophisticated and subtle, or they may be crude, overt, and direct. They are used to secure economic gain through a monopoly in illegal goods and services, as well as to infiltrate legitimate enterprises and to corrupt public officials. As part of this strategy, the application of blackmail, violence, or threats is particularly effective after victims are led to believe that the relationship could be handled at purely an economic level in an "honor among thieves" atmosphere. As one study points out, "When organized crime embarks on a venture in legitimate business it ordinarily brings to that venture all the techniques of violence and intimidation which are employed in its illegal enterprises."

5. By experience, custom, and practice, organized crime's conspiratorial groups are usually very quick and effective in controlling and disciplining their members, associates, and victims. Therefore, organized crime participants are unlikely to disassociate themselves from the conspiracies and are in the main incorrigible.

The President's Commission on Law Enforcement and Administration of Justice remarked that organized crime members are "subject to laws more rigidly enforced than those of legitimate governments." The individuals involved know that deviation from the terms under which they operate will evoke a prompt response from the other participants. This response may range from a reduction in rank to a death sentence.

6. Organized crime is not synonymous with the Mafia or La Cosa Nostra, the most experienced, diversified, and possibly best disciplined of the conspiratorial groups.

The Mafia image is a common stereotype of organized crime members. Although a number of families of La Cosa Nostra are an important component of organized crime operations, they do not enjoy a monopoly on underworld activities. Today, a variety of groups is engaged in organized criminal activity.

7. Organized crime does not include terrorists dedicated to political change, although organized criminals and terrorists have some characteristics in common, including types of crimes committed and strict organizational structures.

Although violent acts are a key tactic of organized crime, the use of violence does not in itself mean that a group is part of a confederacy of organized criminals. Organized crime groups tend to be politically conservative, desirous of maintaining the status quo in which they succeed, contrary to terrorist groups dedicated to radical political change through violent acts.

THE PROFITS AND COSTS OF ORGANIZED CRIME

The profits made by and costs of organized crime are staggering. Though it is impossible to state the figures involved with precision, the following estimates highlight the enormous magnitude of the sums involved. In 1972 the Attorney General estimated the net worth of organized crime to be as high as $150 billion. He estimated its annual net profit to be as high as $50 billion. If these figures are correct, organized crime nets a higher income than any other single industry in the United States. A recent report on organized crime[5] outlines the economic and social costs of organized crime in some detail. According to this report:

The most serious threat to society from organized crime comes when criminal syndicates use vast sums of money gained from illicit enterprises to undermine legitimate business enterprises and political institutions. Organized crime has infiltrated labor unions, the entertainment business, manufacturing, real estate, and even the stock market. To measure its impact in terms of dollars would be a formidable, if not prohibitive task.

In 1972 the stock brokerage industry alone estimated that stolen or missing securities of 1.2 billion dollars were being utilized in illegal operations around the world. The loss of income tax revenue from organized crime operations is incalculable. It has been estimated that illegal betting on horse racing, lotteries, and sporting events alone totals at least $20 billion a year with the syndicate taking about $6 to $7 billion as its share (this is about three times the amount of the annual budget of U.S. foreign aid). Loan sharks have been known to charge interest rates as high as 500 percent. Millions of dollars of cargo are pilfered from airports and piers by trucking companies and union locals working for a criminal group. Labor union pension funds have been used for loans to finance illegal or questionable enterprises, and construction companies have used shoddy materials and workmanship through kickback arrangements. What this means, translated to the level of the everyday citizen, is higher prices through the monopolistic practices of organized crime, shoddy merchandise, poorly constructed and unsafe buildings, and higher taxes. More important is the threat to the free enterprise system. Organized crime operates on the local level as well, controlling businesses such as laundries, taxicab companies, paving-contract firms, travel agencies, insurance underwriting firms, vending machine companies, and restaurants. The social costs of political corruption by organized crime are even more difficult to assess. Organized crime needs the involvement of the political system to profit from economic opportunities. The President's Commission concluded that "all available data indicate that organized crime flourishes only where it has corrupted local officials." Over and over again, investigations into criminal activities have turned up close connections with respectable persons in business and public officials at all levels of government. Corruption is achieved through bribes and contributions to political campaigns; a police officer is bribed or overlooks gambling and a state or Federal legislator's vote on a bill is bought by the criminal organization that contributed heavily to the person's campaign through a front organization. Hence, organized crime is, in part, a subversion of the democratic process which ultimately will produce a political system where the strong and powerful exist at the expense of the weak.

BRIEF HISTORY

The Immigrant Origin

The origins of present-day organized crime in this country[6] date back to the period of massive immigration that began in the late nineteenth century and lasted until the onset of World War I. During that period hundreds of thousands of immigrants came to the United States in response to a seemingly limitless demand for labor as well as to escape political persecution and upheaval at home. Most of these newcomers settled, at least for a while, in teeming immigrant communities in such major port cities and transportation hubs as New York City, Boston, Baltimore, New Orleans, and Chicago. And it was in these cities that the seeds of organized crime as we now know it first took hold in America.

Though most of the people who lived in these immigrant communities were honest and hard working, there were those among them who were not. These few quickly settled into lives of crime. Their efforts in general were directed toward members of their own community. Only in rare instances did they move against the native-born population. As a result, their activities for the most part were concealed from the general population by an ethnic curtain of secrecy.

Gangs and Secret Societies

The criminal elements that existed among the various ethnic societies soon found it to their advantage to band together in gangs and secret societies. As always, there was strength in numbers. Soon each ethnic neighborhood was preyed upon by its own gang. Some of these groups amounted to small armies. Monk Eastman's powerful East Side gang in New York City numbered over 1,200 men during its apex of power in the 1890s.

Two of the most notorious secret societies that blossomed in this era were the Chinese Tongs and the Italian Mafia, or "Black Hand," organization. The Tongs surged into the public eye during the early 1900s when a bloody war broke out among rival factions seeking to gain control of vice operations in New York's Chinatown. Finally, a truce was established by the authorities, and Tong activities once more slipped from public attention.

The roots of the Italian Mafia extend back to Sicily. There, because of abject poverty and the almost total breakdown in the social order, bands of brigands and robbers became all-powerful. In actuality these early Mafiosi controlled all aspects of Sicilian business and government. Members of the Mafia who came to the United States saw the packed Italian communities of this country as ideal locations to continue their criminal careers.

Gambling, prostitution, drugs, and extortion all provided rich opportunities for these early Mafia gangs. They too confined their activities to the immigrant community. Consequently, they were not regarded as much of a threat by the general population. However, from time to time their actions did outrage the local population outside the ethnic communities. When this happened, the retaliation was usually swift and sure. For example, when the popular New Orleans Police Chief, David Hennesy, was murdered in October 1890, eleven Italian suspects were promptly lynched—an act that was thoroughly applauded by the local populace and much of the rest of America.

Prohibition

The Prohibition era of the 1920s and 1930s was a godsend to organized crime. America's unquenchable thirst for alcohol provided the underworld with an almost limitless source of income. Gangsters such as Al "Scarface" Capone, Johnny Torrio, and Harry Cox, to name only a few, reaped hundreds of millions of dollars from a thirsty nation. But rum running was not the only activity in which these entrepreneurs were engaged. Drugs, prostitution, gambling, and labor racketeering were all coordinated under the control of the core group (known as the "syndicate" or the "mob") during this period.

As might be expected, the enormous profits that organized crime reaped during these years led to widespread corruption. Many a gangland czar could in all truth boast of "owning" his town. In all too many cases judges, prosecutors, police, and legislators ended up on the mob's payroll. Money or favors given to well-placed individuals allowed gangland leaders to carry on their operation with a minimum of interference.

The Great Depression and World War II

The onset of the Great Depression and the repeal of Prohibition forced a number of changes upon organized crime. New sources of profits had to be found to replace those that illegal liquor had once so bountifully provided. One source that many mob leaders were quick to recognize was drugs. Though drugs had always been a minor source of income to the underworld, it was during the 1930s that it became a thriving, multimillion-dollar business.

Loan sharking became another major source of revenue. During the cash-lean years of the Depression, legitimate businesses by the hundreds turned to underworld figures for loans at absurd interest rates. The result in many cases was that the underworld lords either took the business over when the owner defaulted on the loan or became silent controlling partners in the business.

World War II provided organized crime with lush opportunities in the black market. Millions were made furnishing anything in short supply at a premium price. Everything from butter to gasoline ration stamps could be had from the underworld.

The Postwar Era

The years following World War II saw a major move on the part of organized crime toward an increasing involvement in drugs and gambling. Some underworld lords, such as New York's "Lucky" Luciano, argued strongly against becoming involved with drugs because of the fear that such involvement would bring about stepped-up federal enforcement. But the great profits possible negated the argument, and other leaders sought to expand the enormously profitable trade.

Gambling became a major source of income for the mob during this period. Since its earliest days organized crime had been involved in gambling. However, during the years that followed World War II a major new emphasis was placed on it. Numbers, slot machines, dog- and horse-race betting operations were all streamlined and brought under the mob's iron-fisted control. In December 1945 ground was broken for the Flamingo Hotel in Las Vegas. The brainchild of West Coast mob czar Benjamin "Bugsy" Segal, the Flamingo was the first move on the part of organized crime into what was later to prove to be the immensely profitable domain of legal organized gambling in Nevada.

The 1950s saw the first major public exposure of organized crime in the United States. On May 1, 1950, Tennessee Senator Estes Kefauver opened congressional hearings aimed at determining the power and extent of organized crime in this country. By the time these hearings ended sixteen months later the public had been rudely awakened to the fact that the cancer of organized crime was fast penetrating all aspects of this country's business and commercial life.

The 1960s and 1970s

Throughout the 1960s and 1970s law enforcement agencies actively investigated the activities of organized crime. This, as well as the changing nature of the cities, had a profound effect upon the mob.

At every level of government increased pressure was brought to bear upon organized crime. On the national scene a Senate committee delved deeply into the problem, especially as it related to organized labor. Largely because of the finding of this committee, the Justice Department stepped up its activities against organized crime. Key federal legislation, such as the Organized Crime Control Act of 1970, was passed that greatly expanded the government's powers to combat the problem. Action on the national level was duplicated by many state and local governments. With federal assistance and cooperation they were able to mount their own intensive compaigns against organized crime.

As a result of these efforts, a number of important inroads have been made into the traditional, illegal activities dominated by organized crime. These investigations have also served to focus the public's attention on the continuing penetration of organized crime into many segments of legitimate business.

The violent social unrest of the 1960s was also to have a profound effect on the structure of organized crime. Until then most organized crime activities had been, for all practical purposes, under the direct control of white ethnic groups. However, when the cities went up in flames, so did white control of many of the organized crime activities within them. Blacks and Latins now became dominant urban underworld forces.

Looking to the Future

It is likely that the trends of the last decade will continue. Black and Latin groups will in all probability continue to control such traditional organized crime activities as prostitution, gambling, and drugs at the local level in many of this country's larger urban centers. The traditional white-ethnic organized crime groups will continue to function to some extent in these activities at a national and international level and continue to dominate such areas as loan sharking and the manipulation of stolen bonds and securities. They will also continue to push their drive to penetrate all segments of legitimate business and labor.

ORGANIZED CRIME ACTIVITIES

Organized crime figures are currently involved in a wide range of activities. These vary according to local conditions and the personal preferences of those involved. The most common areas of involvement are the following:

1. Gambling
2. Prostitution and pornography
3. Loan sharking
4. Bootlegging
5. Fencing stolen goods
6. Labor racketeering
7. Legitimate business
8. Drugs

Gambling

Many consider gambling to be the largest single source of revenue for organized crime. It is a cash-only business that supplies much of the capital that is used for such other activities as loan sharking, stock manipulation, and the wholesale purchase of drugs. The kinds of gambling involved include everything from the numbers racket to off-track and sports-event betting. Large sums are also skimmed from legal gambling operations that are either owned or operated by organized crime groups.

Prostitution and Pornography

In the early days of organized crime, prostitution was a major source of profits. In recent years, however, it has largely taken a back seat to other, more profitable enterprises. This does not mean, however, that it has been totally abandoned. In the summer of 1976 a long-time associate of the notorious Genovese "family" was indicted for setting up a prostitution ring designed to cater to workers on the Alaskan pipeline.

The link between organized crime and pornography was documented as far back as the Kefauver hearings of the 1950s. At the present time there is ample evidence that organized crime elements are involved in all aspects of the production, wholesaling, retailing, and distribution of all forms of pornographic films, magazines, and services.

Loan Sharking

A loan shark lends money at interest rates that are far higher than those permitted by law. Typical customers include gamblers who cannot meet their obligations and owners of small businesses who are unable to obtain credit from conventional sources. The interest charged for these loans varies anywhere from 1 percent to an astounding 150 percent a week. The results of this compounding can be staggering. For example, one $13,500 loan ended up as a $515,000 debt to a loan shark. All manner of force is resorted to in order to ensure that borrowers make good on their obligations and stay clear of the authorities.

Bootlegging

Bootleg cigarettes have taken the place of bootleg liquor in many parts of the country as a major source of income for organized crime. The heavy taxes that are placed on cigarettes in many areas make them an ideal item to sell in the illegal market. Cigarettes are either stolen or purchased at a relatively low price in the South and then shipped to cities in the North where taxes on them are high. There counterfeit government tax stamps are applied by members of the syndicate, and the cigarettes are sold through "cooperative" outlets, which often charge a few cents less per pack than the going commercial rate.

Some idea of the scope of these operations can be gained from the statistics for New York City. It is estimated that anywhere from one-third to one-half of the cigarettes sold there are supplied by bootleggers. No one can estimate the profits that organized crime reaps from this trade, but the loss in municipal tax revenues is estimated to be somewhere in the neighborhood of $85 million annually.

Fencing Stolen Goods

There is mounting evidence that a number of organized crime groups are actively involved in the disposal (or as it is called on the street, the "fencing") of stolen goods. This is particularly true of high-value items, such as cameras, TVs, and stereos. The national nature of organized crime makes it a relatively easy matter to arrange for the disposal of goods in areas far from where they were stolen.

In recent years organized crime has also become deeply involved in the theft and subsequent disposal of securities. These are almost the ideal hot item. They can be used to secure bank loans as well as be converted directly into cash through international "laundry" operations. Though exact figures are impossible to obtain, authorities are convinced that security thefts are now a major multimillion-dollar enterprise.

Labor Racketeering

Organized crime's involvement in some segments of the labor union movement goes back to the turbulent industrial strife of the 1920s and

1930s. Since that time organized crime has attempted in every way imaginable to profit from the labor movement. Crime leaders have resorted to all sorts of violence, threats, and extortion schemes to win immense sums from labor and management alike. In situations where they have been able to gain a dominant influence in a union, they have frequently used the pension and welfare funds for their own illegal purposes. They have also been able from positions of power in the shipping, construction, and trucking unions to extort profitable contracts and other benefits from a wide range of legitimate businesses.

Legitimate Business

Much of the profit that organized crime has reaped from its various illegal activities has been invested in a wide range of legitimate businesses. These provide it with a desired cloak of respectability as well as a legitimate source of income that helps to prevent prosecution for tax evasion.

Sometimes organized crime takes over a legitimate business in order to perpetrate a "scam," or illegitimate bankruptcy. The firm will order a large amount of merchandise on credit, dispose of it for quick cash, and then declare bankruptcy.

The full extent of the involvement of organized crime in the legitimate sector will, in all probability, never be known. On the basis of what is known, it can be stated that organized crime's share runs to hundreds of millions, if not billions, of dollars. One syndicate alone is known to have real estate investments worth an estimated $300 million.

Drugs

At the present time a number of organized crime groups are deeply involved in many aspects of the illicit drug trade. This appears to be especially true in the case of heroin and cocaine.

HEROIN.   As mentioned earlier, the heroin trade is ideally suited for organized crime. It requires large amounts of capital, and this is easily supplied from the profits of such other activities as gambling and loan sharking. The demand is enormous. It is estimated that there are anywhere from 250,000 to 600,000 heroin addicts in this country. And the profits are astronomical. A kilo of heroin which costs $25,000 to $40,000 to import will yield over a quarter of a million dollars when sold on the street. Finally, the importation and large-scale distribution of heroin requires the kind of closely knit and well-disciplined group that only organized crime can provide. The evidence which is now available indicates that for the most part organized crime elements have, at least for the last twenty or thirty years, preferred to limit their involvement to the upper rungs of the heroin trade. This includes financing and arranging for the smuggling of large shipments into this country. Lower-level distribution and sales, the most vulnerable sectors of the drug trade, have been left pretty well in the hands of the smaller independent operators.

During the last few years there have been a number of important changes in the heroin trade. Prior to the smashing of the notorious French Connection and the Turkish ban on opium poppy cultivation in the early 1970s, nearly all the heroin used in this country came from Europe. All the evidence points to the fact that its importation and upper-level distribution were ruthlessly controlled by the traditional organized crime families. However, since the major source of heroin shifted to Mexico, the situation is not nearly so clear. It now appears that black and Hispanic organized crime groups are exerting control over a large share of the heroin trade. The narcotics files of the New York City Police Department illustrate this. Of the thirteen top heroin traffickers in New York, five are black, four are Hispanic, and four are of Italian ancestry.

COCAINE. The situation is a good deal clearer in regard to the cocaine trade. It is, for all intents, under the complete control of organized crime groups that are dominated by Colombians, Cubans, Mexicans, Puerto Ricans, and, to a lesser degree, blacks. Considering the Latin American origin of cocaine, this is not hard to understand. At the present time there is little or no evidence that the traditional Italian organized crime groups have any major involvement in the cocaine trade other than occasionally in the role of financiers.

OTHER DRUGS. It is difficult to gauge the involvement of organized crime in other segments of the drug trade. There is some evidence of organized crime involvement in the manufacture of methamphetamine and in the large-scale importation of marijuana. However, for the most part it appears that such activities are the province of independent operators.

LAW ENFORCEMENT COUNTERMEASURES

Over the years a number of countermeasures have been developed by law enforcement agencies to combat organized crime. Though none of these, either by itself or in combination with others, has succeeded in eradicating organized crime, many have had a good deal of success in checking its activities. Some of the more effective tools include the following:

1. Wiretapping
2. Strike forces
3. Special intelligence units
4. Granting of immunity
5. Grand jury investigations
6. Tax investigations
7. Conspiracy charges

Wiretapping

One of the most effective weapons against organized crime has been wiretapping. When used in the proper manner, wiretaps along with other forms of electronic surveillance leave criminals with virtually no defense. After all, how can one deny one's own words? Though wiretapping had been used to a limited degree for years, it came to the forefront of the battle against organized crime during the period when Robert Kennedy served as Attorney General of the United States in the 1960s.

During the three years from 1969 to 1971 the use of wiretaps was instrumental in at least 1,200 organized crime arrests and 100 convictions. This included the shattering of numerous gambling and drug operations as well as the exposure of widespread union corruption.

Strike Forces

Closely coordinated and intensely focused investigations of organized crime targets have proved to be exceedingly fruitful in a number of areas. One way to achieve this is through the use of so-called strike forces. These consist of lawyers, investigators, accountants, and other specialists who combine their efforts against selected gangland targets.

The basic goal of these strike forces is to converge their efforts on major organized targets from as many different enforcement angles as possible. Even the most cautious and crafty criminal is going to find it difficult to escape from the combined resources of such agencies as the Drug Enforcement Administration, the Internal Revenue Service, the Bureau of Customs, the Postal Service, the Bureau of Alcohol, Tobacco, and Firearms, and the Securities Exchange Commission. As one seasoned strike force investigator states, "If we don't get our man one way, we'll get him another."

Another advantage of the use of strike forces is their ability to coordinate investigations that extend across state lines. For example, in one drug case strike forces under the command of the Justice Department's Organized Crime Division participated in simultaneous raids in ten different cities. As a result, 139 suspects were arrested and nearly 100 pounds of heroin and cocaine were seized.

Special Intelligence Units

Accurate, up-to-date intelligence information is one of the mainstays of all investigations. This is particularly true in the case of enforcement activities that are directed against organized crime. It is simply impossible to go after the mob unless the officers and the other people involved know with some degree of certainty what the mob is up to. Some of the innermost secrets of the underworld have been ferreted out by coordinated federal, state, and local intelligence activities. This has enabled enforcement agencies to keep much closer tabs on the movements and activities of organized crime figures than was ever possible before.

Granting of Immunity

It has been a common and popular device for a long time to grant immunity from prosecution to criminals who voluntarily testify against others or who provide valuable information. However, the Organized Crime Control Act of 1970 went even further. It contained provisions for the granting of immunity to individuals who did not want to talk about an offense with which they were suspected of being involved. The act also provided for stiff prison sentences for those who failed to cooperate with investigators or who committed perjury. In addition, it provided for the greatly expanded use of depositions in criminal proceedings. Until the act's passage an all too familiar tactic had been to kill witnesses who might harm the mob before they had a chance to testify. After the act became law, depositions given by witnesses against the mob had legal standing in court. Now, for the first time, it did not do any good to kill witnesses. Their testimony in the form of depositions could still count against an individual.

Grand Jury Investigations

The Organized Crime Control Act of 1970 also provided for special grand juries to sit in major cities for a period of thirty-six months to investigate all aspects of organized crime. These juries were empowered to issue reports dealing with all aspects of organized crime and corruption. They proved to be a powerful weapon against organized crime. No matter how corrupt local conditions proved to be, able prosecutors in cooperation with hard-working grand juries of ordinary citizens were still able to achieve a startling number of indictments against many figures of organized crime, from the lowest to the highest echelon.

Tax Investigations

Since the days of Al Capone, tax investigations have proved a powerful weapon against the lords of organized crime. Many an underworld czar (including Capone himself) ended up behind bars because of the astute work of the Internal Revenue Service. In recent years the pace of these investigations has been accelerated with continuing success. Although gangland figures can still avoid successful prosecution for many of their crimes, convictions on tax charges climb from year to year.

Conspiracy Charges

For years enforcement agencies have found it difficult, if not impossible, to reach the upper rungs of the organized crime hierarchy. The bosses have been careful to see that layer upon layer of underlings separate them from actual criminal activities. They keep their hands clean and enjoy the rewards while the underlings, the "soldiers," do the dirty work.

The conspiracy laws offer enforcement people a way to reach the crime lords. These laws provide for the prosecution of those who are in any way involved in the *planning* of a crime.

IN CONCLUSION

The problems of organized crime and the drug trade go hand in hand. The enormous profits that the underworld reaps from such activities as gambling and loan sharking are used to finance large-scale drug transactions. The profits that these produce are in turn used to finance still other mob activities. This vicious cycle can be broken only by concerted enforcement efforts aimed at all the various activities through which the underworld provides the financial footing for their illicit empire.

NOTES

[1]President's Commission on Law Enforcement and Administration of Justice, *Task Force Report: Organized Crime* (Washington, D.C.: GPO, 1967), p. 4.

[2]National Advisory Committee on Criminal Justice Standards and Goals, *Report of the Task Force on Organized Crime* (Washington, D.C.: GPO, 1976), p. 213.

[3]National Advisory Committee, pp. 213–214.

[4]National Advisory Committee, pp. 7–8.

[5]Law Enforcement Assistance Administration, *Basic Elements of Intelligence* (Washington, D.C.: GPO, 1976), p. 2.

[6]Humbert S. Neilli, *The Business of Crime* (New York: Oxford, 1976). This work provides an excellent overview of the history of organized crime in this country.

Part 3
TREATMENT

Chapter 16

UNITED STATES SYSTEM OF TREATMENT

In many ways the drug problem can be regarded as a classic example of the laws of supply and demand in action. Abusers demand drugs; dealers supply them. A need exists that suppliers all too happily (and profitably) fill. Thus it becomes apparent that if we are ever to bring this country's drug problem to manageable proportions, we must attack both sides of it. Along with doing all that is possible to cut off illicit drug supplies, we must also do all that we can do to reduce the demand for them.

History too aptly demonstrates the folly of assuming that enforcement efforts directed only at shutting off supplies can be successful. No matter how much time, effort, and money we devote to the effort, we can never be absolutely successful in eliminating all the sources from which illicit drugs spring. Our past experience with the shift in heroin production is an excellent example. Traditionally, authorities considered the heroin problem in this country in terms of the infamous Turkish-French Connection. The heroin that satisfied the demands of America's addicts originated in the windswept poppy fields of Turkey's Anatolian Plateau. The opium collected there was shipped to the labs of Marseilles, where it was converted to heroin and then smuggled into the United States. For years it was an article of faith among U.S. officials that if the Turkish-French Connection could only be smashed, America's heroin problem would fast fade away.

By the early 1970s the impossible dream had been accomplished. The Turkish-French Connection had been broken, many of its key figures were behind bars, and Turkey, bowing to extraordinary pressure from the U.S. government, had outlawed opium poppy cultivation. The "good guys" had finally won. Now, at long last, officials felt, heroin supplies were cut off. For a brief moment it appeared that we truly had turned the corner on drug abuse in America. Then the roof caved in.

Once more the laws of supply and demand demonstrated their age-old validity. As always, wherever a demand exists, if the profits are large enough, someone will come forth with a supply. That is exactly what happened with heroin. As soon as Turkish supplies were cut off, production in Mexico surged. By 1975 Mexican brown heroin was almost as freely available in the United States as Turkish-French white had ever been.

Examples such as this do not mean, however, that enforcement efforts aimed at cutting off illicit drug supplies are useless. Far from it. Such efforts have made and, in many instances, continue to make illicit drugs more difficult to find and more hazardous to buy. This, in turn, drives up the prices of the drugs and makes them less attractive to occasional users and experimenters, thereby diminishing the number of users. There will, nevertheless, always be those compulsive abusers who are prepared to run any risk or to pay any price to obtain their supplies.

Thus, the importance of those efforts that are directed at reducing the demand for illicit drugs becomes apparent. Every drug user who can be turned away from his or her habit represents one less source of profit for underworld drug traffickers, one less burden for America's law enforcement and public health authorities, and one less social misfit.

Several approaches are being used in an attempt to reduce the demand for illicit drugs in this country. Some are primarily educational in nature. Their purpose is to inform potential abusers, especially school children and young adults, of the extraordinary hazards involved in drug abuse. Other programs emphasize vocational education in an attempt to provide abusers with a productive alternative lifestyle. Some programs emphasize research in order to discover the basic causes and the nature of drug abuse. Others attempt to free individuals from the bondage of drug abuse through a variety of different treatment alternatives. It has been the latter approach, treatment, that has received by far the greatest emphasis and funding. Because of this and because of the not always happy relationship that exists between law enforcement and treatment efforts, this chapter is devoted to an examination of the more important approaches to treatment in the United States.

Since most of the treatment efforts have been directed at heroin addiction, the discussion concentrates on these programs. However, in the final section of the chapter, techniques for treating the abuse of such nonopiates as the hallucinogens, marijuana, barbiturates, cocaine, and amphetamines are reviewed.

BACKGROUND

The problem of drug abuse has plagued this country for more than a century. Ever since the widespread abuse of opiates that characterized the latter half of the nineteenth century first caught the public's attention, numerous cures have been tried.

During the nineteenth century and well into the 1920s, the proper approach to the treatment of opiate abuse was thought to be abstinence. The root cause of addiction was held to be the addict's lack of will power. If addicts really wanted to, it was reasoned, they would stop using drugs, particularly if they were supervised by professionals. For the most part, treatment during this period consisted of gradual withdrawal lasting perhaps a week or so, followed in some cases by a brief period of aftercare. By the turn of the century America's burgeoning addict population was supporting numerous private sanatoriums where addicts (or at least the more affluent of them) could go for such "cures" (Figure 16-1).

Needless to say, the success rate of these programs was almost nil. Those in charge of such treatment efforts did not, of course, consider their methods of treatment the cause for the dismal failure rate. Instead, they reasoned that it merely proved that most addicts did not really want to be cured. Obviously, with such logic prevailing, those who ran the treatment programs could hardly be called to fault.

Public alarm about drug abuse reached new heights in the first years of this century. The passage of the Harrison Narcotics Act in 1914 represented the culmination of the prohibitionist approach to the problem of narcotic addiction. The rationale behind this act was the essence of simplicity. Narcotics are harmful; therefore, their use should be prohibited. Once this is done, people will stop using them because they are

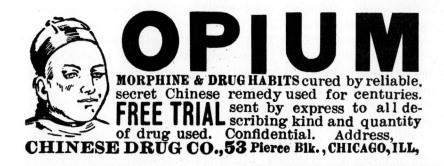

OPIUM
MORPHINE & DRUG HABITS cured by reliable, secret Chinese remedy used for centuries. FREE TRIAL sent by express to all describing kind and quantity of drug used. Confidential. Address, CHINESE DRUG CO., 53 Pierce Blk., CHICAGO, ILL,

FIGURE 16-1
By the end of the nineteenth century, numerous "cures" for addiction were advertised in the popular press.

scarce and expensive and because people will be subjected to heavy penalties if caught.

Some users, especially those with relatively mild habits, did, indeed, give up drugs after the act was passed. But others more desperate or bold merely turned to illegal sources for their supplies. As a result, it was not long before a flourishing black market in drugs existed.

Alarmed by the mounting evidence of the link between addiction and criminality, a number of cities tried to provide treatment in the form of free clinics. These supplied maintenance doses of opiates to addicts under medically supervised conditions. The first clinics opened their doors in the early teens; others followed during the early twenties.

In the beginning the federal government lent its support to this effort. Almost as soon as they opened, however, the clinics were caught in a whirlwind of controversy, not unlike that which surrounds many of today's methadone maintenance programs. Some clinics did do a creditable job. Others, however, were plagued with mismanagement, establishment hostility, political intrigue, and dishonesty. Needless to say, it was the more troubled of the programs that the press brought to the public's attention. As a result, the federal government, almost at the same time that it gave its support to the clinic approach to treatment, withdrew it. This brought about the hurried demise of the public clinics. By 1925 the last of them had closed its doors.

During the next decade, for all practical purposes, no treatment alternatives were available to addicts. If they could not find a sympathetic physician who was willing to risk violating the provisions of the Harrison Act, the addicts were simply out of luck.

The mid- and late thirties saw the opening of the U.S. Public Health Service hospitals at Lexington, Kentucky, and Fort Worth, Texas. These were the federal government's first true steps into the drug treatment field. The methods and treatment philosophies of these facilities were in actuality a continuation of the withdrawal approach, the mainstay of drug treatment since the mid-nineteenth century. Until 1952, these two hospitals were the only public treatment facilities available. In that year New York City opened a treatment center for youthful addicts at Riverside Hospital, but this facility closed a few years later after proving to be an almost total failure.

By the mid-1950s it became obvious that the drug treatment methodologies this country had pursued for the last century were almost totally useless. No matter what it was called, where it was carried out, or how it was managed, the basic approach of supervised withdrawal just did not work. Time and time again the same sad pattern of treatment and relapse was repeated. In almost every instance addicts returned to drug use as soon as they were released from treatment facilities.

However, in 1958 the founding of this country's first therapeutic community, Synanon, opened a new era in the treatment of addiction. Here, at last, was a different, and from all initial signs, promising approach to treatment. In the years that followed literally hundreds of other therapeutic communities modeled after Synanon sprang up across the country.

In 1964 another importance advance was made in the treatment of narcotic addicts. It was in that year that Drs. Vincent P. Dole and Marie Nyswander began their pioneering work on methadone. The impact that their labors were to have on the direction that drug-abuse treatment took in this country cannot be overestimated. Once the initial success of methadone maintenance was demonstrated, those involved in the management of treatment programs felt that for the first time they really had a methodology that would work. They thought it would allow the relatively simple and relatively inexpensive (when compared to other approaches) treatment of a large and apparently rapidly expanding addict population. Unfortunately, as we shall see later, this early optimism had not been fully borne out by the events that followed.

Today the most widely used types of treatment to combat narcotic addiction in this country are the following:

1. Therapeutic communities
2. Methadone maintenance and detoxification
3. Forced institutionalization
4. Drug-free outpatient services
5. Narcotic antagonists
6. Centers for treatment of nonopiate drug abuse

THERAPEUTIC COMMUNITIES

By the mid-1950s an all-pervasive gloom had spread over the drug treatment community, for by then it had become obvious that the traditional approaches to narcotics treatment were almost complete failures. The most that could be hoped for as the result of any of them was a temporary respite from drug use. As soon as treatment was over and the addict returned to the street, past abuse patterns were almost sure to be resumed. It was an endless merry-go-round that no one knew how to stop.

It was against this background that Charles Dedrich began meeting with a small group of alcoholics in his California home. A former alcoholic himself, Dedrich conducted group sessions in the hopes that his "clients" would come to an understanding of the inner problems that contributed to their drinking habits. Dedrich's group was soon joined by a number of drug addicts who were trying to break their habits. After a short while it became obvious that a larger facility was needed to accommodate Dedrich's "family," and the group moved to Santa Monica, where they established Synanon, this country's first permanent therapeutic community.

Many similar facilities soon were formed. Some of the better known include Phoenix House, Odyssey House, and Daytop Village in New York; Rubicon in Richmond, Virginia; Integrity House in Newark, New Jersey; and Gardenzia, Inc., in Philadelphia. Today it is estimated that there may be as many as 500 therapeutic communities now operating in the United States with a total clientele of approximately 100,000[1] (Figure 16-2).

In general, the term "therapeutic community" refers to a residential treatment facility in which the residents live and work under an intensely demanding set of social relationships designed for their mutual benefit. Though there are many variations on Dedrich's original theme, most of the therapeutic communities have the same basic assumptions.

1. Drug abuse, in and of itself, is not an illness.
2. Drug abuse is a symptom of an underlying emotional disorder and/or immaturity.
3. In order to escape from the bondage of addiction, individuals must learn an entirely new set of coping skills which will then allow them to remake their lives along more productive lines.

Second Genesis, a highly regarded East Coast therapeutic community, in literature explaining its program, summarizes well the philosophy common to most therapeutic communities.

The Second Genesis program has often been described as a school which educates people who have never learned how to live and feel worthy without hurting themselves and others. Second Genesis helps people who have tried again and again to get what they wanted from life and have continually defeated themselves. The principle combines the basic and universal human values of knowledge, love, honesty, and work with the dynamic instrument of intense group pressure in order to recognize and

FIGURE 16-2
Typical therapeutic community. (*Drug Enforcement Administration*)

help correct the personality defects which prevent people from living by these values. The results are rehabilitation so that the individual may re-enter his or her community as an independent and productive person.[2]

The treatment used in therapeutic communities is primarily based on two techniques that are fundamental to psychotherapy: encounter group therapy (or as it is sometimes called, "confrontation group therapy") and milieu therapy. During the encounter group sessions, addicts meet in a confrontation setting. At these meetings they are forced to acknowledge their own shortcomings to the group as a whole. In this way it is hoped that they will come, in time, to recognize their own weakness and lack of maturity (Figure 16-3). Once this is accomplished, they are then helped and encouraged by the group to develop an entirely new set of living skills. Ideally, these new skills will assist them to cope in a mature, reasonable manner with the problems and frustrations that are a part of life.

The entire milieu or setting of the community also contributes to the therapeutic processes. Typically, therapeutic communities are rigidly structured, closed social environments. The status of each res-

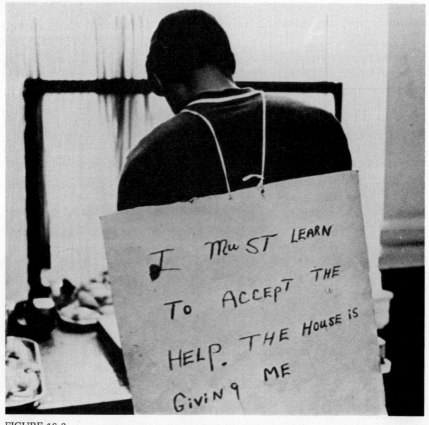

FIGURE 16-3
The primary aim of treatment as practiced in therapeutic communities is for drug abusers to recognize their own weakness and lack of maturity. Once this occurs, they can develop a new set of living skills. (Drug Enforcement Administration)

ident is determined solely by his or her progress. This is measured in terms of a willingness to assume increasing responsibility, the demonstration of improved self-discipline. The greater the progress made in these areas, the higher the status that is awarded within the community.

Though the methodology employed varies considerably from community to community, the following is representative. When residents are first admitted to a community, they go through a period of isolation. Their ties with the outside world are completely severed. They are not permitted to make or receive phone calls, send or receive mail, have visitors, or leave the premises.

During the initial isolation period the new residents assume the role of "low man on the totem pole." They are given the most mundane and tedious housekeeping assignments, such as washing dishes, taking out the garbage, and sweeping floors, and they are allowed few if any privileges. As one counselor observed, "When they first come in here, we make them think they are dirt. No, it's worse than that. We let them know they are nothing—with a capital N."

As the novice residents begin to acknowledge their own shortcomings and seek to assume more responsibilities, they are granted a greater number of privileges and given more desirable work assignments. Their status within the community increases. At any point that it is felt that an individual is backsliding or not making satisfactory progress, his or her status within the community is lowered with an accompanying loss of privileges and responsibilities.

As with all the other modes of treatment, it is extremely difficult to give a meaningful evaluation of the effectiveness of therapeutic communities. There is no doubt that they have made the difference between a new life and a living death for many individuals. The young lady who typed a large segment of this manuscript is a graduate of one such community. Now happily married and with a new baby, she represents almost the ultimate in successful rehabilitation. After several years in a therapeutic community she went from being a mainline addict with a felony criminal record to becoming a responsible, well-adjusted, and productive member of society. In the language of the street, she "made it."

Despite such success stories, however, therapeutic communities have been criticized on several grounds. One of the most serious problems with them, from a public health point of view, is that they have proved to be a suitable treatment alternative for only a very small number of addicts. In order to survive their rigors, especially during the early stages of the regimen, individuals must be highly motivated, and this is a quality for which addicts are not particularly noted. It has been estimated that as many as 75 percent of the individuals who enter therapeutic communities leave within one month.[3] Another drawback is the selectivity of these communities. Many feel that because of their close, communal nature, they must be extraordinarily selective in admitting residents. This immediately limits their ability to be a significant factor in treating a rapidly expanding addict population.

Another criticism frequently voiced is that such programs are far too expensive on a per patient basis to be useful in treating great numbers of abusers. A 1975 White House report on drug abuse placed the average yearly cost per patient in a therapeutic community at $4,500. This is compared to an average yearly cost per patient of $1,700 for outpatient programs.[4] Obviously, in these days of skyrocketing inflation and shrinking municipal tax bases, such cost differences are of critical concern.

METHADONE MAINTENANCE AND DETOXIFICATION

At the close of World War II the U.S. Department of Commerce sent a team of investigators to study the German pharmaceutical industry. One of the new drugs that this team brought back to the United States was a synthetic opiate—methadone hydrochloride. It had been produced as an alternative for the pain-killer morphine, which was not available in Germany due to the hostilities. After its introduction to this country, methadone was used to a limited extent as an obstetric anesthetic, a cough suppressant, and a pain-killer. However, once its addictive potential became fully understood, its use in medicine was severely limited.

Methadone was first tried in the treatment of narcotic addicts during the late 1940s. At the federal hospitals in both Lexington and Fort Worth, doctors administered subcutaneous injections of it to help wean addicts from their craving for heroin. The customary procedure was to provide two injections a day over a seven- to ten-day period.

The first use of methadone in the maintenance of heroin addicts is credited to Dr. Vincent P. Dole. In the 1950s, Dr. Dole conducted a series of studies on the metabolism of overweight individuals. During the course of this research he was impressed by the number of similarities between an addict's craving for drugs and an obese person's obsession with food. Later, in collaboration with Dr. Marie Nyswander, Dr. Dole began a series of studies into the metabolic aspects of morphine abuse. During these studies a number of experimental subjects, all of whom were confirmed narcotic addicts, were maintained on methadone for an extended period of time while additional metabolic tests were run. Much to everyone's surprise there was a dramatic change in the behavior of these individuals. Instead of sitting around in the listless haze characteristic of narcotic addicts, the individuals who were being maintained on methadone began to show a marked interest in their own welfare and what was going on around them.

Their hopes and curiosity aroused by these preliminary results, Dole and Nyswander tried methadone maintenance with several hard-core heroin users. During the first phase of this experiment the addicts were hospitalized; while in the hospital they were stabilized on daily doses of methadone. Once this was accomplished, they were released from the hospital and required to return daily for their methadone. Those receiving the maintenance program were once again able to function in the outside world. As the program began to show signs of success, it was expanded until it soon included almost 4,000 addicts. In 1967 an exhaustive evaluation was made of Dole and Nyswander's work, and it was found that some 80 percent of those enrolled in the program remained and showed "significant improvement in social functioning."[5]

Encouraged by these findings, the federal government allowed other experimental methadone treatment programs to be established. These programs were the subject of numerous studies. It was found that the initial period of hospitalization for stabilization was not necessary. Without hospitalization the cost of programs could be greatly reduced, which, in turn, made them increasingly more attractive to municipalities across the country reeling under the impact of the drug-use explosion.

Over the next few years massive federal funding was committed to methadone maintenance. This, combined with encouraging research and clinical findings and the fact that no other treatment alternative was available that showed promise in treating the enormous number of addicts, led to a rapid expansion of methadone programs. By 1975 it was estimated that over 100,000 addicts were involved in them nationwide.[6]

At the present time methadone is used in two types of treatment programs.

1. DETOXIFICATION. In these programs methadone is used as a substitute narcotic to help dry out heroin addicts. It is provided in decreasing doses until the addict reaches a drug-free state, which generally takes from two to three weeks. In addition, addicts undergoing detoxification are usually provided with such services as group and individual rehabilitation. Such assistance, it is hoped, will help them to remain drug-free once they have been detoxified.

2. MAINTENANCE. These programs are geared toward the long-term, continued use of methadone as a substitute for illicit narcotics such as heroin.

Experience indicates that, of the two, maintenance programs are the most successful in treating the majority of addicts. Most heroin addicts who participate in detoxification programs either relapse into their old drug-abuse patterns or, fearing that, switch to long-term maintenance programs. An analysis of one detoxification program found that at the end of a six-month period, only 9.5 percent of those who had completed the program remained drug-free.[7]

The basic principle behind maintenance treatment is simple. One narcotic, methadone, is substituted for another, heroin. Addicts are provided free daily doses of methadone. The methadone prevents them from suffering the discomforts of withdrawal. It satisfies their craving for narcotics. In addition, if the methadone dose is properly adjusted, it blocks or prevents them from experiencing any pleasurable sensation from the use of heroin.

As a result of this substitution, addicts no longer need to live drug-centered lives. Their lives need no longer be dominated by the "steal–buy–shoot-up" cycle that characterizes that of the mainline heroin addict. It is hoped that once this cycle is broken, the addict, with appropriate rehabilitative assistance, will develop a productive, crime-free lifestyle.

At the present time methadone maintenance programs are limited to addicts sixteen years old and older who have been dependent on opiates for a minimum of two years. Addicts between sixteen and eighteen years of age must have a parent's permission to join. In addition, they must have failed in at least two prior attempts at detoxification.

In most of the programs, when the addict's condition has been stabilized, he or she is required to return to a clinic on a daily basis. There the individual is given an oral dose of liquid methadone mixed with a carrier, such as orange juice. This must be consumed in the presence of a member of the clinic's staff. Once addicts have demonstrated their reliability, some programs allow them to take enough methadone home to last for several days. This reduces the interruption to their daily schedules caused by the daily visits to the clinic.

Unfortunately, some addicts enrolled in methadone maintenance programs "cheat" and continue to use heroin and other drugs. This is especially true of individuals who are participating in the programs as the result of some form of coercion, such as those who are enrolled in lieu of going to jail. For this reason most programs administer laboratory tests to spot cheaters. The most common are urine tests. A test is given on a periodic and unannounced basis. The more sensitive urine tests can spot the use of heroin up to a week after the heroin was used (Figure 16-4).

The stabilization of addicts on maintenance doses of methadone is, of course, just the beginning of the rehabilitative process. Once the need for getting and using heroin has been removed, in-depth rehabilitative programs aimed at helping the addicts become productive members of society can start. To this end, federal regulations require that all maintenance programs provide their clientele with at least a

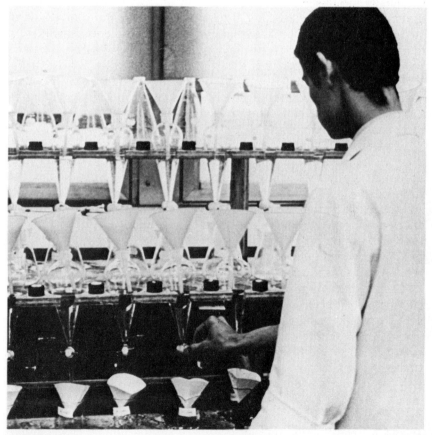

FIGURE 16-4
Frequent urine tests are one of the ways in which drug treatment programs attempt to spot those patients who continue to use illicit drugs. (Drug Enforcement Administration)

minimal level of supportive services, such as group therapy, vocational training, social services, and family counseling.

When it first became available, methadone maintenance was hailed as the answer to America's drug-abuse problem. Here, at last, was, as one instructor called it, "the chemical cure to original sin." But, as history has so often shown, it is rare indeed that complex social problems such as drug abuse lend themselves to simple solutions. Since the mid-1970s the concept of methadone maintenance has been subjected to increasing criticism. One of the most frequently voiced dissatisfactions is that while methadone maintenance may be good for society as a whole because it reduces the need for drug abusers to commit crime to support their addiction, it does nothing to help the individual addict to become drug-free. In short, the end result of methadone maintenance is to substitute a socially sanctioned addiction to methadone for an illicit one to heroin. Among critics who are members of minority groups, this substitution is frequently viewed as deliberate genocide. That is, it is seen as a means by which the white majority can, on a continuing basis, emasculate and render impotent a large segment of this country's minority population by keeping them enslaved to methadone.

In addition, long-term methadone maintenance programs have also been criticized on medical grounds. The criticism is certainly valid in that we do not yet know the long-range health effects. Methadone simply has not been used long enough for us to know what its effects are after extended periods. Though the clinical results have been quite encouraging, no one can state with certainty what the results will be on individuals after many years of continual use.

The diversion of methadone into illicit channels has also been the grounds for heated criticism. As might be expected, as soon as methadone became widely used, a thriving illicit market developed for it. In some cities where maintenance programs were hastily put together and poorly administered, substantial quantities of the drug were stolen or diverted from treatment facilities and doctor's offices. However, a changeover from tablet to liquid dosage as well as a general tightening of security and administrative requirements has gone a long way toward easing this problem in many areas.

FORCED INSTITUTIONALIZATION

We have already noted that for many years the principal thrust of narcotics treatment in this country was based on the compulsory institutionalization of addicts. The programs conducted at the federal facilities in Lexington and Fort Worth exemplify this approach.

Treatment at these hospitals consisted of three phases. First, addicts were withdrawn from heroin by giving them gradually decreasing doses of morphine. This usually took a week or two. Next followed a period of intensive inpatient care. During this time addicts remained isolated from their former environments and cut off from all sources of illicit drugs. Various forms of family, group, and individual therapy were provided in an attempt to prepare the addicts for their eventual release. Finally, when considered able to cope with a normal lifestyle, the addicts were returned to their home communities, where they underwent a period of outpatient care. During this time they continued to receive counseling, therapy, and other rehabilitative services.

Unfortunately, the records of the Lexington and Fort Worth efforts speak only too clearly of the dismal failure of this approach to the treatment of drug abuse. Though thousands of addicts went through the cure, for all but a mere handful the process was a waste of the government's time, money, and effort. However, the obvious failure of Lexington and Fort Worth did not bring about the abandonment of the basic approach of forced institutionalization. Various state and federal agencies continued to rely on so-called modified Lexington methods of treatment.

During the 1960s the Narcotic Addict Rehabilitation Act (NARA) was passed. Among other things, it provided for the civil commitment of addicts both in lieu of prosecution for federal offenses and after conviction of federal offenses. At the state level, both New York and California embarked on ambitious new civil commitment programs. In the years that followed several other states followed suit. All these treatment programs were essentially based on the fundamental concept of "incarceration for rehabilitation," and each of them tried to learn from the lessons of Lexington and Fort Worth.

The administrative details varied from state to state, but in general all provided that addicts could be ordered into the programs in lieu of criminal sentencing or prosecution. Addicts could also volunteer for treatment or be committed by their families or the authorities. After an initial period of inpatient care at a designated rehabilitation center, the clients were returned to the community. There they were closely supervised. If they returned to drug use, they were recommitted to the rehabilitation center.

There is a good deal of disagreement about just how successful these forced institutionalization programs were. Some contend that even though they did not produce a significant number of long-term cures, at least they did manage to get a relatively large number of addicts off the streets. This is itself a plus. Critics, however, point out that such gains are at best temporary. As soon as the overwhelming majority of the recipients of such cures are allowed to return to their old stomping grounds, they resume their old drug habits.

DRUG-FREE OUTPATIENT SERVICES

During the last few years a number of groups have attempted to assist addicts by offering such rehabilitative services as counseling, psychotherapy, and vocational training on a drug-free outpatient basis. As is implied, these programs do not sanction methadone as a substitute drug, though there are centers that do approve of its use for short-term detoxification.

The scope and nature of the assistance provided by these programs varies enormously. Some are tightly structured and have a complete range of services such as group and individual counseling, vocational rehabilitation, family guidance, and medical and psychiatric care. Others are run in a much looser manner with far fewer professional services available to their clients.

At present there is not sufficient data about the results of the drug-free outpatient approach to treatment to make a meaningful evaluation. From past experience it would seem likely that such an approach is more effective with youthful experimenters than with hard-core addicts.

NARCOTIC ANTAGONISTS

Antagonists are drugs with a chemical structure that is almost identical to that of the opiates. Their use in the treatment of drug abuse rests on the fact that they counteract many of the effects of narcotics without being addictive themselves. After taking an antagonist, addicts no longer experience the rush and euphoria produced by heroin. These effects are said to have been blocked by the apparent ability of the antagonist to occupy the same place in the nervous system as that where narcotics act.

Some researchers feel that drug abuse should be viewed to a large extent in terms of classical conditioning. According to them, the pleasurable sensation that addicts experience when they use narcotics reinforces their addiction. When viewed in those terms, it becomes apparent that narcotics abuse is a vicious cycle. Each time that addicts use heroin, they experience a pleasurable sensation. These pleasurable sensations, in turn, serve to reinforce their drug taking. Anything that can be done to reduce the pleasure that addicts derive from narcotics, such as the use of antagonists, helps reduce drug taking and hence break the cycle.

Most research involving antagonists has been centered on two drugs—cyclazocine and naloxone. Cyclazocine, which has been under study since the mid-1960s, is a moderately long-acting antagonist whose blocking effects last from twelve to fourteen hours. Though clinical experience indicates that cyclazocine may help some former addicts stay away from drugs after withdrawal, there are several serious drawbacks associated with its use. For one thing, it can produce unpleasant side effects, such as dizziness, headaches, and hallucinations. Additionally, if cyclazocine is given to an individual whose system has not been completely cleansed of narcotics, extremely acute withdrawal symptoms can be precipitated.

Naloxone, on the other hand, is almost free from unpleasant side effects. It suffers, however, from several drawbacks of its own. For one, it is extremely expensive, for it must be synthesized from thebaine, an opiate present only in small quantities in raw opium. Another problem is the short duration of its effects; a normal dose lasts only from four to six hours.

CENTERS FOR TREATMENT OF NONOPIATE DRUG ABUSE

The preceding discussion has been concerned with the principal treatment methods for heroin addiction. Because of the explosive growth of the heroin problem over the last decade or so, it is these programs that have received the bulk of federal, state, and local attention and funding. Treatment efforts specifically geared to other drugs, such as the barbiturates, amphetamines, and hallucinogens, by comparison have received meager support indeed. The reason for this situation is one of priorities. As one federal official said, "If I only have so much money and I am faced with spending it to treat either a city full of heroin junkies who are stealing everybody blind to support their habits or a bunch of kids who are sitting around popping pills, you know where that money is going!"

In most localities treatment of nonopiate abusers is limited to so-called crisis-intervention centers that furnish medical and psychiatric services on an emergency, short-term basis. Many of these centers operate in conjunction with hospital emergency rooms; others operate as independent, free clinics. Most of their efforts are directed at the short-term management of drug-precipitated crises—for example, LSD-induced bad trips and psychotic episodes brought on by an overdose of such stimulants as amphetamines or cocaine.

In recent years a number of localities have started to provide nonopiate abusers with long-term treatment alternatives as well as emergency services. At the present time, however, it is too early to assess the effectiveness of these efforts.

IN CONCLUSION

Though it has been plaguing doctors and law enforcement authorities since the Civil War, the question of how to best treat drug abusers remains unanswered. Until it is, we will never be successful in solving the drug problem.

NOTES

[1]Peter G. Bourne and Ann S. Ramsey, "The Therapeutic Community Phenomenon," *Journal of Psychedelic Drugs*, vol. 7, no. 2, p. 203, April–June 1975.

[2]Program *Overview of Second Genesis, Inc.,* unpublished handout, n.d., p. 1.

[3]National Clearinghouse for Drug Abuse Information, *Treatment of Drug Abuse: An Overview,* U.S. Department of Health, Education, and Welfare Report Series 34, no. 1, p. 8 (Rockville, Md.: The Clearinghouse, 1975).

[4]Domestic Council Drug Abuse Task Force, *White Paper on Drug Abuse* (Washington, D.C.: GPO, 1975), p. 71.

[5]National Clearinghouse for Drug Abuse Information, p. 4.

[6]Richard C. Schroeder, *The Politics of Drugs: Marijuana to Mainlining* (Washington, D.C.: Congressional Quarterly Inc., 1975), p. 139.

[7]National Clearinghouse for Drug Abuse Information, *Methadone: The Drug and Its Therapeutic Uses in the Treatment of Addicition,* U.S. Department of Health, Education, and Welfare Report Series 31, no. 1, p. 8 (Rockville, Md.: The Clearinghouse, 1974).

Chapter 17

BRITISH SYSTEM OF TREATMENT

The term "British system" is frequently heard in reference to drug-abuse treatment but rarely understood. Proponents of both "hard" and "soft" approaches to this country's drug problem frequently cite it in support of their particular viewpoints—too often without any real idea of what the British system is or how it operates.

In the most basic terms, the British system of handling narcotic addicts is based on the notion that it is better to supply addicts with drugs than to try to cut off their drugs. In Britain addicts can obtain heroin and some other drugs for a nominal charge simply by applying at one of a number of government-operated treatment centers.

The British cite two theoretical reasons for supplying drugs in this manner. First, it is thought that if addiction is viewed as a medical matter rather than a criminal one, drug users will be encouraged to seek treatment. This, it is felt, will help undermine the drug subculture. Second, it is reasoned that by providing drugs at a minimal cost, the government undermines the profit base of the illicit drug market. This, in turn, removes any incentive for organized crime to become involved in drugs.

Over the years these concepts have continued to serve as the cornerstones of the British approach to the treatment of drug abusers. However, there have been a number of important changes in the approach to accommodate the shifting patterns of drug addiction in Britain. During the early 1920s under certain circumstances any physician was legally entitled to dispurse either heroin or morphine to bona fide narcotic addicts. Now only specially designated doctors who are associated with government-controlled clinics may do so.

For the purposes of discussion the evolution of the British system can be examined in relation to three periods. These are:

1. The First Period: Rolleston Committee (1924)
2. The Second Period: First Brain Committee (1958)
3. The Third Period: Second Brain Committee (1964)

FIRST PERIOD: ROLLESTON COMMITTEE

In 1924 the question of supplying heroin to addicts came up as a possible violation of the International Opium Act of 1912. The British Minister of Health appointed a committee of distinguished physicians headed by Sir Humphrey Rolleston to review the problem. This group conducted an extensive review of the legislation then in force concerning the treatment of narcotic addicts (the Dangerous Drug Act of 1920). In 1926 the committee issued a report which stated in part:

> Morphine or heroin may properly be administered to addicts in the following circumstances, namely a) where patients are under treatment by the gradual withdrawal method with a view to cure, b) where it has been demonstrated that after a prolonged attempt at cure, the use of the drug cannot be safely discontinued entirely, on account of the severity of the withdrawal symptoms produced, and, c) where it has been similarly demonstrated that the patient, while capable of leading a useful and relatively normal life when a certain minimum dose is regularly administered, becomes incapable of this when the drug is entirely discontinued.[1]

The conclusions reached by the Rolleston Committee had a fundamental influence on how narcotic addicts were viewed by the law and treated. To a very large degree, they set the tone of all subsequent legislation.

It is reasonable to assume that the response to the narcotics problem that is exemplified by the Rolleston Report was greatly influenced by the nature of the drug problem in Britain at that time. Addicts were few and far between. Until the 1960s the total number of registered addicts averaged fewer than five hundred a year. In addition they were not drawn from "threatening segments of society." Indeed data reveals that prior to World War II most were professionals such as doctors and nurses. In addition they tended, more often than not, to be middle-aged females.

SECOND PERIOD: FIRST BRAIN COMMITTEE

During the 1950s profound changes took place in the nature of Britain's addict pattern. In many ways these changes mirrored those that had taken place in the addict population in the United States in the decades immediately following the passage of the Harrison Narcotics Act. Britain's middle- to upper-class, largely female, addict population was replaced by one that was made up of young, mainly urban, males. At this time the greatest concentration of addicts seemed to be within the avant-garde world of London's notorious jazz clubs.

This shift in the composition of the addict population had the inevitable effect of producing numerous calls for the authorities to "do something" about Britain's drug problem. In February 1955 the government responded by announcing that it intended to refuse to allow further production of heroin. The hue and cry that this announcement produced from the medical community embroiled the government in a controversy. Finally bowing to extreme pressure, the government rescinded the order. However, this did little to defuse the now raging controversy.

It was against this background that a committee, under the chairmanship of the late Lord Brain, was appointed in 1958. Its stated purpose was twofold: to consider whether new methods of treatment had rendered the recommendations of the Rolleston Committee obsolete and to consider whether the newer synthetic analgesics such as methadone should come under stricter control or review.

In 1960 the Brain Committee published its final report. Its principal findings were that the incidence of narcotic addiction was small in England and that there was no substantial illicit trade in narcotics. Among other conclusions and recommendations the report stated that:

1. addiction should be regarded as an expression of mental disorder and not as a criminal act;
2. compulsory detention of addicts is not desirable for successful treatment;
3. specialized institutions for the treatment of addiction are not necessary;
4. registration of addicts is neither desirable nor helpful;
5. irregularities in the prescribing of dangerous drugs are infrequent and do not warrant further statutory control; and
6. there is no need to initiate special prescription policies and forms for dangerous drugs.[2]

THIRD PERIOD: SECOND BRAIN COMMITTEE

During the 1960s Britain's drug problem worsened noticeably. For any number of still-debated reasons, the number of narcotic addicts rose alarmingly. During the previous decades the number of narcotic addicts in Britain consistently numbered less than 500. And of those, heroin addicts accounted for only some 50 to 60 cases. By 1967 the count of narcotic addicts had mushroomed to 1,729, and of these, almost 1,300 were using heroin.[3]

This same period saw other troublesome changes in the composition of Britain's addict population. As the epidemic progressed, the average age of British heroin addicts dropped sharply. In the past they had tended to be middle-aged. In 1960 the first person under twenty years old addicted to heroin was reported.[4] In the years that followed, the proportion of known addicts under twenty continued to increase. In 1963 they constituted 7 percent of the addict population. By 1966 they represented an alarming 35 percent. And as might be expected, many of this new generation of youthful addicts were highly unstable personality types with past histories of social maladjustment, sociopathic behavior, and delinquent behavior.[5]

From the middle 1960s an increasing number of Britain's addicts began to use powerful stimulants such as methamphetamine and cocaine in addition to narcotics. The high doses of these drugs that were commonly used took their toll in an increasing number of incidents of paranoid and otherwise delinquent or disturbed behavior.[6]

Although in some ways the explosive increase in narcotics abuse which occurred in Britain was similar to its counterpart in the United States, there were a number of important differences. In the United States the use of all narcotic drugs and in particular heroin had been for the most part confined to minority groups such as blacks, Mexican-Americans, and Puerto Ricans. In addition, the use of such hard drugs as heroin (in contrast to soft drugs such as marijuana and LSD) had usually been associated with urban slum areas. This was not the case in Britain. Narcotic addicts in Britain were drawn from a much more heterogeneous cross section of the population. Lawyer and laborer alike succumbed to the magic of the fix.

It was against this setting that the Second Interdepartmental Committee on Drug Addiction (the Second Brain Committee) met in 1964. Its task was to "consider whether in the light of recent experience the advice they gave in 1961 in relation to the prescribing of addictive drugs by doctors needs revising."

From the evidence gathered, it appeared that there was little if any organized importation of or trafficking in narcotics. Instead, it became obvious that most of Britain's expanding addict population obtained their drug supplies as the direct result of overprescribing by a handful of physicians. During 1962, for example, 1,000,000 heroin tablets were prescribed for all of Britain's narcotic addicts. Of these, 600,000 tablets were prescribed by one doctor in London. On one occasion this doctor prescribed 900 tablets of heroin for a single addict. Then a mere three days later he prescribed another 300 tablets to the same addict to replace those "lost in accident."[7]

Fortunately, the committee found that such abuses were limited to a small number of doctors, six or seven at the most. Still, the handwriting was on the wall for all to see. Clearly, more effective controls were needed. When the report was released in July 1965, it called for sweeping revision of the British drug program. The controls proposed were far more rigorous—far more in the nature of a formal system—than anything that had existed up to that time. The committee's most important conclusions and recommendations were that:

1. centers should be organized to treat addiction problems;
2. only doctors at centers should be authorized to prescribe heroin and cocaine to addicts;
3. a system of the nótification of addicts, more stringent than that which existed, should be established;
4. doctors at centers should be given advice in cases where addiction was in question; and finally
5. doctors at centers should be given the power to detain addicts in inpatient facilities without the addict's consent.[8]

All but the last recommendation was passed into law by the spring of 1968.

THE PRESENT SYSTEM

At the present time addicts can obtain drug supplies at a number of special clinics, facilities, and outpatient departments scattered throughout England and Wales. Each of these facilities has a wide latitude in determining its own staffing approach and treatment philosophy. Though this latitude exists, there are certain basic similarities in the way addicts are treated.

In general, once an addict reports to one of the clinics or other treatment facilities, an effort is made to determine accurately the type and amount of drugs that are required for stabilization. Once the addict has been stabilized on the smallest possible dose, every effort is made to encourage the individual to reduce his or her drug taking. Eventually it is hoped that the addict can be induced to undergo withdrawal and forgo drugs altogether.

Each week the staff reviews the amount of drugs called for or the addict's prescription. This is then mailed to a retail pharmacy. This procedure is followed to eliminate the possibility of altered prescriptions. The addict then goes to the pharmacy each day to pick up his or her daily ration of drugs.

EVALUATING THE BRITISH SYSTEM

American reactions to the British methods of dealing with narcotic addicts have always been mixed. On the one hand there are those observers who claim that the British approach has had "truly magnificent results." An equal number of commentators take a totally different tack. To them the results have been nothing short of disastrous. Those in favor of British methods point to the relatively small number of British addicts and the insignificant level of illicit drug trafficking found in Britain. Detractors tend to single out the "explosive" increase in the number of addicts which occurred during the 1960s as proof of an underlying fallacy in the British approach.

Some critics of the British approach also raise the fundamental question (much as critics of methadone maintenance in this country do) of whether it is morally acceptable for the government to provide addicts with the drugs they crave. These reservations are encapsulated in the words of two American physicians, Drs. Granville Larimore and Henry Brill, who made an exhaustive study of British methods of handling addicts: "It might be noted in passing that the concept of providing an addicted individual with a plentiful supply of the noxious agent with which to seal his doom is, in certain aspects at least, ethically and morally repugnant, whether that agent be alcohol, a narcotic or some other substance."[9]

And so the arguments go. But the real question, as far as Americans are concerned, is whether a method that has proved useful in Britain will prove equally so in the United States.

IN CONCLUSION

Drug abuse as a phenomenon does not exist by itself. It does not exist separate from the culture in which it is found; rather it is an integral part of that culture. It acts upon and with it, and in turn it is shaped and molded by the culture it affects. While it is true that there are many similarities between British and American cultural patterns, there are also enormous differences. Britains and Americans are not interchangeable parts stamped out by the same Anglo-tradition. With that in mind, the question to be answered is, even if the present British approach to narcotic maintenance proves successful, will it work in the United States?

Until narcotic maintenance is tried in the United States, we will never know the answer. At the present time it appears that that day may not be too far off. During the past few years a number of different proposals for experimental heroin programs have been put forth. Perhaps the boldest up to date was that made by a special blue ribbon grand jury in San Diego, California. Though none of these plans has come to fruition, it is reasonable to assume that some form of heroin maintenance plan will be put into effect in the United States within the foreseeable future. Then, and only then, will we be able to truly evaluate the wisdom or folly of the British system.

NOTES

[1]National Clearinghouse for Drug Abuse Information, *The British Narcotics System*, Report Series 13, no. 1, p. 2 (Washington, D.C.: GPO, 1976).

[2]Ministry of Health, Department of Health for Scotland, *Drug Addiction Report of the Interdepartmental Committee* (First Brain Report) (London: H. M. Stationery Office, 1961).

[3]John B. Williams, *Narcotics and Drug Dependence* (New York: Glencoe Press, 1974), p. 5.

[4]John B. Williams, p. 169.

[5]Pierce I. James, "The Changing Pattern of Narcotics Addiction in Britain, 1959 to 1969," *The International Journal of Addictions*, vol. 6, no. 1, March 1971, p. 120.

[6]Pierce I. James, p. 123.

[7]National Clearinghouse for Drug Abuse Information, p. 4.

[8]Scottish Home and Health Department, *Drug Addiction: The Second Report of the Interdepartmental Committee* (Second Brain Report) (London: H. M. Stationery Office, 1967).

[9]Granville W. Larimore and Henry Brill, quoted in National Clearinghouse for Drug Abuse Information, p. 9.

Appendix A

HEROIN TREND INDICATORS

How many heroin addicts are there in the United States? Is this number increasing or decreasing? These are two of the most basic and yet most difficult questions to answer about today's drug scene.

Until recently there was little or no valid information available about the shifting patterns of drug abuse in the United States. As a result, policy makers were forced to act in an almost perfect factual vacuum. Recently, however, several techniques have been developed for assessing the extent and nature of the drug problem. Some of them are explained in the following excerpt from the *Heroin Indicators Trend Report*[1] published by the National Institute on Drug Abuse.

FOREWORD

The drug abuse explosion of the late 1960's caught most of us off guard. While our knowledge about drug abuse was limited, our speculation about the nature and extent of drug abuse was not restricted. Estimates of the numbers of heroin addicts, speed freaks, acid heads, and hippies in Haight-Ashbury reflected all of the political and social views that searched for a headline. There was no validation. No documentation. No explanation. No verification. Yet one fact was clear: Our national response to drug abuse was handicapped by our lack of an understanding of these issues.

By the early 70's the complex task of counting and sorting and measuring and estimating and figuring and analyzing had begun. The guessing was restricted and the methodologies were debated. By 1973 there was more information—and by the fall of 1973, a Presidential statement of turned corners and unfinished tasks.

The temporary nature of that corner-turning was not understood. Now it is. And sufficient admonition remains to caution the use of any data about a problem as complex as drug abuse. On the other hand, careful review and analysis, coupled with increased knowledge about how to measure drug abuse, has enabled us to gather data that can now serve as a basis for more accurate public policy. . . .

INTRODUCTION

This is the first in a series of reports intended to provide an objective assessment of heroin indicator trend data in this country. The information utilized in this report has been collected from a variety of data sources which are generally considered to have an association with trends in drug use. The absolute nature of this association between drug use and the indicators is not known, although it is generally considered that changes in drug use are reflected by changing values in the indicators. Thus, the indicators should be viewed as relative measures of change rather than absolute measures. The indicators include:

> medical examiner reports on drug-related deaths
> emergency room reports on drug-related episodes
> hepatitis reports
> reports on the drug retail price and purity levels
> State and local law enforcement reports on drug law arrests
> drug abuse treatment program admission records

This first report focuses on patterns of heroin use. The exact relationship between the indicators and the actual number of heroin users in the Nation at any given time and the rate at which this population is increasing or decreasing in size remains undefined. The indicators are thought, nonetheless, to indirectly reflect changes in heroin use trends. The following is a brief description of the rationale underlying the selection of each data source as an indicator of heroin use.

Drug-related Deaths

An increase in the number of active heroin users in the Nation is thought to result in an increase in the number of fatal reactions to the drug. It is believed that the number of deaths would increase as a function of the number of persons who intravenously self-administer heroin of varying quantity and quality.

Drug-related Emergency Room Episodes

Similar to drug-related deaths, the number of nonfatal reactions of heroin is thought to increase as the number of heroin users increases. Thus, the number of individuals who experience heroin overdose and are treated in hospital emergency rooms should vary with the total number of active users.

Hepatitis Reports

Viral hepatitis is transmitted via unsterile syringes shared by individuals who use drugs intravenously, primarily heroin users. Drug-related hepatitis is considered to be an indicator of new heroin use since it typically occurs only once, usually during the first year or two of use. Changes in the number of hepatitis cases should reflect changes in the number of new users of heroin.

Drug Price and Purity

Changes in the retail purity or potency of heroin and changes in price are generally considered a measure of heroin availability. As the purity of heroin increases and the price declines, availability of heroin increases: Increases in availability are believed to be associated with increases in the total number of heroin users. It also seems apparent that when heroin becomes more available, the number of heroin-related deaths and emergencies increases since these fatal and nonfatal reactions are assumed to be primarily dose related.

Drug Law Arrests

The number of arrests by State and local law enforcement authorities for drug law violations is thought to bear a relationship to overall drug use in the Nation. It is assumed that as drug-related activity increases, public concern also increases, resulting in more law enforcement activity and a greater number of arrests for drug-related offenses.

Treatment Program Admissions

Treatment admission data are considered to be related only partially to the extent of the drug-using population. They probably reflect treatment funding levels more than they describe trends in heroin use. However, admission data are included in this report as an indirect indicator of the treatment delivery system and to provide trend information regarding individuals who have identified themselves as having a serious problem associated with heroin use requiring immediate treatment.

It is generally assumed that medical examiner, emergency room, and law enforcement data reflect rates of change in the prevalence of heroin use, while hepatitis data are considered to be measures of heroin incidence. In this report, the term prevalence refers to the total number of heroin users in a specific population during a specific period of time. Incidence refers to the number of new users of heroin in a specific population who began use during a specific period of time. Thus, the prevalence of heroin use in a specific community during a given year would be equal to the total number of established users present at the beginning of the year plus all those who began using during the year (annual incidence) minus those who terminated use during the year (as a result of treatment, incarceration, etc.). For a detailed discussion of heroin incidence and prevalence methodologies, the reader is referred to Drug Incidence Analysis, and Estimating the Prevalence of Heroin Use in a Community, two monographs available from the National Clearinghouse for Drug Abuse Information.*

Trends based on data from each of these sources will be discussed in this report. The format will be a brief discussion of each specific data source and the major limitations in interpreting the data from each source. A graphic and tabular presentation of the data will follow with a general description of the trend suggested by the data. In addition, survey data will be included as a supplement of this report. Surveys provide a unique source of information regarding prevalence of heroin use in a broader population which is not likely to be reflected in the indicators.

Caution. Most of the data sources presented are still in a process of refinement as they relate to heroin use. In subsequent reports, any changes which may occur in the data reporting, collection, calculation, or interpretive process affecting current or previous data will be discussed.

It should be noted that the indicators described are believed to have a distinct, albeit indirect, relationship with heroin trends. Although the exact association among the various indicators or between the indicators and heroin use or activity is unknown, the indicators are thought to reflect general variation in heroin trends. Each indicator provides a unique set of data regarding the consequences or correlates of heroin use or activity, i.e., deaths, emergencies, hepatitis, availability, arrests, and treatment. None of the indicator trends is intended to represent a one-to-one relationship with heroin trends or to measure the overall prevalence of heroin use in the Nation. The illegal nature of heroin use and the unresolved problems in reporting systems preclude statistical precision at present. However, it is suggested that the indicators reported represent the major data systems currently available regarding heroin trends and, considered as a whole, are useful in providing a general reflection of heroin use and activity.

NOTE

[1]National Institute on Drug Abuse, Heroin Indicators Trend Report (Washington, D.C.: GPO, 1976).

*National Clearinghouse for Drug Abuse Information, Post Office Box 1908, Rockville, Maryland 20850.

Appendix B

SUMMARY EXCERPTS FROM DAWN III REPORT [1]

DAWN is a nationwide data collection system designed to monitor the trends in problem use of more than 2,000 drugs. More than 1,200 hospital emergency rooms, medical examiners, and crisis centers in 29 Standard Metropolitan Statistical Areas (SMSA's) provide data to DAWN on a monthly basis.

DAWN is funded and operated jointly by the Drug Enforcement Administration (DEA) and The National Institute on Drug Abuse (NIDA), and represents a major step forward in cooperation among Federal agencies to monitor drug abuse trends associated with harm to individuals and society.

INTRODUCTION

The Drug Abuse Warning Network (DAWN) is a nationwide program that:

identifies drugs currently abused or associated with harm to the individual and society;

determines existing patterns of drug abuse in 29 Standard Metropolitan Statistical Areas (SMSA's);

monitors national drug abuse trends, including detection of new abuse entities and new combinations;

provides current data for the assessment of the relative hazards to health and relative abuse potential for substances in human experience; and

provides data needed for rational control and scheduling of drugs of abuse, both old and new.

DAWN is utilized by the Drug Enforcement Administration (DEA) and the National Institute on Drug Abuse (NIDA) for the purpose of gathering, interpreting, and disseminating data on drug abuse from selected sites within the continental United States. The Drug Enforcement Administration directs the information to its enforcement, compliance, and scheduling programs, and the National

Institute on Drug Abuse applies the information towards forecasting, education, prevention, treatment, and rehabilitation programs.

DEFINITIONS

1. *Drug Abuse* is defined as: the non-medical use of a substance for any of the following reasons: psychic effects, dependence, or self destruction (attempt and/or gesture). For the purposes of this definition, non-medical use means:
   a. The use of prescription drugs in a manner inconsistent with accepted medical practice.
   b. The use of OTC (over-the-counter) drugs contrary to approved labeling.
   c. The use of any other substances, heroin, marijuana, peyote, glue, aerosols, etc., for the reasons cited above.
2. A *drug related death* is defined as:
   a. Any death involving a drug "overdose" where a toxic level is found or suspected.
   b. Any death where the drug usage is a contributory factor, but not the sole cause, i.e., accidents, diseased state, withdrawal syndrome, etc.
3. *Psychic effects*—include euphoria, high, kicks, mood alteration, sexual enhancement, alleviation of unhappiness, trips; drug experiences, including experimentation and use for pleasure and fulfillment; use for social or recreational purposes or because of peer pressure.
4. *Dependence*—A state, psychic and/or physical, characterized by behavioral and other responses that always include a compulsion to take the drug on a continuous or periodic basis in order to experience its psychic effects; or to avoid the discomfort of its absence.
5. *Suicide attempt or gesture*—successful or unsuccessful suicide attempt or gesture verified by note or other evidence.

GENERAL INFORMATION

This report contains the narrative or description of DAWN data collected during the period April 1974 through April 1975.

An important consideration to keep in mind when using DAWN data is that this system only collects abuse episodes that have resulted in a crisis. The person involved has sought help (or died) and has subsequently been reported by one of the four facility types (emergency room, inpatient unit, crisis center or medical examiner). While this system may be gathering only a portion of data on the actual drug abuse taking place, it appears to be a source of reliable information.

Patient Contact and Drug Mentions by Facility Type

A patient contact (or abuse episode) represents a death, visit to, or other contact with a DAWN facility reported by that facility. In the DAWN context visits are not synonymous with number of individuals involved in that, over time, one person may make repeated visits to an emergency room or to several emergency rooms or have contacts with more than one type of facility. *Inasmuch as no patient identifiers are collected, it is impossible to determine the number of individuals involved in the reported episodes.*

Since DAWN accepts up to six substances per episode (patient contact), each episode generates an average of 1.39 drug mentions (named substances). Drug mentions represent the sum of all substances, in the aggregate, which played a part in causing an abuser to seek treatment or other help. Many episodes are associated with more than one substance, and so the number of mentions exceeds the number of episodes. However, for any given substance, such as heroin, the number of mentions is equal to the number of episodes involving that substance.

TABLE 1
ABUSE EPISODES AND DRUG MENTIONS BY FACILITY TYPE DAWN III

	Abuse Episodes #	% of Total %	Drug Mentions #	% of Total %	Drug Mentions Per Episode #
Crisis centers	62,373	32	76,061	29	1.22
Emergency rooms	115,094	60	167,075	62	1.45
Inpatient units	7,717	4	11,615	4	1.51
Medical examiners	7,196	4	12,129	5	1.69
Total	192,379	100	266,880	100	1.39

As evidenced in Table 1 there appears to be a progression of number of drugs mentioned per episode as the apparent seriousness of the episode increases which is suggested by the facility type.

Drug Classification

The substances reported through DAWN are generally grouped into therapeutic classes such as tranquilizers, narcotic analgesics, non-narcotic analgesics, etc. The miscellaneous class includes marihuana, hashish, drug unknown and substances not assignable to another therapeutic class. Hallucinogens are grouped into one therapeutic class as are substances abused by inhalation.

Within each therapeutic class or category, drugs are grouped generically. Thus, street names, trade names, or both, may be included in these generic groups.

Street names are carried in DAWN due to the inability to reliably identify the compound other than by its street name. Therefore, reference to substances such as speed, uppers, and downers may appear in a table or in the text.

The term "drug unknown" is given in approximately 5% of the drug mentions. This term may occur when the person actually didn't know what was taken or, perhaps, did not wish to reveal what was taken particularly if it was an illicit substance.

Most Frequently Mentioned Drugs

The DAWN system, since its inception, has accumulated a vocabulary of approximately 3,000 substances mentioned in incidents of abuse. Twenty-five of these substances account for 64% of all drug mentions. Drug unknown, as previously mentioned, is named in 5% of all drug mentions bringing the total to roughly 70% of all drug mentions being generated by this very limited number of substances.

It may prove useful in utilization of these data if several items are clarified and kept in mind when reviewing this report.

The first item requiring clarification is the substance "alcohol-in-combination." DAWN does not gather data on alcohol used alone, only alcohol used concomitantly with another abuse substance. Therefore, all alcohol mentions are combination mentions.

The second item concerns heroin and morphine. While heroin may be the ingested drug, it is metabolized to morphine. Therefore, deaths from heroin will appear low, but are, in fact, listed under morphine, as this is the substance identified through laboratory findings. The more reasonable heroin death total should represent the sum of the heroin and morphine drug related death episodes as reported by medical examiners.

System Caveats

As data used in the DAWN III report are raw or sample data, there are certain caveats intrinsic in their utilization. One major factor lies in the differing saturation rates among SMSA's. Since no adjustment has been made to compensate for these varying rates, comparison between SMSA's is not recommended.

The actual number of drug mentions from month to month within an SMSA or between SMSA's potentially is affected by adding or dropping facilities from the DAWN participating group, partial or non-reporting by a participating facility for a given month, and differing numbers of days among months. While no adjustments have been made to take account of the above factors, efforts have been made in the text to identify major reporting changes. One other caveat to keep in mind about inter-SMSA comparison is that the DAWN data were not expressed in proportion to SMSA populations. Thus, while changes in numbers of mentions may reflect real changes in drug abuse episodes, they may also indicate system changes and problems.

DAWN III RESULTS

During the 13 month period, April 1974 through April 1975, 192,379 drug abuse episodes involving 266,880 drug mentions were reported from DAWN facilities.

Demographics

The individuals involved in DAWN reported drug abuse episodes are younger than the general population. The median ages of individuals contacting the various facility types, all facilities and the 1970 U.S. census are:

DAWN Emergency Rooms	26.9 years
DAWN Inpatient Units	26.5 years
DAWN Crisis Centers	21.9 years
DAWN Medical Examiners	29.8 years
Total DAWN System	25.4 years
1970 U.S. Census	28.3 years

In addition to the lower median ages reported for all facility types except medical examiners, DAWN contacts are concentrated in the 10–29 year age groups (ranging from 51% to 90%) compared to the U.S. census figure of 32% for those ages.

Whereas whites constitute 84% of the U.S. population and blacks 14%, the percentage of drug mentions by whites is 76% from the total DAWN system and by blacks 21%.

Male contacts outnumber female contacts in crisis centers and medical examiners offices whereas the reverse is true of emergency room contacts.

Motivation for Use

The major motivations are psychic effects, dependence and suicide attempt or gesture. One problem with interpretation of motivation data is the high unknown* rate for this information in emergency rooms (25%) and medical examiners' offices (32%). Motivation mentions vary considerably by drug; however, only an overview is presented here.

EMERGENCY ROOMS. In total, psychic effects and dependence mentions combined approximately equal suicide attempt/gesture. Whites account for a much higher percentage of suicide mentions than do blacks and other races. Between sexes, the female suicide percentage is more than double that of males. The highest percentage of dependence is found among blacks.

Psychic effects percentages decrease for older age groups. Suicide attempt/gesture percentages increase for older age groups. Dependence percentages decrease for older age groups.

CRISIS CENTERS. Psychic effects is the primary motivation among all race and sex groups. Dependence is reported as a motivation to a greater extent among blacks than for other races or between sexes. Suicide attempt/gesture is reported more frequently by females and whites. Psychic effects shares decrease for older age groups. Dependence shares are highest for the 30–39 year age group. Suicide attempt/gesture shares increase for older age groups.

MEDICAL EXAMINERS. Suicide attempt/gesture percentages are much higher for whites and females while dependence shares tend to concentrate in blacks and males. The percentages for psychic effects are higher for non-whites and for males.

Psychic effects shares are lower for older age groups. Dependence shares are highest in ages 20–39 years. Suicide attempt/gesture shares tend to be higher for older age groups.

Source of Substance

Source information was collected only from emergency rooms and crisis centers. For emergency room mentions, the most frequently reported source was legal prescription; from crisis centers, street buy.

EMERGENCY ROOMS. Considerable difference is seen in the pro-

---

*The unknown/no response answers are those for which the reporting facility was unable to obtain information. Either the patient did not know the answer or was reluctant to give the information.

portion of different prescription drugs obtained by legal prescription. Phenobarbital is reported to have been obtained by legal prescription to a greater extent than secobarbital or the secobarbital/amobarbital combination. Within the non-barbiturate sedative class, flurazepam was obtained by legal prescription in 63% of the mentions, whereas methaqualone was obtained by legal prescription in only 33%. Methaqualone was obtained by street buy in 10% of mentions, flurazepam in 1%.

The highest percentage of "gift" as a source is reported for LSD, marihuana, and hashish. Percentages reported for stolen, forged prescription, and other are generally negligible.

CRISIS CENTERS. Methaqualone, amphetamine, secobarbital, and secobarbital/amobarbital are prescription drugs for which the most frequently mentioned source is street buy. Speed is reported to have been obtained by legal prescription in a limited number of mentions.

Forged prescription admitted as a source of a substance is only 1% in total, but reaches 5–7% for secobarbital, chlordiazepoxide, and the secobarbital/amobarbital combination.

Gift is mentioned most frequently for marihuana and hashish (9% and 10%). The propoxyphenes are reported as stolen in 7% of cases compared to not more than 5% for other drugs reported by crisis centers.

LEADING DRUGS

Table 6 provides the rank, number of mentions and percentage of total mentions for 35 selected drugs by facility type. [Table 7 provides a ranking of the leading drugs of abuse in DAWN II and DAWN III surveys.] Because approximately two-thirds of all drug mentions are provided by emergency room reports, the all drug figures are significantly influenced by emergency room data.

The only substance which ranks among the top 10 in emergency room, but does not rank among the top 10 overall, is flurazepam (8th). In contrast, several drugs rank among the top 10 in crisis centers, but do not rank among the top 10 overall. They are speed (5th), amphetamine (6th), cocaine (9th), and methaqualone (10th). Three of these 4 drugs are stimulants which account for 15% of the crisis center mentions and only 2% of emergency room mentions. Other differences in ranking include:

1. The number one ranking for morphine as reported by medical examiners. This generally reflects the impact of heroin abuse. Heroin metabolizes in the human body and appears as morphine when

TABLE 6
SELECTED LEADING DRUGS OF ABUSE IN EACH FACILITY TYPE.
ALL FACILITIES COMBINED AND % SHARE OF MENTIONS

Total DAWN System
April 1974–April 1975
DAWN III

All Drugs	All Facilities			Emergency Rooms			Inpatient Units			Medical Examiners			Crisis Centers		
	Rank	# of Mentions 266,880	% of Total 100	Rank	# of Mentions 167,075	% of Total 100	Rank	# of Mentions 11,615	% of Total 100	Rank	# of Mentions 12,129	% of Total 100	Rank	# of Mentions 76,061	% of Total 100
Diazepam	1	27,271	10	1	23,046	14	3	1,036	9	6	461	4	7	2,728	4
Alcohol-in-Combination	2	21,602	8	2	15,133	9	4	694	6	2	1,622	13	4	4,153	5
Heroin	3	20,206	8	3	10,637	6	1	1,939	17	15	106	1	2	7,524	10
Marijuana	4	11,021	4	14	1,837	1	5	340	3	27	13	*	1	8,781	12
Aspirin	5	9,243	3	4	8,490	5	6	252	2	11	248	2	28	253	*
LSD	6	8,797	3	10	2,723	2	9	226	2	30	5	*	3	5,843	8
Secobarbital	7	7,030	3	7	3,911	2	7	238	2	4	630	5	8	2,251	3
d-Propoxyphene	8	6,040	2	6	4,304	3	10+	211	2	5	587	5	14	938	1
Chlordiazepoxide	9	5,812	2	5	4,627	3	10+	211	2	17	84	1	15	900	1
Methadone	10	5,634	2	9	2,954	2	2	1,073	9	3	1,065	9	18	542	1
Speed	11	4,699	2	24	835	*	20	100	1	32	2	*	5	3,762	5
Amphetamine	12	4,579	2	18	1,517	1	13	206	2	18	82	1	6	2,774	4
Flurazepam	13	4,221	2	8	3,473	2	15	161	1	20	57	*	19	530	1
Secobarbital/Amobarbital	14	4,053	2	11	2,651	2	8	236	2	14	128	1	13	1,038	1
Methaqualone	15	3,921	1	15	1,759	1	17	146	1	19	68	1	10	1,948	3
Phenobarbital	16	3,684	1	12	2,645	2	10+	211	2	8	355	3	20	472	1
Hashish	17	3,256	1	16	1,675	1	22	82	1	33	1	*	12	1,497	2
Cocaine	18	3,069	1	25	784	*	16	147	1	22	53	*	9	2,085	3
Pentobarbital	19	2,922	1	17	1,644	1	18+	120	1	7	423	3	17	735	1
Amitriptyline	20	2,912	1	13	2,194	1	14	196	2	10	272	2	29	250	*

TABLE 6 (cont.)
SELECTED LEADING DRUGS OF ABUSE IN EACH FACILITY TYPE.
ALL FACILITIES COMBINED AND % SHARE OF MENTIONS

Total DAWN System
April 1974—April 1975
DAWN III

All Drugs	All Facilities			Emergency Rooms			Inpatient Units			Medical Examiners			Crisis Centers		
	Rank	# of Mentions 266,880	% of Total 100	Rank	# of Mentions 167,075	% of Total 100	Rank	# of Mentions 11,615	% of Total 100	Rank	# of Mentions 12,129	% of Total 100	Rank	# of Mentions 76,061	% of Total 100
PCP	21	2,758	1	22	902	1	23	69	1	29	11	*	11	1,776	2
Morphine	22	2,099	1	34	173	*	31+	24	*	1	1,641	14	26	261	*
Meprobamate	23	2,083	1	19	1,477	1	18+	120	1	16	103	1	22	383	1
Codeine	24	1,617	1	21	1,022	1	25+	48	*	12	146	1	21	401	1
Glutethimide	25	1,570	1	20	1,083	1	21	100	1	13	131	1	27	256	*
Methamphetamine	26+	1,137	*	32	241	*	29	30	*	25	20	*	16	846	1
Pentazocine	26+	1,137	*	26	709	1	27	43	*	24	35	*	24	350	*
Clorazepate	28	1,125	*	23	879	1	30	27	*	28	12	*	31	207	*
Meperidine HCl	29	1,007	*	28	522	*	25+	48	*	21	56	*	23	381	1
Amobarbital	30	780	*	33	235	*	33	17	*	9	300	2	30	228	*
Oxazepam	31	737	*	27	564	*	31+	24	*	31	3	*	33	146	*
Methylphenidate	32	728	*	29	432	*	28	34	*	—	—	—	25	262	*
Hydromorphone	33	472	*	31	245	*	24	63	1	26	19	*	34	145	*
Butabarbital	34	403	*	30	297	*	34	12	*	23	41	*	35	53	*
PCP Combinations	35	175	*	35	26	*	—	—	—	—	—	—	32	149	*
Total—35 Drugs		(177,800)	(67)		(105,688)	(63)		(8,484)	(73)		(8,780)	(72)		(54,848)	(72)

*Less than 0.5%
+Denotes equal rank

toxicological laboratory examination is subsequently performed.
2. The high rankings among medical examiners for pentobarbital (7th), phenobarbital (8th), amobarbital (9th), and amitriptyline (10th).
3. The number two ranking of methadone within inpatient units.

TABLE 7
RANKING OF LEADING DRUGS OF ABUSE
DAWN II (July 1973–March 1974) and
DAWN III (April 1974–April 1975)

	DAWN III (N = 266,880)		DAWN II (N = 167,759)	
	Rank	% of Mentions	Rank	% of Mentions
Diazepam	1	10	1	8
Alcohol-in-Combination	2	8	2	7
Heroin	3	8	3	7
Marijuana	4	4	4	5
Aspirin	5	3	6	4
LSD	6	3	5	4
Secobarbital	7	3	7	3
d-Propoxyphene	8	2	12	2
Chlordiazepoxide	9	2	10	2
Methadone	10	2	9	2
Speed	11	2	11	2
Amphetamine	12	2	13	2
Flurazepam	13	2	19	1
Secobarbital/Amobarbital	14	2	15	2
Methaqualone	15	1	8	2
Phenobarbital	16	1	17	1
Hashish	17	1	14	2
Cocaine	18	1	18	1
Pentobarbital	19	1	16	1
Amitriptyline	20	1	22	1
PCP	21	1	21	1
Morphine	22	1	23	1
Meprobamate	23	1	26	1
Codeine	24	1	32	1
Glutethimide	25	1	31	1

NOTE

[1]National Institute on Drug Abuse, *Summary Excerpts, DAWN III Report* (Washington, D.C.: GPO, July 8, 1976), pp. 1–11.

Appendix C
EMERGENCY MEDICAL TREATMENT TECHNIQUES

Drug overdoses present serious problems. Because law enforcement officers are often the first to arrive at the scene of a crisis, it is vital that they know how to render the correct emergency medical aid. Their actions may spell the difference between life and death for the victim.

The treatment techniques that are given in this section are emergency measures. They are not designed in any way to take the place of or substitute for professional medical assistance. Rather, they are intended to keep the victim alive until he or she can receive the proper medical attention. With that thought in mind, it is vital to emphasize two key rules to follow when dealing with drug overdoses:

1. Do not overestimate your own capabilities. A drug overdose is a complex medical phenomenon, and as such it requires professional medical treatment.
2. Get medical assistance as soon as possible. Any delay in getting medical assistance to the victim may have grave medical consequences.

Drug-related emergencies are not all the same. Some are far more serious and difficult to deal with than others. In the following sections, the symptoms associated with the treatment for overdoses of the more commonly encountered drugs are explained. In addition, step-by-step instructions are given for ways in which to administer artifical respiration.

HEROIN AND SIMILAR NARCOTICS

Medical emergencies involving heroin and related narcotic drugs are comparatively common. The exact cause of the phenomenon known popularly as a heroin overdose is not completely understood. However, experience has shown that the lifesaving steps outlined below can greatly increase the victim's chance of survival.

Symptoms

One or more of the following symptoms is usually associated with heroin overdoses:

Constricted pupils (except in the case of meperidine)

Needle marks, scars (tracks), or abcesses

Depressed breathing

Unconsciousness, coma

Profuse sweating

Convulsions (especially in cases involving codeine, Demerol analgesic, and apomorphine)

Cold, clammy skin

Muscle relaxation

Treatment

Take the following steps if you suspect a narcotic overdose:

1. Try to arouse the victim. One of the best ways to do this is to lightly slap the victim with a cold, wet towel. If possible get the victim on his or her feet.
2. Keep the victim's airway clear. Administer artificial respiration if needed. (See Mouth-to-Mouth Resuscitation.)
3. Keep the victim warm.
4. Do not treat the victim roughly.
5. Reassure the victim.
6. Get medical assistance as soon as possible.
7. If possible, take a sample of the drug with you to the hospital.

STIMULANTS

Stimulants include amphetamine, dextroamphetamine, methamphetamine, cocaine, and similar drugs.

Stimulant abuse is widespread in this country. It ranges in severity from occasional pill popping by students before examinations to the repeated intravenous abuse that characterizes today's speed freak.

Symptoms

Symptoms increase in severity as the dosage increases. They include:

Hyperactive behavior

Restlessness

Talkativeness

Feelings of extreme elation

Compulsive repetitive behavior

Confusion

Rapid changes in mood

Suspiciousness

Fear that can become panic

Paranoid delusions that can result in seriously antisocial behavior

Fever

Convulsions and coma

Treatment

The emergency treatment of stimulant abuse is largely supportive. Specific procedures include:

1. Maintain an open airway. Administer artificial respiration if the victim stops breathing. (See Mouth-to-Mouth Resuscitation.)
2. Protect the victim against self-injury and prevent injury to others.
3. Keep the victim warm.
4. Try to quiet the victim by talking to him or her in a calm, reassuring manner.
5. Seek medical assistance at once.
6. If possible, take a sample of the drug with you to the hospital.

DEPRESSANTS AND TRANQUILIZERS

Some of the more commonly encountered of these drugs are the barbiturates, glutethimide, chloral hydrate, and such minor tranquilizers as meprobamate (Miltown, Equanil), chlordiazepoxide (Librium), and diazepam (Valium). The abuse of these drugs is widespread. It is also extremely dangerous. They are also frequently used as a means of committing suicide.

The effects of many of these drugs are greatly potentiated by alcohol. A normal dose of barbiturates can prove fatal if taken in conjunction with even moderate amounts of alcohol. In addition, the abrupt withdrawal from barbiturates is extremely dangerous and can, under some circumstances, prove fatal.

Symptoms

Some of the more common symptoms associated with depressant overdoses include:

Disorientation

Staggering and stumbling

Slow, shallow respiration

Constricted pupils (Dilation may occur later. Dilation is also characteristic of glutethimide poisoning.)

Depressed circulation

Unconciousness, coma

Treatment

Take the following steps if you suspect some form of depressant overdose:

1. Keep the victim's airway open. Administer artificial respiration if needed. (See Mouth-to-Mouth Resuscitation.)
2. Try to arouse the victim. One of the best ways to do this is to lightly slap the victim with a cold, wet towel. If possible get the victim on his or her feet and walking.
3. Keep the victim warm.
4. Get medical assistance as soon as possible.
5. If possible, take a sample of the drug with you to the hospital.

HALLUCINOGENS

These include LSD, STP, MDA, mescaline, and similar drugs. A number of hallucinogenic drugs are currently popular. All of them are capable of producing bizarre changes in the way in which victims sense their surroundings. In some cases they can also trigger violent mood changes and panic.

Symptoms

Hallucinogen abusers may exhibit one or more of the following symptoms:

Dilated pupils

Flushed face

Rapid changes in mood

Blurred vision

Distortion of the sensory impressions

Panic

Hallucinations

Treatment

Treatment of an overdose of hallucinogens is for the most part supportive. Specific steps include:

1. Talk the victim down in a calm, reassuring manner.
2. Protect the victim from self-injury and from injuring others.
3. Get medical assistance as soon as possible.
4. If possible, take a sample of the drug with you to the hospital.

MARIJUANA, HASHISH, AND SIMILAR DRUGS

It is rare that marijuana and similar drugs precipitate medical emergencies. However, it is becoming increasingly popular to "doctor" them with such hallucinogens as LSD, STP, and PCP. The resulting "killer weed" can cause serious medical complications.

Symptoms

Some of the signs that may be associated with the abuse of marijuana include:

Reddening of the eyes
Intoxicated or disturbed behavior
The odor of burning rope

Treatment

There is no specific emergency medical treatment for marijuana abuse.

In instances where psychotic reactions occur, the approach is the same as that used in treating hallucinogen abusers.

INHALANTS

These include glue, cleaning fluids, nitrous oxide, ether, and similar substances.

At the present time glue sniffing and other forms of inhalant abuse are quite popular. Because of the ever-present danger of suffocation, these practices are a clear menace to health.

Symptoms

Some of the more common signs of inhalant abuse include:

Drunken behavior such as slurred speech and staggering

A strong chemical odor on the victim's breath and/or clothing

Lethargic behavior

Unconciousness or coma

Paraphernalia such as glue tubes, solvent bottles, and paper or plastic bags.

Treatment

Emergency treatment includes:

1. Clear the victim's airway. If the victim is found with a bag or some other device over his or her head, remove it at once.
2. Provide artificial respiration at once if breathing stops.
3. Get medical assistance at once.
4. If possible, take a sample of the drug with you to the hospital.

MOUTH-TO-MOUTH RESUSCITATION

In terms of emergency care, one of the most serious consequences that can result from a drug overdose is that the victim stops breathing. When this happens artificial respiration must be administered at once. The mouth-to-mouth method has been shown to be the most effective way of doing this.

Mouth-to-mouth resuscitation is easy to administer. The steps involved are:

1. Lay the victim on his or her back.
2. Clear any foreign material that may be present in the victim's mouth.
3. Place one hand under the victim's forehead and the other under the neck. Then tilt the head back so as to open the airway (Figure C-1).

FIGURE C-1
Positioning the victim's head to open the airway.

FIGURE C-2
Pinching the victim's nostrils together
with thumb and index finger.

    (This step helps to open the airway by moving the victim's tongue away from the back of the throat.)

4. Now check to see if the victim is breathing. Look at the victim's chest and abdomen to see if they are rising and falling. Listen and feel for exhaling air. If there is no evidence of respiration, begin mouth-to-mouth resuscitation by going on to step 5.
5. Continue to exert pressure on the victim's forehead and, with the same hand, pinch the victim's nostrils together with your thumb and index finger (Figure C-2).
6. Take a deep breath, make a tight seal with your mouth, and blow into the victim's mouth (Figure C-3).

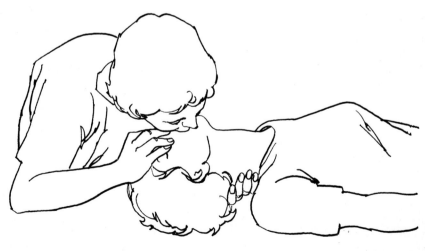

FIGURE C-3
Administering the first breath to the victim.

FIGURE C-4
Allowing the victim to exhale.

7. Remove your mouth and let the victim exhale (Figure C-4). *Note:* When you first begin mouth-to-mouth resuscitation, you should use four quick full breaths without allowing time for the full deflation of the victim's lungs between breaks.
8. Begin the cycle again. It should be repeated every 5 seconds until either *(a)* medical assistance arrives, or *(b)* the victim begins to breath again.

Though the procedure used in the mouth-to-mouth resuscitation of infants and small children is the same in many respects as that used with adults, there are some differences:

FIGURE C-5
Mouth-to-mouth resuscitation of infants.

Cover the child's mouth and nose with your mouth (Figure C-5).

Use small breaths with less volume and inflate the child's lungs every 30 seconds.

Tilting a small child's head too far back may obstruct his or her airway. Therefore you should not make the tilt too extreme. It sometimes helps to place your hand under the child's shoulders.

GLOSSARY

A   Amphetamine.

A-bomb   A mixture of marijuana and cocaine.

abscess   An infection that is a localized collection of pus with inflamed tissue around it; can be caused by injection of impure drugs or barbiturates subcutaneously.

abstinence syndrome   A state of altered behavior observed following cessation of drug administration.

abuse   To use wrongly or improperly; to misuse.

acapulco gold   High-grade marijuana (derived from the flowering parts of the female *Cannabis* plant).

acetylcholine (ACh)   A neurotransmitter in the central and peripheral nervous systems.

acid   LSD, LSD-25 (lysergic acid diethylamide).

acid head   Frequent user of LSD.

addiction   A condition resulting from repeated use of a drug in which physical dependence is established because of biochemical and physiological adaptations to the drug.

addictive effect   An increased effect observed when two drugs having similar biological actions are administered. The net effect is the sum of the independent effects exerted by each drug.

alcohol   Ethyl alcohol, ethanol—a widely used sedative-hypnotic drug.

alcohol dehydrogenase   An enzyme that carries out a specific step in alcohol metabolism of acetaldhyde to acetate. This enzyme may be blocked by the drug disulfiram (Antabuse).

alfalfa   Marijuana.

amine   A basic compound derived from ammonia by replacing one or more atoms of hydrogen.

amino   A prefix indicating the presence in a compound of the group NH_2.

amnesia   Loss of memory or loss of a large block of interrelated memories.

amphetamine   A central nervous system stimulant.

analgesic   A chemical or drug that has the ability to relieve pain.

anesthetic   A chemical, substance, or agent that produces loss of feeling or sensation.

angel dust   Phencyclidine (PCP), a hallucinogenic drug.

antagonists   Opposing or counteracting drugs or medicines.

antianxiety agent   A sedative-hypnotic compound used in subhypnotic doses.

antidepressant A drug that counteracts the feelings of depression (absence of cheerfulness or hope), with reduction of the functional activity of the body.

antiemetic A drug, medicine, or substance that prevents vomiting or relieves nausea.

antipsychotic drugs Psychoactive drugs that have the ability to calm psychotic states and make the psychotic patient more manageable.

artillery Equipment for injecting drugs.

ascending reticular activating system (ARAS) An area of neurons located in the brain stem and thought to function in arousal mechanisms.

autonomic nervous system The part of the nervous system that controls involuntary action, made up of the sympathetic and parasympathetic nervous systems.

babo Morphine-related substance used to treat narcotic poisoning from heroin, methadone, or morphine. It is called "babo" since it takes the user to the "cleaner."

baby Small habit.

backtrack To withdraw the plunger of a syringe before injecting drugs to make sure needle is in proper position.

bad trip A panic reaction while under the influence of drugs.

bag A packet of drugs.

bagman A drug supplier.

ball Absorption of stimulants and cocaine via genitalia.

bam A mixture of stimulants and depressants.

bang To inject drugs.

banger A hypodermic needle.

barbecue A fatal drug dose.

barbiturate A central nervous system depressant.

barbs Barbiturates.

bean Benzedrine stimulant.

beast LSD.

beat Swindle someone out of narcotics or money.

been had Been arrested or cheated out of something.

bent High from a hallucinogen or narcotic; also perverted.

benny Benzedrine stimulant.

Benzedrine Trademark for a specific amphetamine.

benzodiazephine A class of chemically related sedative-hypnotic agents of which chlordiazepoxide (trademark Librium) and diazepam (trademark Valium) are examples.

bernice Cocaine.

bhang Marijuana.

big D   LSD.
Big John   Police.
big O   Opium.
bindle   A packet of narcotics.
biochemical   Pertaining to the chemistry of living matter.
biz   Equipment for injecting drugs.
black   Opium.
black and white   A patrol car.
black beauty or **black bomber**   Benzedrine stimulant.
blackout   Temporary loss of consciousness. When used in reference to
    alcoholism, a period of temporary dulling or loss of memory, vi-
    sion, or consciousness occurring while drinking.
black stuff   Opium.
blank   Extremely low-grade narcotics.
blanks   Capsules of nonnarcotic powder used to deceive an addict.
blast   Strong effect from a drug.
blasted   Under the influence of drugs.
block   An ounce of hashish.
blow   To smoke a marijuana cigarette.
blow it   To lose one's self-control (cool).
blow lunch   To vomit.
blow pot   To smoke marijuana.
blow your cool   To lose self-control.
blue angel, blue devil, or **blue heaven**   Amytal sedative, a barbiturate.
blue bird   Sodium Amytal, a barbiturate.
blue   Numorphan analgesic; also, paying one's dues.
blue velvet   A paregoric and an antihistamine.
bomber   Benzedrine stimulant.
bombido   Injectable amphetamine.
bombita   An amphetamine injection, sometimes taken with heroin.
boo   Marijuana.
boost   To steal.
boost and shoot   To steal in order to support a narcotic habit.
boxed   Jailed.
boy   Heroin.
bozo   A completely uncouth, bumbling individual, worse than a dil-
    do; also a swindle artist.
bread   Money.
brick   A kilogram of marijuana.
bring down   To depress.
brown   Benzedrine stimulant.
brown shoes   Name for squares.

brown stuff Opium.

bud Marijuana cluster.

bufotenine A psychoactive drug obtained from the mushroom *Amanita muscaria*.

bull A federal narcotics agent.

bullet A capsule.

bummer A bad experience with psychedelic drugs.

bum trip A bad experience with psychedelic drugs.

bundle A packet of narcotics.

bunk Bad dope of any kind; anything misrepresented.

burn To swindle someone out of narcotics or money.

burned Having obtained badly diluted or nonactive drugs.

burned out Having the sclerotic condition of the vein present in most conditioned addicts.

business Equipment for injecting drug.

businessman's special Dimethyltryptamine (DMT).

bust An arrest.

busted Arrested.

buttons The dried tops of the peyote cactus.

buy The purchase of a drug.

buzz on To feel good.

C Cocaine.

caffeine A behavioral and general cellular stimulant found in coffee, tea, cola drinks, and chocolate.

candy Barbiturate.

California sunshine LSD.

can A container of marijuana; term derived from the Prince Albert tobacco can in which marijuana was commonly sold in the past.

Cannabis Marijuana; the hemp plant genus that is the source of marijuana.

cap A capsule.

cap-up To put drugs into capsules.

cardiovascular Pertaining to the heart and blood vessels.

carry in To carry narcotics on the person.

cartwheels Amphetamine tablets.

cat Fellow; also, heroin.

cent A unit of money; one cent equals one dollar.

charged up Under the influence of drugs.

champ Drug abuser who will not reveal his or her supplier.

chemotherapy Treatment of disease by the administration of chemicals, medicines, or drugs.

chief LSD.

chipping Taking narcotics occasionally.

chippy Drug abuser taking small, irregular amounts.

chiva Latino term for heroin.

chloral Chloral hydrate, a hypnotic drug.

chlordiazepoxide hydrochloride A benzodiazephine, a sedative-hypnotic drug (trademark Librium).

chlorpromazine A phenothiazine, an antipsychotic drug (trademark Thorazine).

Christmas trees Dexamyl appetite suppressants in Spansule sustained release capsules, which contain a mixture of dextroamphetamine sulfate and amobarbital.

chronic Continuing for a long time; more specifically, used to describe condition of body or disease that is of long duration.

chuck To eat excessively, especially candy, after recovery from withdrawal.

chump An idiot or punk.

Cibas Doriden, trademark for glutethimide, a sedative-hypnotic drug with high potential for abuse.

cirrhosis Disease of the liver involving progressive destruction of liver cells, accompanied by excessive increase in connective tissue, resulting in contraction of the organ.

clean To remove stems and seeds from marijuana; also to be free from incriminating evidence of drug use.

clean up To withdraw from drugs.

clomiphene An ovulation-inducing agent thought to act by blocking the inhibitory effect that estrogens exert on the hypothalamus (trademark Clomid).

coast To become drowsy while on heroin; also to lie back or take it easy—not necessarily while high.

coasting Under the influence of drugs.

cocaine A behavioral stimulant derived from coca leaves.

cocktail A regular cigarette with marijuana inserted into the end which is to be lit.

codeine An analgesic, hypnotic, sedative drug derived from opium, classified as a narcotic.

coke Cocaine.

coke freak or **coke head** A habitual user of cocaine.

coke time Ready for a snort.

cokie A habitual user of cocaine.

cold Tough deal, as cold-hearted.

cold-shake or **cold-cook** To prepare drugs for injection, usually pills that are hard to dissolve without the use of heat.

cold shot   A bad drug deal.

cold turkey   Sudden withdrawal from drugs.

collar   A piece of paper wrapped around the end of an eyedropper to make the needle fit tighter into the makeshift hypodermic needle apparatus.

coma   Abnormal, deep stupor or sleep.

comatose   In a coma.

comedown   Recovery from a trip.

conditioned reflex   Learned response to a specific stimulus that has been repeated until it appears automatic.

connect   To buy drugs.

connection   A drug supplier.

contact high   A high achieved merely by interacting with one who is high.

convulsions   Contortions of the body caused by violent involuntary muscular contractions.

cook   To heat a solution of heroin; also an underground chemist.

cook up   To mix heroin with water and heat for an injection.

cook up a pill   To prepare opium for smoking.

cooker   Small pan, spoon, or other handy container used to heat a drug for injection.

cookie   A habitual user of cocaine.

cop   To obtain drugs.

copilots   Amphetamine tablets.

cop out   To quit, take off; to confess, defect, inform.

Corine   Cocaine.

cotics   Narcotics.

cotton   A piece of cotton used to strain a drug before shooting it, sometimes saved for later or for someone else.

cotton fever   Chills and fever resulting from using impure or poor quality cotton to strain drug. The fever could be septicemia if cotton was contaminated with bacteria.

crack   Methamphetamine.

crackers   LSD, in Boston.

cracking shorts   Breaking into automobiles.

crank   Methamphetamine.

crap   Highly diluted heroin.

crash   The effects of stopping the use of drugs.

crash pad   The place where the user withdraws from amphetamines.

crib   The apartment where one lives; also the place where addicts go to inject themselves (shooting gallery).

croaker A doctor.

cross-dependence A condition in which one drug can prevent the withdrawal symptoms associated with physical dependence on a different drug.

crossroads Amphetamines.

cross-tolerance A condition in which tolerance of one drug results in a lessened response to another drug.

crutch A holder (matchbook, tweezers, hairpin) for marijuana.

crystal Methamphetamine, speed.

cube A cube of morphine or LSD.

cube head A frequent user of LSD.

cut To adulterate narcotics.

dabble To take small amounts of drugs on an irregular basis.

deal A narcotic transaction; also to be a drug supplier.

dealer A drug supplier.

deck A packet of narcotics.

deeda LSD, in Harlem.

delirium tremens (DTs) Psychic disorder involving visual and auditory hallucinations, delusions, incoherence, anxiety, and trembling found in habitual (addicted) users of alcoholic beverages and some other drugs.

denature To change the nature of a substance. In reference to alcohol, to make it unfit for human consumption without affecting its usefulness for other purposes.

depersonalization Loss of the sense of personal identity or of personal ownership of the parts of one's body.

depressant A chemical, substance, or agent that has the ability to reduce the functional activity of the body.

depression A state of sadness, marked by inactivity and inability to concentrate; reduction of the functional activity of the body.

desoxyn Trademark for methamphetamine tablets.

DET Diethyltryptamine.

Dexedrine Trademark for dextroamphetamine, a stimulant.

Dexies Dexedrine, appetite suppressants, which are amphetamines.

DFP Diisopropyl fluorophosphate.

diazepam A benzodiazepine derivative, an antianxiety drug (trademark Valium).

dicarbamate A class of chemically related sedative-hypnotic agents of which meprobamate (Equanil, Miltown) is an example.

diethylstilbestrol A synthetically produced estrogen occasionally used in high doses as a postcoital contraceptive.

diethyltryptamine (DET)   A hallucinogenic drug found in many South American snuffs.

diisopropyl fluorophosphate (DFP)   An irreversible acetylcholine-sterase (AChE) inhibitor.

dildo   An idiot; sometimes a term of affection.

dilly   Dilaudid, trademark for hydromorphone, a sedative and analgesic.

dime   Ten dollars.

dime bag   Ten-dollar package of narcotics.

dimethyltryptamine (DMT)   A psychedelic drug found in many South American snuffs, such as yopo (prepared from the beans of the tree *Piptadenia peregrina*); known as the businessman's special.

dirty   Possessing drugs, liable to arrest if searched.

disinhibition   A physiologic state within the central nervous system characterized by decreased activity of inhibitory synapses, which results in a net excess of excitatory activity.

disorganization   A state of impaired and inefficient emotional organization resulting from a person's inability to cope with internal conflicts and external reality.

distillation   The process of vaporizing a liquid and then condensing the products of vaporization into a liquid in order to purify or abstract a specific substance from the original liquid.

DMT   Dimethyltryptamine; also called the businessman's special.

dollies   Dolophine, trademark for methadone.

dolls   Barbiturates.

DOM   4-Methyl-2, 5-dimethoxyamphetamine, a hallucinogenic drug; also known as STP.

domino   To purchase drugs.

doojee   Heroin.

doomed   Under the influence of a drug.

doo-wah-diddy   If you don't know by now, don't mess with it.

dope   Any narcotic.

doper   An addict.

double blue   Amphetamine and barbiturates.

double trouble   Tuinal, trademark for a hypnotic barbiturate.

doup   To smoke a joint; to take an injection of heroin.

down habit   Extreme addiction.

downers   Sedatives, tranquilizers, narcotics, and alcohol.

downs   Depressants—barbiturates or tranquilizers.

drag   To smoke marijuana.

dreamer   Morphine.

dried out   To be withdrawn or detoxified from a drug.

dripper   A dropper.

drivers   Amphetamines.

drop   To swallow a drug.

drop a dime   To inform.

dropped   Arrested.

dropper   Usually a medicine dropper for administering heroin or other drugs into the skin or vein.

drug   Any chemical substance used for its effects on bodily processes.

drug dependence   Condition resulting from repeated use of a drug in which an individual must continue to take a drug to avoid abstinence syndrome (physical dependence) or to satisfy strong emotional need.

drug interaction   The modification of the action of one drug by the concurrent or prior administration of another drug.

drug misuse   The use of any drug (legal or illegal) for a medical or recreational purpose when other alternatives are available, practical, or warranted, or when drug use endangers either the user or others with whom the user may interact.

drug receptor   The specific molecular substance in the body with which a given drug interacts in order to produce its effect.

drug tolerance   A state of progressively decreased responsiveness to a drug.

dry   Having no dope available.

DTs   Delirium tremens.

dubbe   A butt of marijuana.

duck   An easy person to hustle.

dues   Learning, through experience, the price one has to pay.

dummy   A purchase that did not contain narcotics.

dust   Cocaine.

dynamite   High-grade heroin.

ego   According to Freudian theory, the one of the three major divisions of the psychic apparatus that consciously acts as mediator for the impulses of the id, the prohibitions of the superego, and the demands of reality.

egocentric   Regarding one's self as the center of all things.

eighth   An eighth of an ounce of heroin (two spoonfuls).

electrophysiological   Pertaining to the electrical reactions of the body.

endocrine   Any of the glands of internal secretion that produce hormones; also the secretion produced by any of these glands.

enzyme induction   The increased production of drug-metabolizing enzymes in the liver stimulated by certain drugs such that use of these drugs increases the rate at which the body can metabolize them.

epinephrine Monoamine hormone secreted by the adrenal medulla, responsible for transmission of nerve impulses to organs of the sympathetic nervous system.

estrogen A body hormone secreted primarily from the ovaries of females in response to stimulation by a follicle-stimulating hormone (FSH) from the pituitary gland.

euphoria A feeling of well-being; in psychiatry, an abnormal or exaggerated sense of well-being.

explorers club A group of acid heads (LSD users).

factory The equipment for injecting drugs.

fall To be arrested.

Fed Federal narcotic agent.

felony An offense punishable by death or imprisonment for more than a year.

fine stuff Narcotic of unusually good quality, only slightly adulterated.

fink An informer; a phony.

fish An easy person to hustle, a duck.

fit Equipment used for injecting drugs.

five-dollar bag A packet of heroin sold for $50.

fix An injection of a narcotic.

flake Cocaine.

flaked out Unconscious.

flash The initial pleasurable feeling after injection of a drug.

flea powder Poor-quality narcotic.

flip To become psychotic.

flip out To exhibit irrational behavior as a result of drug usage or as a result of any trauma or heavy trip.

floating Under the influence of drugs.

flying High on a drug, relating only to positive energy.

football An amphetamine.

forwards Amphetamines.

fours Codeine pills with a number 4 on them.

frantic Nervous, jittery state; in need of a fix.

freak A person who is dependent on a drug; hippie dope smoker; a nonconformist; a peer; sexual pervert.

freak out To have a bad trip.

freeze Numbness of gums and nasal passages due to cocaine; just enough coke to freeze your gums; a situation where no dope is available.

fresh and sweet   Out of jail.

front money   Advance payment.

fuzz   The police.

gage   Marijuana.

ganja   Dried leaves of the finest female marijuana plants, used for smoking primarily.

garbage   Highly diluted heroin, generally a bad batch.

gasing   Sniffing gasoline fumes.

gastritis   Inflammation of the stomach.

gatekeeper   One who initiates another into the use of LSD.

gauge   Marijuana

gee head   A paregoric abuser.

geetis   Money.

geeze   To shoot a drug.

geezer   A narcotic injection.

get down   To shoot dope or express yourself; to get off on your main trip.

ghoar (the)   LSD.

gimmicks   Equipment for injecting drugs.

girl   Cocaine.

glad rag   A piece of cloth saturated with glue or gasoline, usually a sock; also known as wad.

gluey   Glue sniffer.

go in   To put one's money with someone else's money in order to obtain drugs.

gold dust   Cocaine.

good H   Heroin of good quality, approximately 50 percent pure.

goods   Narcotics.

good trip   A happy experience with psychedelic drugs.

goofballs   Barbiturates.

goofed up   Under the influence of drugs.

goofer   One who swallows pills.

goofing   Under the influence of a barbiturate or just hanging out.

gow head   An opium addict.

gram   A gram of heroin, approximately 10 capsules; 0.035 ounce.

grass   Marijuana.

grasshopper   A marijuana user.

gratification   Source of pleasure or satisfaction.

greasy junky   An addict who relies on others for getting drugs.

greeny   Dextroamphetamine sulphate with amobarbital.

griefo   Marijuana.

grooving   Becoming high on a drug; having a good time.

ground control   The caretaker in an LSD session.

guide An experienced LSD user who supervises others while they are on a trip (rarely used, almost obsolete term).

gun A hypodermic needle.

guru A companion on a trip who has tripped before.

gutter junkie An addict who relies on others for getting drugs.

H Heroin.

habit Addiction to drugs.

habituation Condition resulting from repeated use of a drug in which a psychic, not a physical, dependence is established.

half-load A packet of a narcotic.

hallucination Perception of objects or experience of sensations with no real external cause.

hallucinogen A chemical, substance, or agent capable of producing distortions of the senses that may include hallucinations.

Haloperidol An antipsychotic drug chemically classified as a butyrophenone (trademark Haldol).

hand-to-hand The direct delivery of a narcotic person to person.

hang tough Encouragement to an addict to "keep it together."

hang-up A personal problem.

hard drugs Narcotics—heroin, opium derivations, or cocaine.

hard stuff Heroin.

harmine A psychedelic agent obtained from the seeds of *Peganum harmala*.

Harry Heroin.

hash Hashish.

hashish An extract of the hemp plant (*Cannabis sativa*).

Hawaiian sunshine LSD.

hawk (the) LSD.

hay Marijuana.

head A person dependent on drugs.

hearts Amphetamines; trademark Dexamyl.

heat The police.

hedonistic Pertaining to pleasure.

heeled Possessing narcotics or a weapon.

hemp Marijuana.

hep Understand; being a part of the current scene.

her Cocaine.

heroin A semisynthetic opiate produced by a chemical modification of morphine.

high Under the influence of drugs.

him Heroin.

hip Understand; being a part of the current scene.

hippie or **hippy**   A person who rejects the establishment's standards of ethics, dress, etc. and who often is a drug user; a beatnik.

hit   A puff of a marijuana cigarette; a direct injection in a vein assuring proper injection of a drug; to steal; to adulterate a narcotic.

hocus   A narcotic solution ready for injection; also morphine.

hog   An addict who uses all the drugs that he or she can obtain.

holding   Possessing narcotics.

hooked   Addicted.

hop head   An addict.

hopped up   Under the influence of drugs.

horning   Sniffing narcotics through the nose.

horse   Heroin.

hot   Wanted by the police.

hot load   An overdose, may result in death.

hot shot   A fatal drug dose.

hustle   An activity involved in obtaining money to buy heroin.

hustler   A prostitute.

hustling   Making money to buy drugs, often by theft.

hydrocarbon   Class of chemical compounds containing only hydrogen and carbon.

hype   A narcotic addict.

hyperalert   Abnormally and excessively watchful of activities around oneself.

hypnotic   A drug that acts to induce sleep.

ice cream habit   A small, irregular drug habit.

id   According to Freudian theory, the one of the three main divisions of the psychic apparatus that harbors the unconscious instinctive desires and striving of the person.

idiot pills   Barbiturates.

intoxication   Literally, a state of being poisoned or drugged; a condition produced by excessive use (abuse) of toxic drugs, alcohol, barbiturates, and so forth.

intracellular   Within a cell or cells.

intravenous   Entering into the body by way of a vein.

irritability   Quick anger, excitability; unusual excitability of a body part; ability to respond to stimuli.

J   A joint; a marijuana cigarette.

jacked up   Interrogated or arrested.

jacks   Heroin tablets.

jaundice   A liver disease that makes the skin (and even the eyes) yellowish in color.

jay   Marijuana cigarette.

Jim Johnson   Equipment used to prepare and inject a drug.

jive   Bad quality of anything; phoniness.

jive stick   Marijuana cigarette.

job   To inject drugs.

joint   Marijuana cigarette.

jolly beans   Pep pills.

jolt   An injection of a narcotic.

jones   A habit.

joy dust   Vietnamese heroin.

joy pop   Occasional injection.

joy powder   Heroin.

junk   Heroin.

junkie   A narcotic addict.

kee   A weight measure of 2.2 pounds (1 kilogram).

kef   Marijuana.

ketamine   A psychedelic surgical anesthetic; trademark Ketalar.

key   A kilogram (2.2 pounds) of a drug.

kick   To abandon a habit.

kick back   To relax with no hassles.

kick the habit   To stop using narcotics.

kilo   Kilogram (2.2 pounds).

king kong   An excessive drug habit (over $200 per day).

kit   A narcotic paraphernalia set.

L   LSD.

lactose   Sugar found in milk.

lady snow   Cocaine.

laid back   Feeling good about time, place, and situation.

lame   A dumb or stupid move.

latency   Period of time between the administration of a drug and the beginning of response.

layout   Equipment for injecting drugs.

leapers   Stimulants; amphetamines.

legal stuff   All narcotics that may be legally purchased.

lemonade   Poor heroin.

length of action   Period of time when a drug is effective.

leukopenia   Reduction of the number of white blood cells (leukocytes) in the blood.

lid   One ounce of marijuana.

lid poppers   Amphetamines.

lift   To steal (Rx pads, doctors' bags, anything.)

lift a script   To change the number on a prescription; for example, in "10 Desoxyn tablets," to change the figure 10 to 20 so that it would read "20 Desoxyn tablets."

line Line of snortable dope; usually cocaine on a shiny surface such as a mirror.

Lipton tea Poor-quality narcotic.

lithium An alkalai metal effective in the treatment of mania and depression.

lit up Under the influence of drugs.

load Stock of illegal drugs.

loaded Full of drugs.

locoweed Marijuana.

looking In the market for heroin.

LSD Lysergic acid diethylamide; a semisynthetic psychedelic drug.

lude Methaqualone.

luding out Using methaqualone plus wine (or other alcohol-containing beverage).

lysergic acid diethylamide (LSD) A semisynthetic psychedelic drug.

M Morphine.

machinery Equipment for injecting drugs.

magic mushrooms The hallucinogenic drugs psilocybin and psilocin.

mainline To inject drugs directly into a vein.

mainliner An addict who injects directly into the vein.

maintaining Keeping at a certain level of drug effect.

major tranquilizer (antipsychotic tranquilizer) A drug used in the treatment of psychotic states.

make a buy To obtain or purchase drugs.

malnutrition The lack of proper nutrition; the lack of adequate food or proper food.

Man (the) The police.

mania A phase of mental disorder characterized by an expansive emotional state, elation, hyperirritability, overtalkativeness, flight of ideas, and increased motor activity.

manicure To remove the dirt, seeds, and stems from marijuana.

MAO inhibitor A drug that inhibits the activity of the enzyme monoamine oxidase.

marijuana or marihuana A wild tobacco; a drug that is a mixture of both male and female individuals of the hemp plant (*Cannabis sativa*); also the name of the hemp plant that is the drug's source.

marijuana cigarette Joint, reefer, roach.

marijuana terms A kilogram of pot, lid of grass, manicured tea, toke up, and weed head.

Mary Jane Marijuana.

matchbox Small container of marijuana.

MDA Methylenedioxyamphetamine.

medicinal Having healing qualities.

meet   To buy drugs.

mellow   Happy; relaxed.

melter   Morphine.

meperidine   A synthetically produced opiate narcotic; (trademark Demerol).

meprobamate   A sedative-hypnotic agent frequently used as an anti-anxiety drug; (trademark Equanil).

mesc   Mescaline.

mescaline   A psychedelic drug extracted from the peyote cactus.

metabolite   Any substance produced by metabolism (the living functions of the cells and the body).

meth   Methamphetamine.

methadone   A synthetically produced opiate narcotic; (trademark Dolophine).

methamphetamine   An amphetamine used medically in weight reduction and as a stimulant.

methaqualone   A sedative-hypnotic compound of relatively low potency.

Methedrine   Trademark for methamphetamine, a stimulant.

meth head   Habitual user of methamphetamine.

methylenedioamphetamine (MDA)   A hallucinogenic drug.

methylphenidate   A CNS stimulant chemically and pharmacologically related to amphetamine; trademark Ritalin.

Mexican mud   Heroin imported from Mexico.

mezz   Marijuana.

Micky Finn   Chloral hydrate.

mike   A microgram of LSD.

minibennies   Small tablets of amphetamines.

minor tranquilizer   Any sedative-hypnotic drug promoted primarily for use in the treatment of anxiety.

misdemeanor   A criminal offense defined as less serious than a felony; usually punishable by less than one year in jail.

Miss Emma   Morphine.

mojo   Narcotics.

monkey   A drug habit where physical dependence is present; also morphine.

monoamine oxidase (MAO)   An enzyme capable of metabolizing norepinephrine, dopamine, and serotonin to inactive products.

mor a grifa   Marijuana.

morf   Morphine.

morphine   Widely used analgesic and sedative; classified as an opiate narcotic.

mota   Marijuana.

motor   In physiology, pertaining to a movement of a muscle or nerve that affects or produces movement in the body.

Mr. Man   Bozo with badge.

mucous membrane   The membrane that secretes the viscous fluid called mucus; the internal linings of the body.

mule   A person who transports narcotics, not necessarily a peddler.

muscarine   A drug extracted from the mushroom *Amanita muscaria* that directly stimulates acetylcholine receptors.

mushrooms   Psilocybin mushrooms.

mutah   Marijuana.

mutha or **mother**   A seller of drugs; anybody dangerous.

myristicin   A psychedelic agent obtained from nutmeg and mace.

narc   Narcotics officer.

narco   Narcotics officers.

narcolepsy   Sleeping sickness.

narcotic   A drug; having the power to produce a state of sleep or drowsiness and to relieve pain.

needle   A hypodermic syringe.

needle freak   An individual who enjoys injecting almost anything, who gets a sexual flash from the injection.

Nemby, Nimby, or **Nobbie**   A Nembutal sedative (pentobarbital) capsule.

nickel   Five dollars; five-year jail sentence.

nickel bag   five-dollar packet of drugs.

nicotine   A behavioral stimulant found in tobacco.

nod   Drowsiness resulting from drug use.

nod out   To pass into a euphoric state in which the head nods to the chest and is jerked back repeatedly.

norepinephrine (NE)   A synaptic transmitter in both the central and peripheral nervous systems.

number   Marijuana cigarette.

number five   Number five capsules.

O   Opium.

OD   An overdose of a narcotic.

off   Withdrawn from drugs; to kill someone; to have gotten high.

ololiuqui   A psychedelic drug obtained from the seeds of the morning glory.

on a trip   Under the influence of LSD.

on the nod   The drowsy, stuporous state that a drug user is in when on drugs.

on the street   Out of jail.

opiate Any drug containing or derived from opium; a true narcotic.

opiate narcotic A drug that has both sedative and analgesic actions.

opium A crude resinous exudate from the opium poppy.

oranges Dexedrine appetite suppressant, an amphetamine.

organotropic Having an attraction for certain organs or tissues of the body.

outfit Equipment used for injecting drugs.

overamp An overdose of amphetamines.

Owsley's stuff LSD manufactured by Owsley Stanley.

oxidation Combination with oxygen or removal of hydrogen from a compound by the action of oxygen; one means by which the body disposes of foreign substances such as alcohol.

oz An ounce.

pad An apartment or any place to live.

paddy Caucasian.

Panama red Red marijuana from Panama.

panic Shortage of narcotics on the market.

panup To put a drug in the cooker.

paper A paper of heroin (bindle); also, a prescription for a narcotic.

paraldehyde A hypnotic drug derived from alcohol.

parasympathic nervous system The branch of the autonomic nervous system that consists of a group of cranial nerves that leave the spinal column in the sacral area of the body. These nerves generally are related to the automatic functions of the body.

paregoric Camphorated tincture of opium.

Parkinson's disease A disorder of the motor system characterized by involuntary movements, tremor, and weakness.

partying Sharing heroin; "just getting it on."

PCP Phencyclidine, a hallucinogenic drug.

peaches Benzedrine stimulant.

peanuts Barbiturates.

peddler One who sells narcotics.

penned Sentenced to a federal penitentiary.

pentylenetetrazol A convulsant drug; trademark Metrazol.

pep pills Amphetamines.

permeability Ability to allow passage, as through a cell membrane.

peyote Common name for the cactus *Lophophora williamsii*.

PG Paregoric.

pharmacology The branch of science that deals with the study of drugs and their actions on living systems.

phencyclidine A psychedelic surgical anesthetic; trademark Sernylan.

phenothiazine A chemical class of antipsychotic drugs.

physical dependence A state in which the presence of a drug is required in order for an individual to function normally. Such a state is revealed by withdrawing the drug and noting the occurrence of withdrawal symptoms (abstinence syndrome). Characteristically, withdrawal symptoms can be terminated by readministration of the drug.

physiological Pertaining to the functioning of the body.

physostigmine An acetylcholinesterase (AChE) inhibitor.

picrotoxin A convulsant drug.

piece One ounce.

pig A police officer.

pill freak, pill head, or **pilly** An amphetamine or barbiturate user.

pinks Seconal, a sedative-hypnotic, or secobarbital capsules.

pinned Having the pupils of the eyes contracted from heroin.

pipe A large vein.

placebo A pharmacologically inert substance that may elicit a significant reaction largely because of the mental set of the patient or the physical setting in which the drug is taken.

plant A cache of narcotics.

poke The puff of a marijuana cigarette.

pons The portion of the brain lying between the medulla oblongata and the mesencephalon, beneath the cerebellum.

pop To inject drugs.

popper Amyl nitrite.

popping Injecting drugs under the skin.

pot Marijuana.

potency A measure of drug activity expressed in terms of the amount required to produce an effect of given intensity. Potency varies inversely with the amount of drug required to produce this effect—that is, the more potent the drug, the lower the amount required to produce the effect.

potentiation Combined action of two drugs that is greater than the sum of the effects of each used alone.

pot head A marijuana smoker.

progesterone A hormone secreted from the ovaries in response to stimulation by luteinizing hormone (LH) from the pituitary gland.

proprioceptive Receiving stimulation from the tissues of the body.

proprioceptor Sensory nerve terminal that gives information concerning movements and positions of the body.

psilocybin A psychoactive drug obtained from the Mexican mushroom *Psilocybe mexicana*.

psychedelic Capable of producing distorted images or states of the mind.

psychedelic drug Any drug with the ability to alter sensory perception.

psychic energizer A drug that acts as a stimulant to the central nervous system and is able to produce an elevation of mood, increased activity, heightened confidence, and an increased ability to concentrate.

psychoactive drug Any chemical substance that alters mood or behavior as a result of alterations in the functioning of the brain.

psychogenic Originating in the mind.

psychological dependence A compulsion to use a drug for its pleasurable effects. Such dependence may lead to a compulsion to misuse a drug.

psychotherapy Treatment of psychological abnormalities or disorders.

psychotoxic Literally, poisonous to the mind; having the ability to modify mood and change behavior.

punk A coward; a stupid, untrustworthy person.

pur Prescription.

pure High-quality or undiluted heroin or other drugs.

purple haze LSD.

purple hearts Dexamyl appetite suppressant, a combination of Dexedrine and Amytal (trademarks).

push To sell drugs.

pusher A drug peddler.

put up To put drugs in capsules.

quacks Methaqualone, after the trademark Quaalude.

quarter A quarter of an ounce of a drug.

quarter bag An ounce of marijuana; a quarter of an ounce of cocaine; a quarter spoon of heroin.

quill A matchbook cover for sniffing Methedrine stimulant, cocaine, or heroin.

raid A surprise invasion of a suspected drug trafficker's quarters by law enforcement officers to arrest the trafficker and seize the trafficker's illicit supplies.

rainbows Capsules of Tuinal sedative-hypnotic (equal parts of secobarbital and amobarbital).

rap To talk.

rat To inform the police.

rat fink An informer for the police.

rationalization   Invention of an acceptable explanation for behavior that has its true origin in the unconscious.

RD   Seconal sedative-hypnotic capsule.

reader   A prescription.

red birds, red devils, or **reds**   Seconal sedative-hypnotic capsules.

reefer   A marijuana cigarette.

reentry   The return from a trip.

reg   Marijuana of regular quality.

regression   The return to a previous state of emotional development.

replacement   Supplement or restorative; a chemical or drug used to restore or supplement some secretion of the body.

reserpine   An antipsychotic drug; trademark Serpasil.

rip off   To steal.

risk-benefit ratio   An arbitrary assessment of the risks and benefits that may accrue from administration of a drug.

roach   A marijuana butt.

roach holder   A device for holding the butt of a marijuana cigarette.

rock   Cocaine in rock form.

rolling dip   Making a marijuana cigarette.

rope   A marijuana cigarette.

roses   Benzedrine stimulant tablets.

roust   An interrogation or arrest.

ruler   A judge.

run   An amphetamine binge.

rush   The initial exhilerating sensation felt after taking a drug.

salt shot   Salt and water injected under the skin when a person takes an overdose of heroin.

Sam   Federal narcotics agents.

satch cotton   Cotton used to strain drugs before injection; may be used again if no other straining material is available.

scag   Heroin.

scam   To hustle whatever one needs or wants, usually resulting in an energy drain.

scene   The place of action.

score   To purchase drugs.

scrath   Money.

script   A prescription.

seccy   Seconal sedative-hypnotic.

sedative   A depressant drug that allays excitement; quieting.

sedative-hypnotic drug   Any chemical substance that acts as a non-selective general depressant upon the central nervous system.

seeds   Marijuana seeds.

Seggy   Seconal sedative-hypnotic.

serotonin   Neurohormonelike substance found in many cells and organs of the body, responsible for activation of the trophotropic system in the brain, transmitting nerve impulses to the parasympathetic nervous system.

serum   Clear, liquid portion of an animal fluid separated from the solid elements; often, blood serum.

shine on   To put off or ignore.

shit   Heroin.

shmeck   Heroin.

shoot   To inject a drug into a vein or under the skin.

shooting gallery   The place where addicts go to inject themselves.

shoot up   To inject drugs intravenously.

short   A car.

short sled   A vehicle.

sick   To need heroin.

side effect   Any drug-induced effect that accompanies the primary effect for which the drug was administered.

sister   Any female, usually black or chicano; also, cocaine.

skag   Heroin.

skin pop   To inject the drugs under the skin.

slammed   In jail.

sleepers   Barbiturates.

smack   Heroin.

smoke   Wood alcohol.

sniff   To inhale drugs, particularly heroin or cocaine, through the nose.

sniffing   Inhaling drugs.

snitch   A police informer.

snort   To inhale drugs, particularly heroin or cocaine, through the nose.

snorting   Inhaling drugs.

snow   Cocaine.

snowbird   A cocaine user.

soaper   Methaqualone, after the trademark Sopor.

somnolence   Sleepiness; unnatural drowsiness.

speed   Methamphetamine.

speedball   A powerful shot of a drug, usually heroin and cocaine combined.

speed freak   Habitual user of methamphetamine.

spike   A hypodermic needle.

splash   Methamphetamine.

split   To break away, exit, leave.

spoon   One-sixteenth to one-quarter of an ounce of a drug, usually cocaine.

spores   Psilocybin spores.

square   A nonuser of drugs.

stardust   Cocaine.

stash   A cache of narcotics.

step on   To adulterate narcotics.

stick   A marijuana cigarette.

stimulant   A chemical, substance, or agent that has the ability to increase the functional activity of the body.

stoned   Exhibiting the effects of marijuana.

stool or **stoolie**   An informer for the police.

STP   DOM, a hallucinogenic drug.

straight   A person holding or under the influence of a narcotic.

street (the)   The immediate outside world.

strung out   Addicted.

strychnine   A convulsant drug.

stud   A fellow; a junk; a gigolo.

stuff   Narcotics.

stumblers   Downers; central nervous system depressants.

subcutaneous   Under the skin.

suede   A black person.

sugar   Powdered narcotics.

superego   According to the Freudian theory, one of the three main divisions of the psychic apparatus; associated with ethics, standards, and self-criticism, which help form the conscience.

sweets   Benzedrine stimulant; amphetamine sulfate.

swingman   A drug supplier.

sympathetic nervous system   A branch of the nervous system consisting of a pair of long nerve trunks located on either side of the backbone that supply the visceral organs, generally causing an excited or ready reaction in the body.

sympathomimetic   Mimicking the effects of impulses affecting the sympathetic nervous system; producing effects similar to stimulation of the sympathetic nervous system.

synergism   Effect of a combination of drugs taken simultaneously, which is greater than the sum of the effects of the same drugs when taken separately.

synthetic   Formed by a chemical reaction in a laboratory.

T   Marijuana.

tab Tablet (pill).

take off To experience the high of a drug; to steal from somebody; to kill a person.

taste Sample of a narcotic.

tea Marijuana.

tea head Marijuana user.

ten-cent bag A ten-dollar unit of drug.

teratogen Any chemical substance that may induce abnormalities of fetal development.

testosterone A hormone secreted from the testes that is responsible for the distinguishing characteristics of the male.

tetrahydrocannabinol (THC) A major psychoactive agent found in marijuana, hashish, and other preparations of hemp.

Texas tea Marijuana.

THC Tetrahydrocannabinol.

thing Heroin.

thoroughbred A high-type hustler who sells pure narcotics.

tie Any cord to tie around the arm or leg to make a vein stand out for easy injection.

tie off To apply pressure on a vein so it will stand out and injection of the drug will be easier.

together In control of oneself or a situation; cool.

toke A puff of a marijuana cigarette.

toke up To smoke marijuana cigarettes.

tolerance Increasing resistance to the usual effects of a drug.

Toolies Tuinal sedative-hypnotics.

tooter An instrument that supposedly dispenses just the right quantity of cocaine for a snort.

toss To search a person or place.

toxic effect Any drug-induced effect that is either temporarily or permanently deleterious to any organ or system of an animal or patient to which the drug is administered. Drug toxicity includes both the relatively minor side effects that invariably accompany drug administration and the more serious and unexpected manifestations that occur in only a small percentage of individuals taking a drug.

toxicity Poisonousness.

tracked up Having numerous injection marks along a vein.

tracks Scar along a person's veins after many injections.

tranquilizer A drug that acts to relieve an overactive, anxious, or disturbed emotional state; a central nervous system depressant.

travel agent An LSD supplier.

trey   Three-dollar bag of heroin.

trick   A person who is an easy mark; a sucker; a fool.

trip   A psychedelic experience.

tripping out   High on psychedelics.

truck drivers   Amphetamines.

Tueies   Tuinal sedative-hypnotics.

turkey   A capsule with a nonnarcotic powder.

turned off   Withdrawn from drugs.

turned on   Under the influence of drugs.

turps   Elixir of terpin hydrate with codeine, a cough syrup.

25   LSD.

Uncle   A federal narcotics agent.

unit   Equipment for injecting drugs.

unkie   Morphine.

up   Under the influence of a drug, usually an amphetamine; feeling positive.

ups or **uppers**   Stimulants; amphetamines.

user   A person who uses heroin.

using   The use of drugs.

vaccine   Preparation of killed or weakened microorganisms for use in immunization.

vasodilator   Causing the blood vessels to dilate (expand in size).

volatile solvent   Easily vaporized substance capable of dissolving something; specifically, chemicals contained in lighter fluid, model airplane glue, and other common substances that produce a state of intoxication when inhaled.

wad   A piece of cloth saturated with glue or gasoline, usually a sock; also known as glad rag.

wake-up   First shot of heroin of the day, sometimes saved from the night before.

wake-ups   Amphetamines.

wallbanger   An individual intoxicated and staggering under the influence of alcohol or another downer.

washed up   Withdrawn from drugs.

wasted   Under the influence of drugs.

water   Methamphetamine.

weed   Marijuana.

weed head   A marijuana user.

weekend habit   A small irregular drug habit.

West Coast turnarounds   Amphetamines.

What's happening?   Do you have any narcotics?

whiskers   Federal narcotics agents.

white girl Cocaine.

whites Amphetamine sulfate tablets.

white stuff Morphine.

works Equipment for injecting drugs.

write To write prescriptions for dope.

yellow jacket or **yellow** Nembutal sedative, a barbiturate.

yen sleep A drowsy, restless state during the withdrawal period.

yesca Spanish terminology for marijuana.

zonked Under the influence of a drug.

INDEX